Jay E Hulot

THE HOLY SPIRIT IN THE GOSPELS

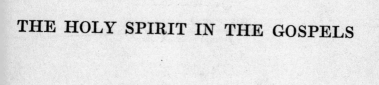

THE HOLY SPIRIT IN THE GOSPELS

THE MACMILLAN COMPANY
NEW YORK · BOSTON · CHICAGO · DALLAS
ATLANTA · SAN FRANCISCO

MACMILLAN & CO., Limited
LONDON · BOMBAY · CALCUTTA
MELBOURNE

THE MACMILLAN CO. OF CANADA, Ltd.
TORONTO

THE HOLY SPIRIT
IN THE
GOSPELS

BY

J. RITCHIE SMITH, D.D.

PROFESSOR OF HOMILETICS IN PRINCETON THEOLOGICAL
SEMINARY. AUTHOR OF "THE TEACHING OF
THE GOSPEL OF JOHN"; "THE WALL
AND THE GATES."

New York
THE MACMILLAN COMPANY
1926

Printed in the United States of America by
THE FERRIS PRINTING COMPANY, NEW YORK

To My Children

PREFACE

This volume comprises a series of exegetical studies, in which every passage of the four Gospels relating to the Holy Spirit is examined that its precise significance may be discovered. Abundant use has been made of the labour of many scholars in this field; but it has been the constant endeavour to ascertain by the close and direct study of the text, in humble reliance upon the promised guidance of the Holy Spirit, what He has chosen to reveal of his nature and his office. Every earnest student of the Word knows how inadequate is our poor thought to penetrate and our poor speech to utter the deep things of God; yet it is by constant and diligent study that the truth is apprehended and interpreted, the truth by which we live.

May He, to whom alone is due whatsoever of truth and wisdom this book may contain, pardon all that has been spoken amiss; and apply the truth with quickening and sanctifying power to the hearts of those who read.

And to God, Father, Son, and Holy Spirit, shall be all the praise.

TABLE OF CONTENTS

PART ONE

THE HOLY SPIRIT IN THE OLD TESTAMENT

PART TWO

THE HOLY SPIRIT IN THE LIFE OF JESUS.

A—IN THE SYNOPTIC GOSPELS.

CONTENTS

PART ONE

THE HOLY SPIRIT IN THE OLD TESTAMENT

CHAPTER I

THE HOLY SPIRIT IN THE OLD TESTAMENT

Every form of religion known to history contains elements of truth to which it owes its vitality and power. It would be difficult indeed to frame an affirmative creed which should be wholly false. Heresy does not create, it perverts and corrupts. Error is the shadow of truth, grotesque, distorted, deformed, as shadows are, yet preserving in some strange, misshapen fashion the likeness of the original. The most widely diffused of all religious systems, polytheism, is the perversion of a great truth, the truth of the variety and fulness of the divine nature. Lacking the conception of a God everywhere present and active, men were forced to assume a host of divinities, between whom the attributes and energies of the Deity may be distributed, and who by virtue of their number may accomplish the works of creation and providence.

This does not purport of course to be a complete account of the genesis of the system, for there are various reasons that lead men to the worship of many gods. But in so far as polytheism was a serious attempt to account for the tokens of the divine presence and power that are manifest on every side, this thought enters into and underlies every form in which it appears. It is the distinctive mark of polytheism that it sacrifices the unity to the variety of the divine nature. Against this error the Old Testament everywhere contends. Not until it was extirpated from the minds of the chosen people, and the taint of idolatry purged away in the furnace of affliction, was the truth revealed in all its fulness that polytheism vainly strove to express. The Old Testament overthrows the error, the New Testament brings to light the truth, of polytheism. It is true that the lawgiver, psalmist, prophet constantly insist upon the infinite riches of wisdom, power, and grace which are found in· God; but the crowning disclosure, the ultimate revelation, of the divine nature is made in Christ alone, to whom all authority is given, in whom are hid all the treasures of wisdom and knowledge, in whom dwelleth all the fulness of the Godhead bodily, in such form that it may be apprehended and embraced by men. The fulness and variety that men seek in many gods are found in one. The doctrine of the Trinity at once preserves the unity and discloses the fulness of the divine nature. God is one, is the message of the Old Testament; God is one in Three Persons, is the message of the New; and the revelation is complete. God is one, distinguishes the religion of the Bible from every form of polytheism; God is one in Three Persons, distinguishes it from that hard and barren monotheism which speaks in the Koran.

The truth revealed to the men of the Old Covenant was the unity, spirituality, and sovereignty of God. The Old must furnish a point of attachment for the New. The Gospel must rest upon the foundation of the law and the prophets, for they proclaim the same God. There is no doctrine of the New Covenant which is not potentially and germinally contained in the Old. We find, accordingly, hints and suggestions in the earlier record which are seen in the light of the New Testament to be adumbrations of the Trinity. There are plural forms of the divine name with which singular verbs and adjectives are usually joined:[1] Elohim; Adonai; the Holy One;[2] Creator;[3] Maker.[4] These are sometimes represented as survivals of the polytheism which was the primitive religion of mankind, but they are more frequently and properly regarded as the plural of eminence or majesty.[5]

No sufficient reason has been shown why we should set aside the Scripture representation that the worship of the one living and true God was the primal religion of the race. Man has not risen from the false to the true; he has fallen from the true to the false. Decaying monotheism crumbles into polytheism.[6] Israel kept alive the knowledge of the truth, and these plural forms indicate that the attributes which polytheism distributed among a host of deities are all found in their perfection in one God. Similar is the use of the phrase *seven spirits* in Rev. i. 4; iii. 1; iv. 5; v. 6 to express the manifoldness of the divine Spirit.

The plural in such passages as Gen. i. 26—"Let us make man in our image," and Gen. xi. 7—"Come, let us go down and confound their language," is sometimes interpreted to mean that God addresses the angels who form his court. But they are not his counsellors, but his ministers. He does not consult with them, he commands. "With whom took he counsel?"[7] God communes with himself. In Gen. iii. 22—"Behold, the

---

[1] Exceptions to the rule, as in Gen. xx. 13; xxxv. 7; Ex. xxii. 8; Deut. v. 26; xxxii. 15; Josh. xxiv, 19; I Sam. xvii. 26, 36; II Sam. xvii. 23; Ps. lviii. 11, are commonly explained from the context; but it is sometimes difficult to see why the plural is preferred. *Gesenius' Lex. Elohim.* Delitzsch, on Isa. liv. 5.

[2] Prov. ix. 10; xxx. 3. Hos. xi. 12.

[3] Eccles. xii. 1.

[4] Job xxxv. 10. Ps. cxlix. 12. Isa. liv. 5.

[5] Oehler, *O. T. Theol.* § 36; Schultz, *O. T. Theol.* II. 126; Davidson, *O. T. Theol.* p. 40; Driver, on Genesis Excursus 1. Delitzsch, on Genesis i. 1. Toy on Proverbs ix. 10.

[6] Orr, *Problem of the Old Testament,* ch. v.

[7] Isa. xl. 14.

man is become as one of us, to know good and evil,"
God apparently associates with himself the angels, who
like him possess the knowledge of good and evil to
which man has just attained. In Isa. vi. 8—"Whom
shall I send, and who will go for us?"—the alternation
of singular and plural is not easily explained. There
are those who think that God addresses the seraphim
who stand above him; [8] but it is better to recognize
here as elsewhere the plural of majesty. God speaks
with himself. Why both singular and plural are used
in the same sentence does not appear. Gen. xix. 24—
"Then Jehovah rained upon Sodom and upon Gomor-
rah brimstone and fire from Jehovah"—is sometimes
interpreted as an intimation of the Trinity, but it is
better taken as an emphatic repetition, like Hos. i. 7;
Zech. x. 12; II Tim. i. 18.

There are indications, moreover, of the number of
Persons in the Godhead, and their various character-
istics and offices. Here of course we are reading the
Old Testament in the light of the New. These representations would never of themselves convey the conception of the Trinity, nor is there reason to believe
that the truth was apprehended by the sacred writers
themselves; but it lay in the mind of the Spirit, and
in the light of the event is seen to have a place in the
Old Scripture. If indeed there are Three Persons in
the Godhead, a truth so transcendent could not be
altogether concealed. Gleams of it must break through
the darkness. God could not reveal himself, however
obscurely, for the redemption of men, and give no
intimation of that threefold nature upon which the
work of redemption rests.

The Word of God, the Wisdom of God, the Angel
of God, the Servant of God, the Christ of God, are all
representations or manifestations of the Eternal Son.
In like manner the Spirit appears as the energy, the

[8] Vs. 2.

activity, the agent of Jehovah. The various attributes of God may indeed be personified: light and truth in Ps. xliii. 3; wisdom in Prov. viii.; righteousness and peace, mercy and truth in Ps. lxxxv. 10-13. But this mode of speech is occasional and figurative only; while our study will show that the representation of the Spirit in terms of personality is frequent and consistent. In fact, there is throughout the Old Testament no reference to the Spirit which may not be interpreted literally of a person. He is nowhere called a person, but he is always spoken of in terms that may properly be applied to a person. Personal attributes and acts are ascribed to him, as will presently appear.

Smeaton discovers the doctrine of the Trinity in Gen. i. 26—"Let us make man in our image, after our likeness"; and habitually imports into the Old Testament the distinctive features of the New. He fails to recognize in an adequate way the difference between the two dispensations which is clearly brought out in Jn. i. 17—"The law was given through Moses; grace and truth came through Jesus Christ." He even goes so far as to say, "The Old Testament Church was in many respects different from the New Testament Church; the former being more occupied with externals, the latter being privileged to have a worship which may be described as more in spirit and in truth. But the divine personality of the Spirit, as we have clearly seen, was not less known and not less recognized in the one economy than in the other. He who spoke by holy men from the beginning was in every age recognized as a Divine Person." [9] The truth contained in the first sentence of the citation should have prevented the errors contained in the sentences that follow. We must recognize both the essential unity of the doctrine presented in the Old and New Testa-

[9] *Doct. Holy Spirit*, p. 43.

ments, and the wide difference in the clearness and fulness with which the truth is revealed.

The teaching of the Old Testament upon this as upon every theme was the background and basis of the teaching of Jesus. He regarded the Old Scripture as in all its parts and throughout its whole extent the word of God, and accepted the traditional view of the order and authorship of the various books. Critical questions of dates and authors and authenticity had no place in his thought. To him all Scripture was inspired and authoritative. It may be held that Jesus was mistaken, but that this was his opinion is too obvious to be denied. It is our purpose to study the doctrine of the Spirit in the Old Testament, not from the point of view of modern critical scholarship, but from the point of view of Jesus and his disciples. We are not concerned with the development of the doctrine, but only with the content of the doctrine as Jesus found it. We are interested in the teaching of the earlier record simply as it furnishes the basis for the teaching of the New Testament. What did Jesus learn from the Old Testament regarding the Spirit of God? That question we may now proceed to consider.

The *Journal of Biblical Literature* for 1900, pp. 132-145, contains an article by Prof. C. A. Briggs on the "Use of Ruach in the Old Testament," which is substantially reproduced in the Lexicon of Brown, Driver, and Briggs. The word is said to be used ninety-four times with reference to the Divine Spirit, but the references given seem to fall somewhat short of that number. We take the article as the basis of our study with certain omissions and additions. No list could be prepared that would command universal assent, for many difficult questions of text and interpretation are involved.

Omissions. (1) The allusion to the spirit of the living creatures in Ezekiel i. 12, 20, 21; x. 17. The term is better understood in the same sense as the *spirit of man*, to signify the conscious and controlling life principle, which proceeds indeed from the Spirit of God, but is not to be identified with him.

(2) The references to the evil spirit that came upon Saul,[10] and the lying spirit in the mouth of the false prophets.[11] To the same class of passages, though it is not cited in this sense by the Lexicon, belongs Judges ix. 23—"And God sent an evil spirit between Abimelech and the men of Shechem"; as is recognized by Prof. Moore in *Intern. Crit. Comm., in loc.* In some of these instances, spirit might be taken to mean inclination or disposition, but in other cases a personal agency is evidently affirmed. In I Sam. xvi. 14 the Spirit of Jehovah is expressly distinguished from the evil spirit, and in the light of this distinction all these passages should be interpreted. Evil spirits are subject to the will of God, and may be employed as his ministers; and in this sense an evil spirit may be termed a spirit of God.[12] But the term is parallel with "an evil spirit from Jehovah," [13] and can in no way be identified with the divine Spirit. The statement of Prof. Briggs that "at this period Biblical ethics had not advanced so far as to regard deception and violent deeds as immoral even when instigated by the divine spirit," [14] is doubly incorrect. The Bible never condones deception, and never represents it as instigated by the divine Spirit. Why should it be assumed that the Bible approves of every recorded act which it does not explicitly condemn?

(3) It is not apparent why Job xxxii. 8 should be included—"But there is a spirit in man, and the breath of the Almighty giveth them understanding";

[10] I Sam. xvi. 14, 15, 16, 23; xviii. 10; xix. 9.
[11] I Kings xxii. 21, 22, 23. II Chron. xviii. 20, 21, 22.
[12] I Sam. xvi. 23.
[13] Sam. xvi. 14.
[14] *Cf.* Schultz, *O. T. Theol.* ii, 270.

and Job xxxii. 18 omitted—"The spirit within me constraineth me." In both cases it is better to understand the human spirit than the divine.

(4) Isa. xxxi. 3—"Now the Egyptians are men, and not God; and their horses flesh, and not spirit." The first clause sets in contrast the divine and the human; the second, the animal and the spiritual.

(5) Zech. xii. 10—"And I will pour upon the house of David, and upon the inhabitants of Jerusalem, the spirit of grace and of supplication." Here the word evidently signifies disposition.

Addiions. (1) Genn vi. 3—"My Spirit shall not strive with man forever." The verse is beset with difficulties, but this appears the better rendering. The Lexicon interprets *my spirit* to signify the spirit which I have breathed into man, and renders, though with hesitation, "my spirit shall not abide in man forever." This view is confirmed by the weighty authority of Dillman, Delitzsch, and Driver. But *my spirit* in this sense is without example elsewhere, and no reason is evident from the context why the ordinary meaning *my Spirit* should not be accepted.

(2) Isaiah xl. 13—"Who hath directed the Spirit of Jehovah"; where the Lexicon reads "mind of Jehovah."

(3) Isaiah lix. 21—"My Spirit that is upon thee, and my words which I have put in thy mouth, shall not depart out of thy mouth, nor out of the mouth of thy seed, nor out of the mouth of thy seed's seed, saith Jehovah, from henceforth and forever." Here the Lexicon understands moral character to be signified. But it is the Spirit of God who puts his words in the mouth of his people.

(4) Ezekiel xxxvi. 27—"I will put my Spirit within you"; where the Lexicon interprets the word by moral character.

(5) Ezekiel xxxvii. 14—"And I will put my Spirit in you"; where the Lexicon renders by *breath of life*.

(6) Micah ii. 7—"Shall it be said, O house of Jacob, Is the Spirit of Jehovah straitened?" Briggs renders the passage, "Is the temper of Yahweh impatient?" But Spirit of Jehovah yields an appropriate sense, and no reason is shown why the word may not be so rendered.

Malachi ii. 15 is rendered in the R. V.: "And did he not make one, although he had the residue of the Spirit?" with marginal reading: "And not one hath done so who had a residue of the spirit." The Lexicon understands the word to signify the spirit of man. The passage is so obscure, rivalling in the number of interpretations Galatians iii. 20, that no account is taken of it in our computation.

The difficulty of rendering the word arises, of course, from the wide range of meaning which it exhibits, beginning with mere wind or breath, and rising through the mental and moral nature of man to God, in whose image he was made. The Lexicon gives nine distinct renderings of the word with various shades of significance under each of them, making in all no less than thirty-three different senses that the word may bear.

So closely related are the conceptions of wind or breath and spirit, whether in God or man, that the word may be used in both senses in the same passage, or even in the same verse, as in John iii. 8. Isaiah lix. 19 is rendered by the R. V.: "He will come as a rushing stream, which the breath of Jehovah driveth"; with margin, "When the adversary shall come in like a flood, the Spirit of Jehovah will lift up a standard against him." Here the reading of the text is decidedly to be preferred. In Job xxvi. 13 the R. V. reads "By his Spirit the heavens are garnished," while the preferable reading, "by his breath the heavens are bright," does not even find a place in the margin. The most striking example of the interchange of meanings is furnished by Ezekiel xxxvii. 1-14, where the word is used to signify wind, breath, and Spirit, and the marginal notes indicate the difficulty of deciding between the various meanings. In Job xxxiii. 4 spirit of God and breath of the Almighty are parallel expressions, though the Revised Version reads, Spirit of God.

The Revised Version renders I Chron. xxviii. 12—"And the pattern of all that he had by the Spirit"; but the marginal reading, "in his spirit," is better, as in Ezekiel xi. 5; xx. 32.

The Revised Version renders Isaiah xxxiv. 16—"For my mouth, it hath commanded, and his Spirit, it hath gathered them." The change from the first to the third person suggests a better rendering: "My mouth, it hath commanded, and the breath of it hath gathered them." There is a striking parallel in Psalms xxxiii. 6: "By the word of Jehovah were the heavens made, and all the host of them by the breath of his mouth." The phrase occurs again in Job xv. 38; *breath of his nostrils* is found in I Samuel xxii. 16, Job iv. 9, Psalms xviii. 15; and *breath of his lips* in Isaiah xi. 4. In Psalms cvi. 33—"Because they were rebellious against his Spirit": the connexion favours the reading, Spirit of God, and not of Moses.

Since the spirit of man is the breath of God, it is not always clear whether the Spirit of God or the spirit of man is meant.[15] The same ambiguity is found in the New Testament.[16] These examples, to which many others might be added, may suffice to illustrate the difficulties that beset the interpreter when he attempts to fix the meaning of this elusive term.

With the omissions and additions indicated we have

[15] Gen. vi. 3. Ps. cvi. 33. Mal. ii. 15.

[16] Acts vi. 10; xx. 22. Rom. viii. 6; on which see Sanday & Headlam, *Intern. Crit. Comm.,* p. 199: note on the Person and Work of the Holy Spirit; Jas. iv. 5.

as the basis of our study seventy-eight passages, each of which will find a place in the exposition.

We proceed to consider the *names,* the *nature,* and the *work* of the *Spirit.*

I. Names of the Spirit

(1) He is commonly called the Spirit of God. Sixty-two times he is represented as the Spirit of Jehovah, and twelve times as the Spirit of Elohim. The significance of this will appear when we come to study his work.

(2) Three times he is called the Holy Spirit.[17] The primary meaning of holy appears to be *separated, set apart.*[18] It may be applied to God, as he is removed from the infirmity and imperfection of the creature; and to persons, places, and things as they are set apart to the service of God. The word thus covers a wide range of meaning, embracing both ceremonial and moral distinctions. It may be opposed to common— "There is no common bread under my hand, but there is holy bread";[19] and to sinful—"Ye cannot serve Jehovah: for he is a holy God; he is a jealous God; he will not forgive your transgressions nor your sins."[20]

The holiness or separation of God may be conceived locally or ethically. He is removed from the creature alike in place and character.

(a) Locally. His throne, his dwelling-place, are in heaven. This thought of the divine transcendence is frequently expressed;[21] and is denoted by the term holy.[22]

(b) Ethically. God is distinguished from his crea-

[17] Ps. li. 11; Isa. lxiii. 10, 11.
[18] See Sanday & Headlam, *Intern. Crit. Comm.,* on Romans i. 17; Prof. H. P. Smith, *Presbyterian Review,* 1881, pp. 588-592.
[19] I Sam. xxi. 4.
[20] Josh. xxiv. 19.
[21] Job xxii. 12. Ps. cxv. 3. Eccles. v. 2. Isa. lxvi. 1.
[22] Ps. xx. 6; xlvii. 8. Isa. lvii. 15; lxiii 15.

tures not merely in those attributes which are called
natural, his power, wisdom, majesty, glory, but yet
more in his moral perfections, as he is free from all
infirmity and impurity of character, and possesses truth
and goodness in infinite degree. This ethical quality
is brought out most clearly by the prophets, who insist
that the holiness which God requires is not outward
and ceremonial but inward and spiritual.[23] What God
requires of men is found in him. The holiness of men
must reflect the holiness of God. "Ye shall be holy;
for I Jehovah your God am holy."[24] This ethical
conception of the divine holiness reaches its height in
Isaiah. In Isaiah vi. the moral purity of God is set in
sharp contrast with the sinfulness of his people; and
in Isaiah v. 16 the ethical quality of his holiness is
clearly defined: "Jehovah of hosts is exalted in justice, and God and the Holy One is sanctified in
righteousness."   The name Holy One of Israel
occurs frequently in all parts of the books that bears
the name of Isaiah, and rarely elsewhere in the Old
Testament.

The meaning of the term cannot be restricted, therefore, to moral purity, for it appears at times to embrace
the varied attributes of the divine nature, so that it is
almost equivalent to divine. God hath sworn by his
holiness,[25] and God hath sworn by himself[26] are virtually convertible terms. In Isaiah vi. 3—"Holy, holy,
holy is Jehovah of hosts: the whole earth is full of his
glory"—holiness is one of the elements or attributes of
that glory which is the outshining of his divine perfections. But while the word has this large and varied
significance, yet throughout the Old Testament when
the terms divine and holy are applied to God, the
ethical conception is always present in higher or lower

[23] I Sam. xv. 22. Isa. i. 11-17. Jer. vii. 22, 23. Micah vi. 6-8.
[24] Lev. xix. 2.   [25] Amos iv. 2.   [26] Amos vi. 8.

degree. Never is it forgotten that God is distinguished from the creature, not only by his greatness, but yet more sharply by his moral perfection.

Here again we are not concerned with the development, but only with the content of the doctrine, for we are engaged with the study of Old Testament teaching only in so far as it affected the thought of Jesus. Questions of a critical nature were foreign to his teaching, and therefore do not require our consideration. We ask only what did Jesus find in the Old Testament regarding the Spirit of God.

The Spirit of the holy God is holy. In Isaiah lxiii. 10, 11, he is represented as the guide of the children of Israel in the wilderness, and is called holy because he sought to lead them in the way of holiness, that holiness which consists in obedience to the will of God. In the prayer of Psalm li. 10, 11, which in spite of the trend of modern criticism should be regarded as personal, not national, the Spirit is termed holy as the source and spring of holiness in men. From him proceed the right spirit and the clean heart. "Create in me a clean heart, O God; and renew a right spirit within me. Cast me not away from thy presence; and take not thy holy Spirit from me." As Isaiah lxiii. 10, 11, portrays the work of the Spirit in the nation, Psalms li. 11 portrays his work in the individual heart. This is the closest and clearest approximation to the New Testament doctrine of sanctification by the personal Spirit which the Old Testament affords.

(3) In Neh. ix. 20 he is termed thy good Spirit: "Thou gavest also thy good Spirit to instruct them." And in Ps. cxliii. 10 we read, "Thy Spirit is good." In these passages good is not equivalent to holy, but signifies rather kind, gracious, as the context indicates.

II. His Nature

Here we are concerned with the relation of the Spirit to God.

The breath is conceived as the condition and therefore as the symbol and expression of life, or even as the vital principle itself, as is indicated by the phrases breath of life,[27] or breath of the spirit of life.[28] *Spirit* thus readily assumes the meaning of energy or activity, the exercise and operation of the life. The Spirit of God is the manifestation, the expression, of the divine nature in its various energies and activities. The Spirit of God and the hand of God may be used interchangeably as the instruments of his power[29] so that the inspiration of the prophets may be referred to either.[30] The New Testament presents an instance of the same kind. In Matt. xii. 28 Jesus says, "If I by the Spirit of God cast out demons"; while the parallel passage, Luke xii. 20 reads, "By the finger of God."

The spirituality of God is obscured in the Old Testament by the constant anthropomorphism which distinguishes it from the later revelation. Bodily senses and members are ascribed to him: eyes and ears and nose and hands and feet. The representation is obviously figurative of course, but it throws a veil over the divine nature which was never removed under the old covenant. There are clear indications of his spiritual nature, as in Ps. cxxxix. 7, where *thy presence* and *thy Spirit* are equivalent terms; and in Isaiah xxxi. 3: "Now the Egyptians are men, and not God; and their horses flesh, and not spirit," where the contrast between man and God is parallel to the contrast between flesh and spirit. The second commandment rests upon the assumption, developed by Paul in his discourse at Athens,[31] that God cannot be expressed in visible form.

[27] Gen. ii. 7.
[28] Gen. vii. 22.
[29] Ezek. iii. 14; viii. 3; xxxvii. 1.
[30] Isa. viii. 11. Ezek. i. 3.
[31] Acts xvii. 24, 25, 29.

But side by side with this conception of the spirituality of God is set the constant representation of him in terms of the physical and material. The truth does not stand out, therefore, with the clearness and distinctness given it in the New Testament, where Jesus declared, "God is a Spirit,"[32] and where the anthropomorphisms so frequent in the Old Testament are rarely found.[33]

The clearest evidence of the spirituality of God afforded by the Old Testament is the fact that his activity alike in nature, in providence, in grace, are referred to his Spirit. "Not by might, nor by power, but by my Spirit, saith Jehovah of hosts."[34] If the exercise and operation of the divine nature are spiritual it is easy to conclude that the divine nature is spiritual. Because the Spirit is the manifestation or action of the divine power, he is at once identified with God and distinguished from him. Thy Spirit and thy presence are synonymous terms (Ps. cxxxix. 7). And, on the other hand, there are various passages in which God is said to send or pour out the Spirit. The Spirit is manifestly divine, though he does not yet appear as a Person.

III. His Work

1—in nature. References to the agency of the Spirit in the work of creation are few, and are all given below.

(1) Gen. i. 2—"The Spirit of God brooded upon the face of the waters." This is the rendering of Dillmann, Delitzsch, Driver, and Skinner,[35] and it is admitted by the Lexicon, though *hovered* is preferred. The Revised Version reads *moved*, with *was brooding*

[32] John iv. 24.

[33] See Oehler, *O. T. Theol.*, p. 46; Schultz, *O. T. Theol.*, ii. 110. Davidson, *O. T. Theol.*, p. 106; *HBD.*, II, 206, art. "God in N. T."

[34] Zech. iv. 6.

[35] *Intern. Crit. Comm.*

in the margin. Amid the darkness that shrouded the primeval chaos the Spirit of God is discovered, brooding upon the face of the waters, like a bird upon its nest. God's relation to Israel is illustrated by a similar figure in Deut. xxxii. 11—"As an eagle that stirreth up her nest, that fluttereth over her young, he spread abroad his wings, he took them, he bare them on his pinions." The narrative makes no further allusion to the creative activity of the Spirit, but the figure implies that he was the agent of the divine purpose in imparting life, and reducing the void, waste earth to order and clothing it with beauty. And this is confirmed by the references that follow.

(2) Ps. civ. 30—"Thou sendest forth thy Spirit, they are created; and thou renewest the face of the ground." In the first clause creation is referred to the Spirit, and in the second to God himself. He creates through his Spirit.

(3) Isa. xl. 13—"Who hath directed the Spirit of the Lord, or being his counsellor hath taught him?" It is plain from the context that the work of creation and providence is here ascribed to the Spirit. The preferable renderings of Job xxvi. 13, xxxiii. 4, and Isa. xxxiv. 16 have been given, and they contain no reference to the Spirit.

In these three passages alone is the Spirit represented as the agent of God in the work of creation. Ordinarily creation is referred directly and immediately to God. If an agent is named, it may be his Spirit; his Word; [36] his breath; [37] his hands; [38] his wisdom. [39]

2—the ethical and spiritual is the main sphere of the Spirit's operation. His work in nature is overshadowed by his work in the life and history of man-

[36] Ps. xxxiii. 6, 9; cxlviii. 5. Comp. the phrase *God said* in Gen. i.
[37] Job xxxiii. 4. Ps. xxxiii. 6.
[38] Ps. viii. 3; xcv. 5; cii. 25. Isa. xlv. 12; xlviii. 13.
[39] Prov. iii. 19; viii. 30. Ps. cxxxvi. 5. Jer. x. 12; li. 15.

kind. To his common operation among men, his
agency in the world at large, there is but one distinct
reference in the Old Testament, and that is in dispute:
Gen. vi. 3—"My Spirit shall not strive with man forever." From this time forward throughout the whole
course of the history the work of the Spirit is confined
to the chosen people. There are evidences of his
power, indeed, among the Gentiles, as in the case of
Melchisedec and Ruth, and the repentance of the
men of Nineveh under the preaching of Jonah; but
nowhere is he named. Balaam, indeed, may seem to
furnish an exception, but the Spirit came upon him
for the sake of Israel.[40] The Spirit withdrawn from
the world was not restored until he was sent by the
risen and glorified Christ.[41]

Israel is the sphere of the Spirit's operation. And
it is also true that the Old Testament contains not a
single prediction that the Spirit shall ever be given
to all mankind. Joel ii. 28 is sometimes regarded as a
prophecy of the world-wide effusion of the Spirit, but
his ministry is plainly confined to Israel. The line is
sharply drawn by the prophet between the people of
God and the heathen world, for which he foresees only
judgment.[42] The promise is not that the Spirit
hitherto restricted to Israel shall be poured out upon
all mankind, but that the Spirit hitherto given to a
chosen few in Israel shall be poured out upon all the
people of God, fulfilling the desire of Moses that "all
Jehovah's people were prophets, that Jehovah would
pour his Spirit upon them."[43] When Peter cited the
promise on the day of Pentecost, there is no reason to
believe that he gave it a wider meaning. Those whom
he addressed were Jews and proselytes.[44] "To you is
the promise, and to your children, and to all that are

[40] Num. xxiv.
[41] John vii. 39. Acts ii. 33.
[42] iii. 1, 2, 16, 17, 19-21.
[43] Num. xi. 29.
[44] Acts ii. 10.

afar off, even as many as the Lord our God shall call unto him." [45] The Jews and Jewish proselytes only are represented as the heirs of the promise, those present in Jerusalem, and those dwelling at a distance. Nowhere in Peter's discourse do the Gentiles find a place. It is true that the words of the prophet are capable of a larger application, which lay in the mind of the Spirit, and was declared by the event; but, so far as the record indicates, it was apprehended neither by prophet nor apostle, and the primary reference of the promise is to Israel alone.

Throughout the Old Testament, then, after Gen. vi. 3, with the partial exception of Balaam, the Spirit is represented as exercising his ministry in Israel alone. There are indications of God's gracious working beyond the borders of Israel, but it is nowhere ascribed to the Spirit. So closely is the kingdom of God restricted to Israel that very rarely does his ministry among the Gentiles appear, and his name is never found. The ministry of grace associated with his name is carried on among the chosen people alone. Israel was the channel of God's grace to mankind, and to Israel from the days of Abraham the kingdom of God in its outward, visible, organized form was confined.

We find accordingly that he is much more frequently termed the Spirit of Jehovah, the God of the Covenant, than of Elohim, the God of nature. No rigid line of division, indeed, can be drawn. The Spirit of Jehovah is operative in nature; [46] while the Spirit of Elohim is represented, with the single exception of Gen. vi. 3, as acting in Israel alone. But it was always the Spirit of Jehovah that came upon the judges who were raised up to deliver Israel, and upon the Messiah; and in general upon the prophets, though the Spirit of Elohim came upon Balaam; [47] upon Saul

[45] Vs. 39.   [46] Ps. civ. 30.   [47] Num. xxiv. 2.

and his messengers,[48] and upon Azariah,[49] Zechariah,[50] and Ezekiel.[51] In the case of Saul and Ezekiel Spirit of Jehovah and Spirit of Elohim are used interchangeably.

The work of the Spirit in Israel was mainly to prepare men for service. Personal sanctification, which is his chief office in the New Testament, fills a much smaller place in the earlier record, and is referred to directly only in Ps. li. 11; cxliii. 10; Isa. xxxii. 15; xliv. 3; lxiii. 10, 11; Ezek. xxxvi. 27, xxxvii. 11.

It is characteristic of the Old Testament, as of all ancient civilization, that the individual is subordinated to the organization, the State or the church. Man is estimated primarily as a member of society, and valued by his contribution to the general welfare. Jesus restored to man his rightful place, and made his well-being the end of all organizations and institutions. "The Sabbath was made for man, and not man for the Sabbath," [52] is a principle far-reaching and revolutionary, which has changed the face of the world. In the New Testament, where alone the rights and interests of the individual and of society are fully reconciled and harmonized, sanctification is the main aspect of the Spirit's work. The outward and visible form of the kingdom is prominent in the Old Testament, the inward and spiritual in the New. The dominant figure of the Old Testament is, my people Israel; in the New, the man Christ Jesus. In the Old Testament Jehovah is the Father of Israel; in the New, of the individual believer; in the Old Testament Christ is the King of the Jews; in the New he is the Saviour of the World. Distinctions of this kind are of course misleading, unless it be borne in mind that they are relative only,

[48] I Sam. x. 10; xi. 6; xix. 20, 23.
[49] I Chron. xv. 1.
[50] II Chron. xxiv. 20.
[51] xi. 24.
[52] Mark ii. 27.

not absolute. In the Old Testament the personal element is not wanting, as the Psalms conspicuously and frequently attest. The modern tendency to eliminate from the Psalter the element of personal experience, and make of them merely a monument of church consciousness [53] does violence at once to the spirit and the letter of some of them, and robs them of their proper place in the unfolding of Old Testament history and doctrine.

> Many of the Psalms in their original form were composed as an expression of private devotion. These features remained even after they were adapted by editorial revision for use in the synagogues. [54]

Is it not true, indeed, that all the great hymns and prayers of the church are born of personal experience? How can a man express the hopes and aspirations of the church except as he speaks out of the fulness of his own heart?

In the Old Testament the work of the Spirit is mainly directed to preparing men for public service, and is almost entirely confined to extraordinary persons and events. He intervenes only upon occasions of exceptional interest and importance, and his gifts usually are conferred for a limited time and a particular purpose. His habitual and unceasing activity, so prominent in the New Testament, is rarely brought to light. The nation rather than the individual is the sphere of his operation, and he works in men chiefly to qualify them for the service of the state. To him may be ascribed every gift and talent that is conspicuously useful in the history of the chosen people: the craft of the artificer; [55] the skill of the com-

[53] *H. B. D.*, IV, p. 158a.
[54] Briggs, *Intern. Crit. Comm.*, I, p. CXV.
[55] Exod. xxxi. 3; xxxv. 31.

mander; [56] the wisdom of the ruler; [57] the strength of the hero; [58] the inspiration of the prophet. [59] His power is not limited to distinctively religious acts and exercises, but moves as freely in the sphere of the secular as of the sacred; for whatever form his activity may assume, it is always ethical in aim and motive. He is the Spirit of the holy God, and Israel, the sphere of his operation, is a holy people. Their history in every particular is religious, and the work of the Spirit in shaping their history is religious. All that concerned Israel as a people set apart to God was sacred. The references to the distinctively ethical and religious work of the Spirit are few, because his work, whatever form it might assume, was all ethical in purpose, motive, result. From him proceed all the gifts by which Israel was qualified for its place in the unfolding of the kingdom of God. All the work of the Spirit, however secular it may appear, was in scope and purpose religious, preparing Israel, and through Israel the world, for the coming of the Christ. Thus the book of Esther, in which the name of God does not occur, finds its place in the canon because it discloses the divine hand guarding his people. Even on the bells of the horses shall be written, Holiness unto the Lord, and every pot in Jerusalem and in Judah shall be holy as the pots in the house of Jehovah. [60]

Thus throughout the Old Testament, not personal sanctification, but public service is represented as the chief purpose of the Spirit's ministry.

The Spirit may use even wicked men as his organs and agents. When Saul is said to have become a new man, [61] it is evident that not a change of heart is indicated, but only a temporary exaltation of spirit. Sometimes the Spirit transforms and renews the man, some-

[56] Judges vi. 34; xi. 29.
[57] Num. xxvii. 18.
[58] Judges xiii. 25.
[59] I Kings xviii. 12 and often.
[60] Zech. xiv. 20, 21.
[61] I Sam. x. 9.

times he simply confers upon him new aptitudes and powers, or quickens and strengthens his natural gifts. He is said to have clothed himself with men, Gideon,[62] Amasai,[63] and Zechariah,[64] that is, to take possession of them. He may come even upon the enemies of God and of his people, and speak and act through them, as in the case of Balaam. Holiness is not an indispensable condition of service. In this respect the Old Testament differs from the New, where sanctification always precedes service. If Caiaphas should seem to be an exception,[65] it must be borne in mind that Caiaphas was high priest under the old economy, and the Spirit was not given in the New Testament sense until Jesus was glorified.[66] Personal sanctification is essential to service, so that the Spirit works only through holy men. That is the general rule in the Old Testament, the invariable rule in the New.

There are certain offices of the Spirit which call for special mention.

1—the inspiration of the prophets. The distinguishing mark of the prophet is immediate inspiration. The priesthood was a hereditary office, the prophet was personally called and qualified of God. To him and through him the will of God was made known. "Surely the Lord Jehovah will do nothing except he reveal his secret unto his servants the prophets."[67] The prophet belonged to no particular family or class or tribe; was set apart by no ceremony, bore no outward mark of distinction. Only in the case of Elisha[68] and of the Messiah[69] is the prophet said to be anointed, and in both cases the word appears to be used in a figurative sense. The only qualification required of the prophet is that the word of God should come to him, the Spirit of God rest upon him. The prophet

[62] Judges vi. 34.
[63] I Chron. xii. 18.
[64] II Chron. xxiv. 10.
[65] John xi. 49.
[66] John vii. 39.
[67] Amos iii. 1.
[68] I Kings xix. 16.
[69] Isa. lxi. 1.

is the man that hath the Spirit.[70] In this he was distinguished from the false prophets, who claimed indeed the same inspiration;[71] but followed their own spirit,[72] and spoke from their own heart or like Saul[73] were possessed by an evil spirit.[74]

The prophet is not the passive instrument, but the conscious and willing agent of the Spirit. He may justly, therefore, be held to account for the proper discharge of his mission. The Spirit uses men according to their capacity, temper, experience. After he came upon them, they differ among themselves as widely as before. He does not destroy, but develops and directs the native gifts and energies of men, so that under his inspiration every man becomes more truly and thoroughly himself. The message bears the impress of the personality of the prophet. The substance is communicated by the Spirit; the form is determined by the character and experience of the messenger, acting indeed under the control and direction of the Spirit.

2—the Spirit qualifies the Messiah for his work. This is directly affirmed by Isaiah alone. The Messiah is represented as a branch or shoot of the stock of Jesse, the house of David: "and the Spirit of Jehovah shall rest upon him." When the Spirit is further defined as the Spirit of wisdom and understanding, the Spirit of counsel and might, the Spirit of knowledge and of the fear of Jehovah,[75] he is described by the gracious fruits of his ministry in the lives of men.[76]

Again the Messiah is portrayed as the servant of Jehovah. The term is used in various senses. It may be applied to anyone who serves the purpose of God, even unconsciously. "I will send unto Nebuchadnezzar, King of Babylon, my servant."[77] And Cyrus,

[70] Hos. ix. 7.
[71] I Kings xxii. 24; II Chron. xviii. 23.
[72] Ezek. xiii. 3.
[73] I Sam. xviii. 10.
[74] See Riehm, *Messianic Prophecy*, Part I.
[75] xi. 1, 2. Isa.
[76] *Cf.* Gal. v. 22, 23.
[77] Jer. xxv. 9.

though he is not called my servant, is termed *my shepherd*,[78] *my anointed*,[79] he whom Jehovah loveth.[80] On this theme consult the Comm. of G. A. Smith.[81] The phrase is used more precisely to designate a conscious and voluntary agent of the divine will. In this sense it is applied to Abraham, to Moses, to David, to the prophets. And indeed the whole company of the chosen people are *my servants*.[82]

In Isa. xli. 8 the collective term *my servant* is applied for the first time to Israel as the chosen people: "But thou, Israel, my servant, Jacob whom I have chosen, the seed of Abraham my friend." Henceforth throughout the prophecy the figure of the servant is conspicuous and dominant.[83]

But it soon appears that much is said of the character and office of the Servant that cannot be applied to the Jewish people. He is expressly distinguished from them in several particulars. Isa.

(1) in person. In chapter xlix the Servant speaks: "and he said unto me, Thou art my servant, Israel";[84] "and now saith Jehovah that formed me from the womb to be his servant, to bring Jacob again to him, and that Israel be gathered unto him."[85] Here the Servant is at once identified with Israel and distinguished from them. He bears the name of Israel, but is sent to lead Israel back to God. The Servant is Israel, but not all Israel. He may be an individual, or the righteous remnant of Israel, those who in the midst of a corrupt and rebellious generation hold fast their faith in God and seek to do his will.

But in chapter liii. the Servant can no longer be taken to represent the righteous in Israel, or any one

[78] Isa. xliv. 28.   [79] Isa. xlv. 1.   [80] Isa. xlviii. 14.
[81] *Isaiah* II, ch. x.   [82] Lev. xxv. 55.
[83] Isa. xli. 9; xlii. 1; xliii. 10; xliv. 1, 21; xlv. 4; xlviii. 20; xlix. 3; lii. 13; liii. *Cf.* Jer. xxx. 10; xlvi. 27; Ezek. xxviii. 25; xxxvii. 25.
[84] Vs. 3.   [85] Vs. 5.

of them. As clearly as the godly are distinguished
from the ungodly among the chosen people, so clearly
is the Servant distinguished from all Israel. The
prophet and those for whom he speaks are not the
Servant, but bear witness to him. "Who hath believed
our message?" The notion that it is the heathen who
speak may be dismissed without consideration, as forbidden alike by the text and the context of the passage.
Throughout the chapter the Servant is set apart from
all men besides. *He* and *we* are put in sharp contrast.
He is not the prophet, nor is he numbered among those
whom the prophet represents. He is not one of *us*.

(2) he is distinguished in character. The people
Israel have turned away from God, and suffer the just
penalty of their sin. None among them is found righteous. This is expressly affirmed in lxiv. 6: "For we
are become as one that is unclean, and all our righteousnesses are as a polluted garment: and we all do
fade as a leaf; and our iniquities, like the wind, take us
away. For there is none that calleth upon thy name,
that stirreth up himself to take hold of thee." It is
everywhere taught that the sufferings of Israel are the
just penalty of their sin, and in that sin everyone of
them has a part. The fifty-third chapter makes this
very clear: "All we like sheep have gone astray; we
have turned everyone to his own way." [86] *We*
embraces the prophet and all his people, righteous and
unrighteous alike, and stretches further to include all
mankind. For if the chosen people are sinners, how
much more the heathen. All we Jews, all we men,
have gone astray. It is the confession of Israel, of the
race. The prophet anticipates the word of the apostle:
"For all have sinned, and come short of the glory of
God." [87]

But the Servant is without sin. The Spirit of God
rests upon him. As he is represented under the figure

[86] Vs. 6.   [87] Rom. iii. 23.

of the Branch, his delight shall be in the fear of Jehovah, and righteousness shall be the girdle of his waist, and faithfulness the girdle of his loins.[88] He suffers, but not for his own sins. "He was wounded for our transgressions, he was bruised for our iniquities."[89] Of him alone it may be said that he had no sins for which he must answer to God, and suffered no punishment for his own transgressions.

That a certain relative righteousness may be imputed to the godly in Israel, in comparison with the ungodly, is true; but it is relative only, while the righteousness of the Servant is perfect. "All our righteousnesses are as a polluted garment."[90] It is contrary to the whole tenor of Old Testament teaching to call men holy except in a limited sense by comparison with others. If the Servant is perfect in righteousness, he is more than man.

(3) he is distinguished in office. The righteousness ascribed to the Servant is not relative merely, in contrast with the wickedness of his generation. It is so absolute, so perfect, that it avails for the redemption of others. "Surely he hath borne our griefs and carried our sorrows." "He was wounded for our transgressions, he was bruised for our iniquities; the chastisement of our peace was upon him; and with his stripes we are healed." "Jehovah hath laid on him the iniquity of us all." "He bare the sin of many." The Servant is offered as an atoning and vicarious sacrifice. He takes upon himself the sin of men, that his righteousness may be imputed and imparted to them. Men cannot make atonement for the sins of others, nor even for their own. "None of them can by any means redeem his brother, nor give to God a ransom for him."[91] If this appears to be spoken of the life of the flesh, how much more is it true of life eternal. Israel

[88] xi. 3, 5.   [90] lxiv. 6.
[89] liii. 5.   [91] Ps. xlix. 7. See Delitzsch, *in loc.*

Isa

does not save, but is saved. Salvation is of God alone, and the thought that one may bear the sin of another is contrary to the whole tenor of Old Testament teaching. Israel is a sufferer, righteous Israel a martyr, but in no sense a saviour. The Servant is not only sufferer and martyr, he is an atoning sacrifice, and in this he stands alone.

It is true that men may suffer for the sake of others, may be afflicted for the sins of others, and through their sufferings may procure for others benefits and blessings that they would not otherwise enjoy. In this sense the principle of vicarious sacrifice plays a large part in the relations that men sustain toward one another. But there is another and higher sense in which no man can suffer vicariously for another. He cannot take upon himself the burden of his brother's guilt so that his brother shall go free. He cannot make atonement for sin. That belongs to God alone. If the Servant makes atonement for the sins of others, he is more than man. When Paul affirms "Now I rejoice in my sufferings for your sake, and fill up on my part that which is lacking of the afflictions of Christ in my flesh for his body's sake, which is the church," [92] he does not mean that the atoning work of Calvary would be incomplete without his labours and sufferings; he means that through his labours and sufferings the benefits of that atoning work are made known and applied to believers. He preaches Christ crucified, he bears branded upon his body the marks of the Lord Jesus, the scars which attested his devotion to his Master, and through his preaching and the afflictions which accompany it he brings the church into a clearer knowledge of Christ and a more fruitful fellowship with him.

Who is this Servant of Jehovah? Evidently he is not Israel, nor righteous Israel, nor does any man in Jewish history answer to the description of the prophet. Is

[92] Col. i. 24.

he the genius of Israel, the ideal which Israel represented but never attained? Such abstractions are foreign to Old Testament modes of thought, in which ideals are always embodied in persons. The ideals of God are not barren, nor do they come short of fulfilment.

The meaning of the term rises from Israel to righteous Israel, and from righteous Israel to him whose character and mission alike fulfil the purpose of God. The prophet has drawn the portrait of Jesus the Christ. His character, his work, even the circumstances of his death and burial, the issue of his sacrifice, as they are depicted here, answer precisely and point by point to the representation of the Gospel story. The Servant of the Old Testament is the Jesus of the New.

It is in accord with the tenor of all Old Testament teaching to conceive of Israel as embodied in a Person through whom its divine mission shall be accomplished. There are various lines of prophecy that terminate in Jesus—the seed of the woman, the seed of Abraham, the successor of Moses,[93] the son of David. He is figured by the prophet, priest, and king of the old economy.

Thus the Old Testament presents two apparently discordant pictures of the Messiah. In one he appears as a king, triumphing over his foes and reigning over the people of God with equity and grace. In the other he is a righteous sufferer, put to death for the sin of others. The earlier of these conceptions fills a large place in the Old Testament, and was more in accord with the pride and aspiration of the Jewish people, so that it is not surprising that the sufferer was hidden behind the king in the thought of the people when Jesus came. They looked for a royal but not a suffering and dying Christ.[94] Even the disciples of Jesus

[93] Deut. xviii. 18.
[94] Matt. xvi. 22; Luke xviii. 34; xxiv. 21; John xii. 34.

never grasped the truth until his death and resurrection forced it upon them. It was foreign to all their Jewish habits of thought. The cross was always a stumbling-block to Israel, whether in prophecy or in history. The *Targum* of Jonathan, the pupil of Hillel who was a contemporary of Jesus, refers Isaiah liii. to the Messiah, but when his sufferings are pictured they are referred to Israel.[95] That there were Jewish interpreters who found in Isaiah liii. the suffering Messiah is true, but it is equally true that this was not the prevailing opinion in the time of Jesus.[96]

The representation of the Servant thus appears to waver between Israel, righteous Israel and the Messiah. The picture may be harmonized by regarding the Servant as embracing both the people and the Christ of God. Of this complex Person sometimes the body alone appears, sometimes the Head alone, and again the whole figure is seen. This thought is suggested by the Jewish interpreters, and early Christian writers, and is developed by J. A. Alexander in his *Commentary* on Isaiah, ch. xlii. This, as Alexander observes, is in accordance with the usage of the Old Testament elsewhere. The seed of the woman, the seed of Abraham, the prophet foretold in Deut. xviii. 18, embracing the prophetic order and its divine head, have all this double reference. Of a similar nature is the representation of the church in the New Testament. The church is the body of which Christ is the head.[97]

The representation of Christ as the Servant is taken up by the New Testament. The words of Isaiah xlii. 1 are applied to him: "Behold, my Servant, whom I

[95] *Jewish Interpreters on Isa. liii.*, Driver and Neubauer, ii. 5.
[96] The subject is treated at length in *HBD* art. "Messiah," vol. III, p. 354. Schürer, *Hist. Jewish People in Time of Jesus Christ*, II, ii, p. 184. Driver and Neubauer, as above; see especially vol. II, p. 61, for various interpretations given by Jewish scholars.
[97] See also Delitzsch on Isa. xlii.; G. A. Smith, *Isaiah II*, ch. xvi.

have chosen" [98] πατε is the term used in the LXX to represent the Hebrew *Servant,* and it should be so rendered in Matt. xii. 18; Acts iii. 13, 26; iv. 27, 30, as in the Revised Version, not *son.* The apostles take the word from the prophet, and with him affirm that the Servant is anointed of God,[99] that is, endowed with the gifts of the Holy Spirit. In Acts xvi. 38 it is expressly declared that "God anointed him with the Holy Spirit and with power."

Isaiah has thus portrayed the Messiah as a righteous king and a suffering Saviour, upon whom God has put his Spirit. Again he is presented in lxi. 1, and again the Spirit of God is seen to rest upon him. "The Spirit of the Lord Jehovah is upon me; because he has anointed me"—anointing is the rite of consecration by which priest and king were set apart, and the oil employed is the symbol of the fitness which God imparts. The Messiah is anointed, not with oil, but with the Spirit. His anointing not merely represented qualification and consecration, but accomplished it. And those who believe in him are not only followers of the Anointed One, they are themselves anointed with the same Spirit.[100]

To the Christ the Spirit is given in full measure and in permanent possession. In this he is distinguished from the prophets, upon whom the Spirit came in limited degree, for a special purpose, a particular time. Their inspiration was occasional and particular, upon him the Spirit abides continually. When John the Baptist said, "He whom God hath sent speaketh the words of God: for he giveth not the Spirit by measure,"[101] though he spoke in general terms the reference is plainly to the Son, who alone is capable of receiving the fulness of the Spirit, and upon whom alone the fulness of the Spirit is bestowed.

[98] Matt. xii. 18.
[99] Acts iv. 27.
[100] II Cor. i. 21; I John ii. 20, 27.
[101] John iii. 34.

3—it is foretold that the Spirit shall be poured out abundantly in the days of the Messiah upon all Israel. We have seen that the prophecy has no relation to the world at large, but is restricted to the chosen people.[102] Thus the Spirit not only equips the Messiah for his ministry, but follows up and completes his work, precisely as in the New Testament. In the Old Testament and in the New, the doctrine of the Spirit keeps pace with the doctrine of the Son. Side by side they appear in the story of the creation, for God called the world into being by his Word, and quickened it by his Spirit; side by side they appear in the visions of the prophet. So closely are they related that the same offices of creation, providence, redemption are ascribed to each of them. In the New Testament the Son and the Spirit are so nearly related that at times they are identified. In Rom. viii. 9, 11 the terms Spirit of God, Spirit of Christ, Christ, are used interchangeably. In II Cor. iii. 17 it is written, "The Lord is the Spirit." [103]

Later Jewish writers add nothing to the Old Testament conception of the Spirit, not even Philo, who in many respects represents the highest type of Jewish thought in the time of Christ.[104]

This, then, is the teaching of the Old Testament regarding the Spirit of God, which moulded the thought of Jesus. The Spirit appears as the divine influence or energy, rather than a Person. He is the manifestation or representation of God. But there are intimations of a profounder truth, hints and suggestions of his Personality, of a Trinity of Persons in the Godhead. Jesus and his disciples brought out into

---

[102] Isa. xxxii. 15; Ezek. xxxvi. 27; Joel ii. 28.
[103] See Meyer and Plummer *in loc.*
[104] See "Holy Ghost" and "Philo" in *Dict. Chr. Biog.;* "Holy Spirit" in *HBD,* p. 304.   Schürer II, iii., 369 ff.; art. "Use of Words for God in Apocryphal and Pseudepigraphical Literature of the Jews," by R. D. Wilson, *Princeton Theol. Review,* Jan. 1920, pp. 103 ff.

clear light the truth thus obscurely intimated. The
Spirit is no longer represented as a personification, but
as a Person, one with God in nature, yet distinct from
him in Person and office.

The teaching of the Gospels we now proceed to
consider.

PART TWO

THE HOLY SPIRIT IN THE LIFE OF JESUS

CHAPTER II

THE VIRGIN BIRTH—I.

The story of the virgin birth is told by Matthew and Luke. Neither narrative is complete, for each of them records various details which the other omits; and while they agree upon the essential facts, they differ in many particulars. The simplest explanation of the relation which they sustain to each other, of the points of resemblance and difference between them, is that they were written independently, and that Luke had at his command ampler stores of material than Matthew. If that be true, the narratives were probably written about the same time, for otherwise the later writer would have made use of the work of his predecessor.

A thorough examination of the historical and critical questions involved in the gospel story would carry us too far from our theme; and it must suffice to trace in outline the course of the argument by which the trustworthiness of the record may be put to the test, with references sufficient to guide the student who may wish to pursue the inquiry further.

There is no good reason to doubt that the verses containing the account of the virgin birth belong to the original text of the Gospels. They are found in all Greek manuscripts, and in all the early versions, Syriac, Latin, Coptic, Armenian. The Syriac manuscript discovered by Mrs. Lewis and Mrs. Gibson at

Mt. Sinai in 1892 is probably of the fourth or fifth century, of the same age, approximately, as the oldest Greek manuscripts that we have, and like them represents a much earlier text. In this version Matthew i. 16 reads: "Joseph, to whom was betrothed Mary the Virgin, begat Jesus, who is called the Christ." In his commentary on Matthew, Allen holds that this is probably "the nearest approach now extant to the original Greek." [1] But even if we should set aside all other authorities in favour of this single manuscript, the reading must be regarded as interesting rather than important; for the virgin birth is explicitly affirmed in vs. 18 of the same chapter: "And the birth of the Christ was on this wise: When Mary, his mother, was espoused to Joseph, when they had not come near one to the other, she was found with child of the Holy Ghost." It is obvious therefore, as Allen recognizes,[2] that *begat* in the passage cited expresses a legal relation and not actual paternity. The exception which this manuscript seems to present is therefore apparent only, and the virgin birth is attested by every authority that we possess.[3]

There is, moreover, abundant evidence that the virgin birth was embraced in the creed of the church from a very early date. Near the close of the second century we have the testimony of Clement of Alexandria [4] and Irenæus, who includes "the birth from a virgin" among the articles of the creed which the church had received from the Apostles.[5] About the middle of the century similar witness is borne by the *Diatessaron* of Tatian, the earliest harmony of the Gospels known

---

[1] Page 8.
[2] So also Moffatt, *Int. Lit. N. T.*, p. 251.
[3] On the Sinaitic Ms. see Mrs. Lewis' *The Four Gospels, translated from the Sinaitic Palimpsest.* Burkitt's *Evangelion Da Mepharreshe*, where various questions of textual criticism are treated. Zahn, *Introd. N. T.*, II, p. 565.
[4] *Strom.* vi. 15; vii. 16.
[5] *Her.* i. 10; iii., xxi. 4.

to us, which contains the narratives of both evangelists, except the genealogies; by Justin Martyr [6] and somewhat earlier, perhaps as early as 125, by the *Apology* of Aristides.[7] In the *Epistle* of Ignatius *to the Ephesians*, written about 110, we read, "Now the virginity of Mary was hidden from the prince of this world, as was also her offspring, and the death of the Lord; three mysteries of renown, which were wrought in silence." [8] "This passage," says Bishop Lightfoot, "is more frequently quoted by the fathers than any other in the Ignatian Epistles." [9] [10]

To these witnesses must be added the so-called Apostles' Creed, which for substance of doctrine may be traced as far back at least as the middle of the second century.[11]

This witness is drawn from all parts of the church, from Syria and Gaul and Egypt and Rome. And these men affirm that they do not speak for themselves alone but express the faith of the holy Catholic Church throughout the world.

Within the church the doctrine of the virgin birth was rejected only by a section of the Ebionites, a Jewish party, who maintained the perpetual validity of the Mosaic law and held that Jesus, though he was the promised Messiah, was yet a mere man, the son of Joseph and Mary.[12] Origen says that there were two opinions among the Ebionites, some affirming and others denying the virgin birth.[13] This division among them is attested also by Eusebius.[14] The whole sect soon came to be regarded by the church as heretical.

[6] *I Apol.*, 46; *Dial.*, 43, 66, 85.   [7] Syriac, ch. ii.; Greek, ch. xv.
[8] 19.   [9] *Apost. Fas.*, II, ii, p. 76.
[10] See also, *Ep. to Smyrneans* i.
[11] Harnack, *Schaff—Herzog Ency.*, I, 242.   McGiffert's Euseb., *Ch. H.*, VII, 8, note 3.   Machen, "Virgin Birth in Second Century," *Princeton Theol. Rev.*, 1912, p. 529.
[12] McGiffert's Euseb., *Ch. H.*, III, 27 and notes.   Machen, p. 547. Lightfoot on Galatians, "St. Paul and the Three," p. 159 ff.
[13] *Agt. Celsus*, vs. 61.   [14] *Ch. H.*, III, xxvii. 3.

The Gnostics, like the Ebionites, were divided upon the doctrine of the virgin birth. Gnosticism was not an outgrowth of Christianity, but an independent speculative and philosophical system, which absorbed certain elements of Christian truth.[15] All sects of Gnostics, even though they assumed the name of Christian, were repudiated by the church. Of those who rejected the virgin birth were Cerinthus, probably a contemporary of the apostle John,[16] [17] and Carpocrates;[18] [19] while it was accepted by the ablest and most distinguished of their teachers, of whom were Valentinus, if we may judge from the fragments of his writings which survive, and the teaching of his followers,[20] [21] and Basilides,[22] [23] though they interpreted it of course in their own peculiar fashion. The doctrine is so obviously incongruous with their views of the essential evil of matter and the docetic or phantasmal nature of the body of Jesus that their acceptance of it in any form bears striking witness to the strength of the evidence that compelled belief.

Marcion also may be cited as a witness against the virgin birth. He received as Scripture only ten epistles of Paul and the Gospel of Luke; and the Gospel he mutilated, omitting among other portions of it the first and second chapters. There was no place in his system for the story of Jesus' birth, since he held with the Gnostics the inherent evil of matter, distinguished

[15] McGiffert's Euseb., *Ch. H.*, II, 13, note 17, IV, 7. Lightfoot on Colossians, "The Colossian Heresy." Machen, *Virgin Birth*, p. 541. Moffatt, *Int. Lit. N. T.*, pp. 353, 408, 586. See Index.
[16] Irenaeus, *Her.*, I, xxvi. 1. Hippolytus, *Her.*, VII, 21.
[17] McGiffert's Euseb., *Ch. H.*, III, 28.
[18] Irenaeus, *Her.*, I, xxv. 1. Hippolytus, *Her.*, VII, 20.
[19] McGiffert's Euseb., *Ch. H.*, IV, 7, note 17.
[20] Tertullian Agt. Valent., 27. Hippolytus, *Her.*, VI, 30.
[21] McGiffert's Euseb., *Ch. H.*, IV, 11.
[22] Hippolytus, *Her.*, VI, 30.
[23] McGiffert's Euseb., *Ch. H.*, IV, 7, n. 7. Art. "Basilides" in *Dict. Chr. Biog.*

the God of the Old Testament from the God of the New, and was therefore repelled by the Jewish cast of the narrative.[24]

From this brief review it appears that the doctrine of the virgin birth was so generally held and so firmly established in the church that it was denied only by those who were counted heretical. And it is also evident that those who rejected it, whether bearing the Christian name or not, were led by philosophical and dogmatic rather than critical or historical considerations.

The question now arises whether the text has been interpolated. The most serious attack is made upon Luke i. 34, 35. The matter is treated at length by Prof. Machen in the *Princeton Theological Review* for 1906, p. 50 ff., and the ten reasons adduced by Harnack for rejecting these verses are sufficiently refuted.[25] Here it is enough to say that there is no manuscript authority for the omission; that to omit them requires changes elsewhere in the text, i. 27 and ii. 5, which are wholly unwarranted; that Luke's record here is supported by Matthew; and that the verses in question are in harmony with the fact, serve indeed to explain the fact, that throughout his narrative Luke gives the foremost place to Mary.

Assuming then the authenticity and integrity of the Gospel narratives, may we regard them as trustworthy? Is the record true? Those who reject the supernatural and aver that miracles do not happen, of course cannot accept the account as historical; for the supernatural, the miraculous, is the very soul and substance of the story. But those who find room anywhere in history for the immediate activity of God will readily recog-

[24] Tertullian *Agt. Marcion*, IV, 7; Hippolytus, *Her.*, X, 15; Irenaeus, *Her.*, I, 27.

[25] Moffatt, *Int. Lit. N. T.*, p. 268, leaves the matter in doubt. Burton favours the theory of interpolation. Galatians, p. 413, note 4.

nize that here is a supreme and unique occasion for the exercise of a divine power transcending the ordinary laws and forces of nature.

Certain inconsistencies and contradictions appear in the record, it is affirmed, of which the most important may claim our attention. A valid theory of inspiration must rest upon historical and critical rather than dogmatic grounds. If errors are found in Scripture it is idle to contend that Scripture cannot err. Arguments of an a priori kind will convince none but those who are already persuaded. When errors are alleged, we cannot take refuge in theories of inspiration, but the case must be examined and determined by the laws of evidence. The Scripture invites, challenges, investigations at every point. To inquiry, to doubt, to unbelief, the response is always, Come and see.

With this in mind we may proceed to examine the most serious objections which are proposed to the Scripture story.

(1) In Luke Nazareth is the home of Joseph and Mary, while Matthew regards Bethlehem as their home, to which they would have returned from Egypt if they had not been afraid of Archelaus. Joseph "came and dwelt in a city called Nazareth." [26] The evangelist evidently looks upon Nazareth not as the home to which they naturally returned, but as a place of refuge which was chosen because it was distant from their home.

It is not credible that Matthew, if, as there is good reason to believe, he derived his information ultimately from Joseph, should have been ignorant of the home in Nazareth, nor is it likely that he refused to name it because he shared the Jewish contempt for Galilee; for why then should he call attention to the prophecy, "He shall be called a Nazarene"?

The answer to the apparent contradiction between

[26] Matt. ii. 23.

the Gospels here is that the plan of Matthew's work with its distinctly theocratic and messianic character did not require the early mention of Nazareth, but led him to lay great stress on the birth in Bethlehem. It was of little consequence to him that the home of Jesus' parents was in Galilee, but it was of the utmost consequence that the prophecies of the Christ were fulfilled by the birth of Jesus in Bethlehem, and his later abode in Nazareth.

(2) Luke's account of the census under Quirinius is called in question on various grounds.

(a) History knows nothing of a general census of the empire in the reign of Augustus.

The attempt has been made to meet the objection by limiting *all the world* to Palestine. But the Roman Empire is plainly indicated by the phrase itself and by the reference to the Emperor.

Is this statement of Luke in accord with the facts of history?

As we enter upon our inquiry we must bear in mind the obscurity that broods over this period of Roman history. Prof. Ramsay tells us that "the reign of Augustus, as is well known, is enveloped in the deepest obscurity. While we are usually well informed about the immediately preceding period of Roman history, and for part of the reign of his successor, Tiberius, we possess the elaborate and accurate, though in some respects strongly prejudiced account of Tacitus, the facts of Augustus' reign have to be pieced together from scanty, incomplete, and disjointed authorities." [27] "Evidence about the details of the Augustan system of provincial administration had almost completely perished, until inscriptions began to reveal a few isolated facts." [28] And again, "The latter part of the reign of Augustus, in fact, the whole period from about 15 B. C. to the beginning of the reign

[27] *Was Christ Born at Bethlehem?*, p. 49.   [28] *Id.*, p. 166.

of Tiberius in 14 A. D., is almost completely hidden from our knowledge." [29]

And Mommsen speaks to the same effect:

> The history of Rome under the Empire presents problems similar to those encountered in the history of the earlier Republic. Such information as may be directly obtained from literary tradition is not merely without form and color, but in fact for the most part without substance. . . . The internal development of the commonwealth is perhaps exhibited in the traditional accounts more fully for the earlier republic than for the imperial period; in the former case there is preserved a picture—however bedimmed and falsified—of the changes of political order that were brought at least to their ultimate issue in the open Forum of Rome; in the latter case the arrangements are settled in the imperial cabinet, and come before the public, as a rule, merely in unimportant matters of form. . . . Anyone who has recourse to the so-called authorities for the history of this period—even the better among them—finds difficulty in controlling his indignation at the telling of what deserved to be suppressed, and at the suppression of what there was need to tell.[30]

We need not be surprised, then, if we find statements in the Gospels which are not confirmed by the historians of the time; and we shall be slow to impute error to honest and intelligent writers who treated of matters which happened under their own observation or within the range of contemporary inquiry.

There is no mention of a general census under Augustus in Tacitus or Suetonius; or in Josephus, though he records the later census of 6 A. D., and though, as

[29] *Expositor*, Series 8, Vol. 4, p. 387.
[30] *Provinces of the Roman Empire*, i, pp. 3-5.

Schürer affirms, "In regard to no other period is Josephus so well informed, in regard to none is his narrative so full, as in regard to the last years of Herod." [31] Yet Schürer also observes that the *Antiquities* was evidently much more carelessly prepared than the History of the Wars of the Jews.

> This is specially true about the last books, of which it has been remarked that when writing them the author must have been utterly wearied. And not only is the work carelessly done, but also the sources are often used with great freedom and the utmost arbitrariness, at least where we are in a position to criticize them. This is not calculated to produce much confidence in the use of those sources that we can no longer verify. [32]

If this be true, the silence of the *Antiquities* will not outweigh the affirmation of the Gospel. It is true, however, that the more accurate *Wars of the Jews* contains no reference to the enrolment which Luke records.

Nor again does Augustus make mention of it in the *Monumentum Ancyranum,* the records of those acts and achievements of his reign which he deemed most worthy of commemoration. [33]

We have no explicit confirmation of Luke's record from any source. Yet there are various indications that a census of this kind would have been in harmony with the policy of the sagacious ruler to whom Luke ascribes it. After speaking of Julius Caesar's ordinance providing for a census of Italy Mommsen adds:

[31] *HJP.,* I, 2, 129.

[32] *Id.,* I, 1, 98. In *Schaff-Herzog Encycl.* Schürer indicates that "the last books" referred to are particularly books 18-20, which treat of the period following the death of Herod. *Cf.* Edersheim *Dict. Chr. Biog.,* art. "Josephus," p. 449, pp. 455 ff.

[33] The text of this inscription as restored by Mommsen is given in Wieseler's *Chron. of the Gospels,* p. 88. See also Schürer, I, 1, 115, 354.

That it was Caesar's intention to introduce similar institutions also in the provinces is attested partly by the measurement and survey of the whole empire ordered by him, partly by the nature of the arrangement itself; for it in fact furnished the general instrument appropriate for procuring. as well in the Italian as in the non-Italian communities of the state, the information requisite for the central administration. Evidently here too it was Caesar's intention to revert to the traditions of the earlier republican times, and to reintroduce the census of the empire, which the earlier republic had effected. . . . This had been one of the first institutions which the torpid aristocracy allowed to drop, and in this way deprived the supreme government authority of any general view of the resources in men and taxation at its disposal, and consequently of all possibility of an effective control.[34] The indications still extant, and the very connection of things, show irrefragably that Caesar made preparations to renew the general census that had been obsolete for centuries.[35]

Augustus followed in the footsteps of his uncle. Suetonius tells us that he thrice took a census of the Roman citizens;[36] and that in the third codicil of his will "he had drawn up a concise account of the state of the empire; the number of troops enrolled, what money there was in the treasury, the revenues, and arrears of taxes."[37] In 27 B. C. he made a census of Gaul.[38] Papyri have recently been brought to light in Egypt which show that a census was taken there in the early days of the empire at intervals of fourteen

[34] II, 402.
[35] Hist. Rome, IV, 653, 4.
[36] Aug. 27.
[37] Id., 101.
[38] Mommsen, Prov. R. Emp., 1, 91.

years, and the evidence upon this point goes as far back as 20 A. D.[39]

There are also indications that enrolments were made from time to time in Syria. That a census was taken in 6 A. D. is attested by Josephus,[40] as well as by Luke.[41] Tertullian affirms that "there is historical proof that at this very time"—during the life of Jesus—"a census had been taken in Judea by Sentius Saturninus, which might have satisfied their inquiry respecting the family and descent of Christ."[42] That he names Saturninus instead of Quirinius suggests that he did not rely upon Luke in this matter, but drew his information from other sources. An inscription has been preserved which relates that a Roman officer made an enrolment of the inhabitants of Apamea, in Syria, by order of Quirinius, but no date is given.[43] In 35 A. D. the order to take a census of the Clitae, a people subject to Archelaus, King of Cappodocia, provoked resistance;[44] and the Clitae were of Cilicia, which formed part of the province of Syria.[45] Justin Martyr, about 150, affirms that the birth of Jesus in Bethlehem may be ascertained "from the registers of the taxing made under Cyrenius, your first procurator in Judea."[46] Cyrenius and Quirinius are different forms of the same name. Justin thus appeals to public records still preserved and accessible, which demonstrate the truth of Luke's account. Clement of Alexandria, about 195, says that "our Lord was born in the twenty-eighth year" (of Augustus) "when first the census was ordered to be taken in the reign of Augustus";[47] but he appeals

[38] Art. "Papyri," *HBD.*, extra vol. 356. Ramsay, *Was Christ Born at Bethlehem?*, Pref. x note, pp. 131, 166, 7.
[40] *Ant.*, XVIII, 1, 1.   [41] Acts v. 37.   [42] *Agt. Marcion*, 4, 19.
[43] Ramsay, p. 150, *Expositor*, series 8, vol. 4, p. 406. Schürer I, 1, 357.
[44] Tacitus *Ann.*, 6, 4.   Schürer I, 2, 123.
[45] Schürer I, 1, 352.   [46] *Apol.* 1, 34.   [47] Strom. i. 21.

to the authority of Luke and cannot be cited as an independent witness.

From such facts as these it is not a long or difficult step to infer that a general census of the empire was decreed by Augustus, though it may not have been taken everywhere at the same time or in the same manner. Schürer holds that Luke was mistaken, yet reaches the conclusion "that in the time of Augustus valuation censuses had been made in many provinces." [48]   There is no reason why these enrolments should not have been made in pursuance of a general comprehensive plan, and Luke might well have gathered them up in a single phrase, as the local famines that occurred in the days of Claudius are described as *the famine*.[49] Luke does not affirm that a census was taken at the time throughout the empire, or even that a general census was taken at all. The decree was issued, but circumstances may have delayed or prevented the execution of it in certain districts. He simply affirms that a census was taken in Syria in obedience to the edict of the emperor. Whether the imperial order was actually carried out elsewhere he is not concerned to inquire. He is primarily an evangelist, not a historian, and is interested in the history only as it is related to the gospel. We shall never understand the Gospels if we endeavour to impose upon them the aims and methods of the modern historian.

The judgments of men will always differ in weighing evidence of this kind, which is not demonstrative, but yields only a balance of probabilities, for judgment is swayed by prepossession and prejudice, from which no man is wholly free. But in the case before us it should not be difficult to recognize that while the facts presented do not establish the taking of a general census under Augustus, yet they show that such a census was

[48] *HJP.*, I, 2, 120.   [49] Acts xi, 28.

not impossible, or even improbable, in view of the established policy of the empire. And if we add to this probability the general accuracy of Luke regarding matters in which he may be put to the test, we need have no hesitation in following his guidance here. The word of the Evangelist may reasonably be held to outweigh the silence of Josephus, who may have recorded the second census because of the disorders to which it gave rise, while no such consequences attended the first census, for reasons which will hereafter appear.

(b) If such a census had been taken it would not have extended to Judea, which was at that time an independent kingdom.

It is true that Judea was not formally incorporated with the empire until 6 A. D., but to speak of it as independent in the days of Herod is altogether misleading. He received the kingdom by decree of the Senate through the good will of Marc Antony,[50] and after the battle of Actium his authority was confirmed by Augustus, and the boundaries of his kingdom were enlarged.[51] From time to time he sent ambassadors to Rome and three times went there in person, to avert the anger or win the favour of the emperor. He sought and obtained the permission of Augustus to put his sons to death, and to dispose of his kingdom by will.[52] Near the close of his reign he made war upon the Arabians without asking leave, and incurred the displeasure of the emperor, who wrote to him that whereas he had used him as a friend he should now use him as his subject.[53] About the same time Herod exacted of the Jews an oath of allegiance to Caesar, which some of them refused to take, and were punished for their disobedience.[54] When the kingdom was

[50] Josephus *Ant.* XIV, 14, 4, 5.   [51] *Id.*, XV, 6, 6, 7; 7, 3.
[52] *Id.*, *Wars* XXVII, II, 23; *Ant.* XVII, 11, 4.
[53] *Id.*, *Ant.* XVI, 9, 3.
[54] *Id.*, XVII, 2, 4; Schürer *HJP.*, I, 1, 445, note 94.

divided between the sons of Herod, soon after the birth of Christ, Augustus ordered that the taxes of Idumea, Judea, and Samaria should be reduced by one-fourth, because they had taken no part in the revolt against Varus, the Roman governor.[55]

While this review does not show of course that a census was taken in Judea by order of Augustus in the days of Herod, it does show that Herod enjoyed no real independence and that a decree of the emperor would be as effective in Judea as in any province of the empire.

The position indeed of Herod as an Idumean, hated and feared by the Jews, compelled him to rely upon the support of Rome:

> From the Roman standpoint the conduct of the new dynasty appears correct . . . the fulfilment of duty such as the Roman commonwealth claimed from its subjects, had been satisfied by King Herod to an extent of which nobler and greater natures would certainly not have been capable.[56]

Schürer impugns the accuracy of Luke, chiefly upon the ground that "Josephus characterizes the census of 7 A. D. as something entirely new and previously unheard of among the Jews," and he concludes that "Roman taxes could not possibly have been raised in Palestine in the time of Herod." [57] But the force of the argument is greatly weakened, if not destroyed, by the natural supposition that the census was conducted not by Roman officials after the Roman method, but by Herod according to the custom of the Jews. That is implied in Luke's statement that "all went to enrol

[55] *Ant.* XVII, 11, 4.
[56] Mommsen *Provs.* II, p. 195. See also Schürer *HJP.*, I., 1, pp. 448 ff.
[57] *HJP.*, I, 2, 131, 132.

themselves, every one to his own city," will account for the absence of such disorders as accompanied the later census, and is in harmony with the imperial policy in dealing with the Jews.

(c) The most serious difficulty that Luke's narrative presents at this point is the reference to Quirinius. "This was the first enrolment made when Quirinius was governor of Syria." History seems to allow no room for Quirinius as governor of Syria before the death of Herod in the spring of 4 B. C. Saturninus was governor from 9 to 6 B. C., and Varus from 6 until after Herod's death.[58] [59] In 6 A. D. Quirinius[60] was governor, and under him the census was taken which is recorded in Acts v. 37 and Josephus *Ant.* XVIII, 1, 1. Of the interval between 4 B. C. and 6 A. D. little is known, but it is generally agreed that during part of this time Quirinius was governor of Syria.[61] Yet if this be granted it does not remove the difficulty, for there appears to be no place for Quirinius within the time indicated by Luke. Nor does it avail to throw back the date of Jesus' birth to 8 B. C., as Ramsay does,[62] for then we are confronted by Saturninus.

It is interesting to note in passing that the same volume of the *Expositor* in which this article of Prof. Ramsay's appears contains also a paper by Prof. Kirsopp Lake, in which he suggests 6 A. D. as the probable date of the birth. That such a wide diversity of opinion is possible indicates the obscurity which envelopes the whole period, and suggests that we should be slow to impute error to a writer who was removed at the

[58] Josephus *Ant.* XVII, 9, 3; 10, 1.

[59] The list of Roman governors of Syria is given in Schürer, *HJP.*, I, 1, pp, 328 ff.

[60] The career of Quirinius is sketched by Tacitus *Ann.* III, 48.

[61] The famous argument of Zumpt is given in outline in Wieseler, *Chron. Gospels*, pp. 143 ff.

[62] *Expositor*, 8th series, vol. IV, p. 386.

utmost by a single generation from the events which he relates, and who had at his command sources of information which have long since perished.

In view of this historical situation is it possible to maintain the accuracy of the Evangelist?

We may set aside without hesitation the conjecture that Luke confuses the census taken under Herod with the census of Acts v. 37, as Eusebius does.[63] On the contrary, he expressly distinguishes them—"this was the first." It is simply incredible that he should allude to a census before the death of Herod and to another ten years later, and confound them.

Nor, on the other hand, may we resort to the exegetical shift employed by some scholars, which gives to πρώτη a comparative sense; and reads, "The ἀπογραφὴ took place as the first, and before Quirinius was governor of Syria."[64] It is obviously true that πρῶτος may be used in this sense when it is followed simply by a noun or a pronoun;[65] but no instance has been adduced to show that it may be so used when it is followed by a clause.[66] And if the construction should be admitted Luke has chosen a curiously awkward mode of dating the census. Was Quirinius of such importance from the evangelist's point of view that the name of the governor by whom the census was actually taken should be set aside for his? Luke has not elsewhere shown himself so obtuse as to go out of his way to create a needless difficulty.

Two other methods of meeting the objection are proposed. (1) The census may have been begun under an earlier governor, interrupted by the disorders that followed the death of Herod,[67] and taken up and completed by Quirinius when he assumed office. But again

[63] *Ch. H.,* I, 1, 5.
[64] Wieseler, *Chron. Gospels,* p. 116.
[65] John i. 15, 30.
[66] Winer *Gram.,* p. 244; Robertson *Gram. of Greek N. T.,* p. 669.
[67] Josephus *Wars* II, 1-6; *Ant.* XVII, 9.

we ask, why should Luke pass over the governor under whose rule Jesus was born, and name Quirinius, who came into office after his birth? The fact that the second census was taken during his administration gives no sufficient reason to refer the first census to him, when that census is recorded simply because it gave occasion for the birth of Jesus in Bethlehem. Again it appears that to name Quirinius is to involve the narrative in needless confusion. This solution therefore has little to commend it. (2) The terms *govern* (ἡγεμονεύω), *governor, government* are used in various senses, referring to officers of different rank, proconsuls, propraetors, that is, governors of senatorial and imperial provinces, and even to the emperor himself.[68] Syria was an imperial province, and the legate through whom the emperor administered the government was the governor. In addition to this officer a legate might be dispatched to perform certain specific duties, such as the conduct of military operations, or the care of the finances of the province. While Varus held the office of governor, Quirinius may have been sent upon a particular mission, and might also be termed governor as the personal representative of him to whom the government belonged.

We learn from Tacitus [69] that Quirinius waged war against the Homonadenses, a barbarous people on the frontier of Galatia. The date cannot be precisely fixed, but it was during the administration of Varus, who was without military skill, while Quirinius was a trained soldier. With the conduct of the campaign the taking of the census may have been entrusted to him, and that would furnish sufficient reason to fix the date by reference to him rather than to Varus.

That the administration of the province should thus be divided is in accord with Roman custom. Examples are given by Ramsay.[70] We may add to the instances

<hr />

[68] Luke iii. 1.   [69] *Ann.* 3, 48.
[70] *Was Christ born at Bethlehem?*, pp. 238 ff.

there adduced that according to Josephus the second census, in 6 A. D., was taken by Quirinius as governor of Syria, while Coponius was governor of Judea, which had been added to the province of Syria.[71]   And again he speaks of Saturninus and Volumnius as "the governors (ἡγεμόνες) of Syria."[72]   Here is sufficient warrant for Luke's ascription of the title *governor* to Quirinius even if he discharged simply the duties of a special legate, and in this double office we may find the explanation of Tertullian's statement that the census was taken by Saturninus,[73] if we may suppose that Quirinius began the work under Saturninus and completed it under Varus.

No certainty can be obtained in dealing with matters embraced in this obscure period of history; but if a final solution of the difficulty has not been found, yet it appears that there are ways of solving it which are possible, even probable, in the light of such knowledge as we possess.

(d) It is objected that even if a census were taken in Judea at the time alleged, Joseph and Mary would not have been required to journey to Bethlehem. But there is good reason to believe that the census was taken not according to the Roman but according to the Jewish mode. Augustus and Herod might well respect the prejudices of a people so stubborn as the Jews in order not to provoke such an outbreak as attended the second census. That all should be required to go to their own cities was not strange either to the Roman, since the citizens from all parts of Italy must journey to Rome in order to vote; or to the Jew, who was commanded by the law of Moses to present himself three times every year in the appointed place.[74] And it was in accord with the policy of the emperors to

[71] *Ant. XVIII*, i, 1.
[72] *Id., XVI*, 9, 1.
[73] *Agt. Marcion* IV, 19.
[74] Deut. xvi.

conform to local customs in matters of this kind.[75]
Mary as well as Joseph was of the house and family
of David, and whether women were required to present
themselves or not, her condition would lead her to
accompany her husband. Moreover she was familiar
with the prophecy that the child of whom she was
soon to be delivered should be born in Bethlehem.
Here are surely sufficient reasons for her journey.

(3) The objection is also raised that the slaughter
of the children in Bethlehem by order of Herod is
nowhere recorded in secular history. That is true.
But the number of children of two years old and under
in a village like Bethlehem was very small; and the
deed ascribed to Herod is in entire accord with his
character.

> There is probably no royal house of any age in
> which blood feuds raged in an equal degree
> between parents and children, between husbands
> and wives, and between brothers and sisters; the
> emperor Augustus and his governors in Syria
> turned away with horror from the share in the
> work of murder which was suggested to them;
> not the least revolting trait in this picture of
> horrors is the utter want of object in most of the
> persecutions.[76]

In this orgy of crime is it strange that the death of a
few children in a little town should pass unnoticed by
the historians of the period?

How precarious is the argument from silence, how
an event which attracts world-wide attention in later
days may pass unnoted at the time, is illustrated by
the massacre of Glencoe, Scotland, in 1692.

> It may be thought strange that these events
> should not have been instantly followed by a

[75] Ramsay, *Was Christ born at Bethlehem?*, pp. 185 ff. *Expositor*,
8th Series, vol. IV, pp. 484 ff.
[76] Mommsen *Provs. R. E.*, 2, 196.

burst of execration from every part of the civilized
world. The fact, however, is that years elapsed
before the public indignation was thoroughly
awakened and that months elapsed before the
blackest part of the story found credit even among
the enemies of the government. That the massacre should not have been mentioned in the London
Gazettes, in the Monthly Mercuries, which were
scarcely less courtly than the Gazettes, or in
pamphlets licensed by official censors, is perfectly
intelligible. But that no allusion should be found
in private journals and letters, written by persons
free from all restraint, may seem extraordinary.
There is not a word on the subject in Evelyn's
Diary. In Narcissus Luttrell's Diary is a remarkable entry made five weeks after the butchery.
The letters from Scotland, he says, described that
kingdom as perfectly tranquil, except that there
was still some grumbling about ecclesiastical questions. The Dutch ministers regularly reported
all the Scotch news to their government. They
thought it worth while, about this time, to mention that a collier had been taken by a privateer
near Berwick, that the Edinburgh mail had been
robbed, that a whale with a tongue seventeen feet
long, and seven feet broad, had been stranded near
Aberdeen. But it is not hinted in any of their
dispatches that there was any rumor of an extraordinary occurrence in the Highlands. . . . At
length, near a year after the crime had been committed, it was published to the world."[77]

(4) The genealogies of Matthew and Luke are said
to be hopelessly at variance with each other.

We need not stop to inquire whether both Gospels
give the genealogy of Joseph or Luke traces the line of
Mary. The fathers generally believed that Mary too

[77] Macaulay's *Hist. of Eng.*, Ch. xvii.

was of the family of David.[78] The Syriac Sinaitic manuscript expressly affirms it;[79] and it is clearly implied in such passages as Ps. cxxxii. 11; Acts ii. 30; xiii. 23; Rom. i. 3. Taken in connexion with the promise on which they are based—"I will set up thy seed after thee, that shall proceed out of thy bowels"[80] —these passages may fairly be termed conclusive. Mary's kinship to Elisabeth, who was of the tribe of Levi,[81] presents no difficulty, for marriage between the tribes was not forbidden, as Eusebius affirms.[82] There is no antecedent objection to the view that Luke records the genealogy of Mary, and thus the descent of Jesus from David is traced through both father and mother. Whether this is actually the case must be determined by a careful examination of the genealogies, upon which we cannot enter. For our present purpose the inquiry is unnecessary, for even if both genealogies should be referred to Joseph there is no difficulty in supposing that Matthew pursued the line of legal and Luke of actual descent; one records the succession of legal heirs to the throne of David, through whom the title was transmitted to Jesus, and the other traces the line of the actual progenitors of Joseph, his reputed father.[83] For Matthew is chiefly concerned to present Jesus as the Christ, the heir of David, and Luke to portray him as the Son of man; Matthew therefore traces his descent from Abraham through David, that he may appear to be the heir of the covenant with Abraham and the promise to David; while Luke follows the line of his descent to Adam, father of the race, and beyond Adam to God.

[78] Justin Martyr *Dial.*, 45, 100; Iren. *Her.* III, 21, 5; Warfield *Pres. Rev.*, 1881, p. 388.
[79] Luke ii. 5.
[80] II Sam. vii. 12.
[81] Luke i. 5.
[82] *Ch. H.*, I, 7; McGiffert's note 35.
[83] Andrews' *Life of Christ*, p. 55.

Both evangelists are careful to note that Joseph was not the actual father of Jesus. Matthew breaks the chain of the genealogy when he comes to him, not affirming as in every other case that Jesus was begotten by Joseph, but that he was born of Mary. And Luke calls him the son, *as was supposed*, of Joseph.

Whether then both Gospels furnish the genealogy of Joseph, or Luke records the genealogy of Mary, in neither case can a contradiction be shown. The genealogies differ because, whichever theory be adopted, they employ different methods and pursue different roads.

(5) The most weighty objection to the truth of the narrative is drawn from the silence of the remainder of the New Testament. Neither in the other Gospels, it is asserted, nor in the Acts, the Epistles, the Revelation, may a single clear allusion to the virgin birth be found. Yet if Jesus was really born of the virgin Mary the fact must have been known to many in the early church; certainly to Paul through his intimacy with Luke, and to John through his acquaintance with the earlier Gospels and his filial relation to Mary. Why then does an event of such transcendent importance find no place in their teaching?

Let us first seek to ascertain the facts of the case and then inquire what is the bearing of those facts upon the truth of the narrative.

Certain references to the virgin birth are adduced from various parts of the New Testament, but none of them will bear examination. Mark begins his Gospel with the ministry of John the Baptist. John attests the fact, but says nothing of the mode of the incarnation. "The word became flesh"—how, we are not told. It is in accord with his usual method to omit what has been sufficiently related by the earlier evangelists. It is not surprising therefore that the virgin birth is not recorded in the Second or Fourth Gospel.

Certain passages indeed are cited from John's Gospel as alluding to the virgin birth, but without sufficient warrant. In i. 13 some of the fathers substitute the singular for the plural, reading, "Who was born" instead of "who were born," and refer the passage to the incarnation.[84] Though this reading is accepted by Zahn [85] the evidence against it is so overwhelming that it may be dismissed without further consideration. But it is said that even though we cannot accept the reading yet

> it is on the track of a right idea. It is the mode of Christ's birth which is in view, and which furnishes the type of the (spiritual) new birth of believers. As Paul in Ephes. i. 19 takes God's mighty power in raising Christ from the dead as the type of the quickening of believers . . . so John takes as a pattern the divine begetting of Christ in his conception by the Holy Spirit.[86]

"John described the birth of the children of God according to the analogy of the birth of the only begotten Son of God." [87]

But the thought of Christ's birth as the pattern of the new birth of believers is obviously imposed upon the text rather than drawn from it. The doctrine is beset with difficulties enough without compelling it to bear the burden of a forced and artificial exegesis. The passage simply expresses in another form the truth which Nicodemus learned from the lips of Jesus, "Except one be born of water and the Spirit, he cannot

---

[84] Iren. *Her.* III, 16, 2; 19, 2. Tertullian affirms that the singular was changed to the plural by heretics: *On the Flesh of Christ*, 19.

[85] *N. T. Intro.*, III, p. 266.

[86] Orr, *Virgin Birth*, p. 112. G. H. Box, *Virgin Birth*, p. 146. See in opposition Prof. Machen, *Princeton Theol. Rev.*, 1905, p. 660. His treatment of the silence of Scripture is judicious and satisfactory throughout.

[87] Zahn *Int. N. T.* III, p. 266. See also Allen, *Comm. on Matthew*, p. 20.

enter into the kingdom of God. That which is born
of the flesh is flesh, and that which is born of the
Spirit is spirit." [88]   John's words are in harmony with
the doctrine of the virgin birth, but they do not suggest it or lend it substantial support.

In John i. 14—"We beheld his glory, glory as of
the only-begotten from the Father"—the word *only-
begotten* (μονογενοῦς) is referred by some scholars
to the miraculous birth of Jesus, but it properly relates to his eternal generation. Jesus did not become
the only-begotten Son at his incarnation, for he was
in the beginning with God. He is identified with
men through the incarnation, distinguished from them
by his eternal sonship.

When we turn to Paul we discover nowhere in his
Epistles a clear and distinct allusion to the virgin
birth. It must be borne in mind that the emphasis
of apostolic preaching and teaching was laid upon three
supreme facts, the incarnation, the atoning death and
the resurrection of Jesus.

In Romans i. 3, 4—"concerning his Son, who was
born of the seed of David according to the flesh, who
was declared to be the Son of God with power, according to the spirit of holiness, by the resurrection from
the dead"—Paul has in mind the human and divine
natures of Christ, but gives no indication of the nature
of his birth. If we read, Spirit of holiness, the reference is obviously to the power of the Holy Spirit not
in conceiving Jesus, but in raising him from the dead.
But the antithesis of flesh and spirit shows that the
proper rendering is that which is given by both the
Authorized and the Revised Versions—*spirit of holiness*—signifying the divine nature of the Son, as σάρξ
denotes his humanity. Nor may an allusion to the
virgin birth be found in the representation of Christ
as the second Adam,[89] where Adam and Christ, the

[88] John iii. 5, 6.   [89] I Cor. xv. 45.

heads and representatives of mankind as created and redeemed, are contrasted as created—"a living soul" —and creator—"a life-giving spirit." Here again the phrase is in harmony with the doctrine of the virgin birth, but does not of itself suggest it or indicate that it was known.

In Galatians iv. 4 Jesus is said to have been born of a woman. Similar phrases are used in Job xiv. 1; Mat. xi. 11; Luke vii. 28, and may be applied to every human being. It is true that Matthew and Luke have γεννητοῖς while Paul has γενόμενον, but to find in this difference an allusion to the virgin birth, as Orr does,[90] is wholly unwarranted. The ablest commentators recognize that Paul here affirms the true humanity of Christ, but gives no intimation of the way by which he entered human life.[91]

I Tim. ii. 14, 15—"the woman being beguiled hath fallen into transgression: but she shall be saved through her child bearing; if they continue in faith and love and sanctification with sobriety"—is interpreted by Ellicott and others as referring to the primal promise that the seed of the woman shall bruise the serpent's head;[92] by most scholars as referring to the obedience of woman to the divine law through the discharge of the proper function of her sex, a view which is sustained by the closing words of the verse. But in neither case is there an allusion to the virgin birth.

In the vision of Rev. xii. 1 the woman represents the church, and there is no hint of her virginity.

From this review which embraces the chief passages adduced from all portions of the New Testament to support the narrative of the Evangelists, it appears that beyond the First and Third Gospels there is not a single passage in any New Testament writing

[90] *Virgin Birth*, p. 118.
[91] So Lightfoot, Ellicott, Meyer, Burton.
[92] Gen. iii. 15.

which affirms or even distinctly implies the virgin birth.

We proceed to inquire what is the bearing of this fact upon the credibility of the Gospel story.

(1)   While there is no passage elsewhere in the New Testament which directly confirms the narrative of Matthew and Luke, it is equally true that there is none which contradicts it or is inconsistent with it.

Upon several occasions Jesus is termed the son of Joseph. In Luke iv. 22 the men of Nazareth inquire, "Is not this Joseph's son?" In John i. 45 Philip tells Nathanael, "We have found him, of whom Moses in the law, and the prophets, wrote, Jesus of Nazareth, the son of Joseph." In Matt. xiii. 55 the men of his own country ask, "Is not this the carpenter's son?" While the parallel passage in Mark vi. 3 reads, "Is not this the carpenter?" Both expressions no doubt were used as the people questioned one with another.

Joseph was of course regarded as the father of Jesus by those who were ignorant of his supernatural birth, but their ignorance throws no discredit upon the narrative. It appears moreover that Joseph was called his father even by those who were acquainted with the circumstances of his birth. When Jesus was brought into the temple, Simeon took him in his arms, and blessed God; and Luke adds that "his father and his mother were marvelling at the things which were spoken concerning him." [93] Several times he speaks of the parents of Jesus.[94] And Mary herself said to Jesus when she found him in the temple, "Thy father and I sought thee sorrowing." [95] Joseph is properly called the father of Jesus on the ground of his legal relationship, and the term throws no doubt upon the virgin birth.

(2)   How easily the story of Jesus' birth gave rise

[93] Luke ii. 33.   [94] Luke ii. 27, 41, 43.   [95] Luke ii. 48.

to scandal appears very early in the history of the church in the coarse slander which Celsus puts in the mouth of a Jew.[99] And how even a Christian, with the Gospel narrative to guide him, could profane the chaste mystery of the holy birth is shown by the Protevangelium of James, which is perhaps as old as the second century, with its gross and sensual details. The matter was of such a nature that it must be treated with the utmost delicacy and reserve, lest it should become a scandal and an offence. This phase of the subject is well treated by Allen, *International Critical Commentary,* on Matthew, p. 20. The same difficulty confronts the missionary today. Rev. G. G. Warren, for thirty-five years engaged in mission work in China, writes in the *Biblical Review,* Jan., 1922, p. 49:

> I have intentionally avoided the slightest reference to the doctrine of the virgin birth in all my addresses to non-Christians. One early experience of the unclean reasonings of an unclean hearer who retorted on a Chinese preacher's allusions to the doctrine made an unfaded impression upon me. General church history confirms the individual experience that unbelievers are more likely to blaspheme than to be converted by allusions to the virginity of the mother of our Lord.

(3) The virgin birth could not be established, like the resurrection, by the testimony of eye witnesses. It rested upon the unsupported word of Mary, and by its very nature was incapable of proof. Until the general truthfulness of the Gospel narrative had been demonstrated, an event lying so far beyond the limits of experience might easily become a stumbling-block in the way of faith. The apostles were eye witnesses of the resurrection, but who save Mary could bear

[99] Origen *Agt. Celsus,* I, 28, 32.

personal testimony to the manner of the birth in Bethlehem?

(4)   Evidently the New Testament writers did not hold the virgin birth to be an essential article of saving faith, like the incarnation, the death, the resurrection of Jesus. If they believed that the acceptance of it was necessary to life and godliness, their silence is inexplicable. Paul must have known of it, if it really occurred, and John; and if it had not been disclosed to them in other ways, it would have been communicated to them by special revelation as an essential part of the Gospel message. Among the revelations which Paul declares were granted him, how could this have failed to find a place? In face of all hindrances and dangers it would have been proclaimed, as Paul set the cross in the forefront of his preaching, though it was to the Jews a stumbling-block, and to the Greeks foolishness. But nowhere does he allude to the virgin birth: not in the earliest creed contained in I Cor. xv. 3, 4, which has two articles only, the death and resurrection of Jesus, nor in the fuller statement of doctrine found in I Tim. iii. 16, regarding the mystery of godliness. The fact of the incarnation is of vital importance, the manner of it is not; or Paul, though he affirmed that he shrank not from declaring to men the whole counsel of God [97] has preached a sadly mutilated gospel. The virgin birth cannot be placed beside the incarnation, the sacrificial death, the resurrection of the Son of God as an essential article of saving faith. Nothing may be deemed essential which did not find a place in the preaching and teaching of the apostles.[98] But this is not the whole of the matter.

We must distinguish clearly here, and when we ask whether a doctrine is essential, we must inquire fur-

[97] Acts xx. 27.
[98] Sweet, *Birth and Infancy of Jesus Christ*, pp. 280, 290.

ther, essential to what? A doctrine may not be essential to saving faith, so that none may be saved without the knowledge of it; and yet may be essential to the full exhibition of the truth as it is in Jesus. And that is exactly the position of the doctrine of the virgin birth. It is not essential to saving faith, like the incarnation and the atonement of the Son of God; but it is essential to any system of theology which professes to be based upon the teaching of the Scripture. Those who have never heard of the virgin birth may be saved through the grace of Christ, as is abundantly attested by the whole history of the church from the day of Pentecost to our own time; but once the truth has been made known it cannot be rejected without repudiating the clear teaching of the Word. Fundamentally the question at issue is simply the authority of the Word of God. Are we bound as Christians to accept the teaching of the Scripture, or are we at liberty to sit in judgement upon the Word, and reject whatever does not comport with our preferences and opinions? The doctrine of the virgin birth is essential to a thorough Biblical theology; it is not essential to saving faith.

(5) The virgin birth is as fully attested historically as the nature of the case admits, is in harmony with the whole course of New Testament teaching, has held a place in the faith of the church from the beginning, and is therefore to be accepted as an integral part of the gospel record. We may conjecture that this was not the only way in which the Son of God might have taken upon himself our nature; that as he was born without sin of a human mother, so he might have been born without sin of a human father and mother.[99] This too lay within the power of God. In either case

[99] Turrettin notes four ways in which men are made: Adam immediately by God; Eve from the man without woman; all men since from man and woman; Jesus from woman without man. *Theol. Loc.,* 13. Qu. 16:19.

his birth would be supernatural, for the sinless cannot proceed from the sinful without the direct interposition of the Almighty. We cannot affirm that only in this way could the Son of God become the Son of man. But this was the way divinely chosen and ordained, and it accords with the dignity of his Person and the unique nature of his work that he should enter into human life by a new way, a way which distinguishes him from all men besides. He is at once identified with men through his mother, and set apart from them by his conception through the Spirit.

As we could not apprehend from the Old Testament the personality of the Spirit, yet when that truth is brought to light all the earlier teaching is seen to be in harmony with it; so there is in the New Testament, apart from Matthew and Luke, no clear intimation of the mystery of the birth in Bethlehem: yet when the truth has been revealed the teaching of all the evangelists and apostles is found to be in full accord with it.

Accepting then the authenticity and integrity of the narratives, and having considered the contradictions and inconsistencies which they are alleged to contain, we are prepared to inquire from what sources they have been derived.

There are those who ascribe to them a mythical or legendary origin. The question at once arises, Where shall room be found for the growth of myth or legend? The Gospels were written before the close of the century, and the traditions from which they drew their material, whether oral or written, go back to the time of the events which they relate. But the chronological argument against the mythical theory, whatever weight we may attach to it, cannot be regarded as decisive. The stories of the divine birth of Augustus and the return of Nero indicate how quickly legends may arise and how rapidly they may spread.[100]   And it is also true that legends relating to the birth of Jesus arose at an early date. The Gospel of Thomas as well as the Protevangelium of James is referred by some scholars to the middle of the second century;[101] and if a later date be assigned to these works they bear witness to early traditions. The argument sometimes advanced, therefore, that myth or legend could not have arisen so quickly is too precarious to furnish a foundation for faith. The utmost that may be claimed is that the balance of probability at this point is somewhat in favour of the Gospel story.

There are two forms in which this mythical theory is held:

(1) the myth was of Jewish origin, and the germ of it is the passage which Matthew quotes from Isaiah vii. 14—"Behold, the virgin shall be with child, and shall bring forth a son, and they shall call his name Immanuel." [102]   The precise meaning of these words will be considered hereafter. It may suffice here to observe that there is no reason to believe that the passage was ever interpreted by the Jews in a Messianic sense. It is not named in Schürer's representation of the Messianic doctrine of the Jews,[103] nor in Edersheim's list of Old Testament passages Messianically applied in ancient Rabbinic writings.[104]   Dalman assures us that "no trace is to be found among the Jews of any Messianic application of Isaiah's words [105] concerning the virgin's son, from which by any possibility—as some have maintained—the whole

---

[100] Swete on Revelation, p. cii. Charles, *Intern. Crit. Comm. on Rev.*, 2, 76. Add. note on ch. XVII.

[101] On these writings see Lipsius *DCB.*, art. "Gospels Apoc."

[102] Matt. i. 23.

[103] *HJP.*, II, 2, p. 28 ff.

[104] *Life of Christ*, Appen. 9. See also *Hastings DCGs.*, II, pp. 806, 7. Orr, *Virgin Birth*, p. 288.

[105] Isa. vii. 14.

account of the miraculous birth of Jesus could have derived its origin." [106]   It may also be noted that the Jews were accustomed to exalt the married state above virginity, which was commonly considered a reproach, as Hannah and Elisabeth attest.   There was nothing in Jewish modes of thought or methods of Scripture interpretation to suggest the virgin birth.

So decisive are these considerations that the theory of a Jewish origin has little support among scholars today.

(2) it is affirmed that the myth is of heathen origin, and analogies are sought in pagan mythology, Greek, Roman, Egyptian, Babylonian.   Justin Martyr represents Trypho as comparing the story of the birth of Jesus with the Greek fable that Perseus was born of the virgin Danae.[107]

There are two insuperable objections to the theory in whatever form it may be held:

(a)   There is no real analogy between the pagan myths which are adduced and the story of the Gospels.   In every instance the resemblance alleged breaks down at the decisive point.

There are many tales of men who sprang from the gods, but the gods are conceived as having the parts and passions of men, and they beget children as men beget them.   Whatever form the god may assume, some mode of physical contact is required for generation. No comparison can be drawn between the pure chaste narrative of the Gospels and the filthy stories of heathen mythology.   The word *holy* fixes an impassable gulf between them.   What likeness may be found between the sensual lust of a Greek or Roman or Oriental divinity and the work of the Holy Spirit? What is there to answer to the unsullied virginity of

[106] *Words of Jesus*, X, 2, p. 276.
[107] *Dial.*, 67. See also *I Apol.*, 54.

Mary, or to the child who is called holy? "Who can bring a clean thing out of an unclean?"

(b) It is incredible that the gross and polytheistic myths of heathenism should have taken root in that Jewish soil from which the Gospels sprang. The spirituality and holiness of God were the first principles of the Jewish creed, and chastity held a foremost place among the virtues. By these conceptions the Jew was distinguished from the pagan world; and they were carried over to the Christian church in their highest and purest form. No part of the New Testament is more thoroughly impregnated with the thought and spirit of Palestinian Judaism in its noblest aspect than the stories of the virgin birth, and the conception of holiness dominates them throughout. How could the church suffer legends of the vilest character, degrading alike to God and man, to profane the very sanctuary of Christian truth, and give shape and colour to the representation of him who was adored as Saviour and Lord? How the church in fact regarded these heathen myths is shown in a striking way by the passages which Bishop Lightfoot has gathered from early Christian writers.[108]

Further objections to all forms of the mythical theory may be drawn from the character of the Gospel records, their historical temper, the precise notes of time and place and person and circumstance, the sober and unadorned style, the freedom from puerile conceits and silly superstitions, the elevated tone, the chaste dignity, the celestial atmosphere. And when we consider further their conformity to all that is afterward related of the character and life of Jesus, their aptness as the introduction to the Gospel story, we need have no hesitation in accepting the narrative

---

[108] *Apost. Fas.*, II, 2, 505, note 4. See G. H. Box, *Virgin Birth of Jesus,* ch. VIII.

of Matthew and Luke as a truthful record of the facts.[109]

The only reasonable explanation of the Gospel narrative is that the events here set forth actually occurred. How they came to the knowledge of the evangelists we are not told, but it is quite clear, as is generally recognized by those who accept the truthfulness of the Gospels, that Matthew derived his information ultimately from Joseph and Luke from Mary; for Joseph's point of view is given by one, and Mary's by the other. What is related of the thoughts and feelings of the father and mother must have been derived originally from them. This will appear presently in the clearest way when we set the Gospels side by side, and mark the points of resemblance and divergence which they present.

How the facts communicated by Joseph came to the knowledge of Matthew we can only surmise. Little weight may be attached to the tradition that Joseph was an old man at the time of his marriage to Mary,[110] but as he does not appear in the Gospels after the visit to Jerusalem when Jesus was twelve years old we may presume that he dies before Jesus entered upon his public ministry, and that Matthew did not learn the facts directly from him. It is possible, as some have supposed, that Joseph prepared a document setting forth the facts of the case in order to guard the good name of Mary, and that this in some way came into the hands of the evangelist. Or it may be that Matthew heard the story from some member of the family, to whom Joseph had imparted it, from Mary, from Jesus, from one of the brothers or sisters. We

[109] For further treatment of the various mythical theories see Weiss, *Life of Christ*, I, 2, 2. Gore, *Dissertations*, p. 6, App. Note A; *HDC. Gs.*, Art. "Virgin Birth"; Machen, *Princeton Theol. Rev.*, 1906, p. 66. Orr, *Virgin Birth*, Lect. VI; Allen, *Matthew*, pp. 18 ff.; Scott, *Spirit in N. T.*, p. 68.

[110] *History of Joseph the Carpenter, Antenic. Fas.*, VIII, p. 390.

are left to conjecture, for neither history nor tradition offers us a guide.

If we turn to Luke, the same uncertainty confronts us. It is evident that the primary source of his information was Mary. From whom else could he have learned of the visit of Gabriel, or obtained the key to the heart of the virgin mother? "His mother kept all these sayings in her heart." [111] It is the voice of Mary that speaks in these words, which express at once the awe and the tenderness that filled her soul. Through what channels her knowledge was conveyed to Luke is not disclosed. He may have met her when he visited Jerusalem,[112] if she was still living there at that time; or he may have heard the story from James, the brother of Jesus, whom he knew.[113] It is probable, however, that Luke made use here of written sources such as he indicates in the preface to his Gospel. The facts were made known by Mary, we may suppose, to Elisabeth, to Joseph, perhaps to others, and through them would reach a wider circle. A narrative or narratives prepared by a writer or writers to whom we have no clue preserved the story as Mary related it, and furnished the source from which Luke drew his material. The striking contrast between the preface of the Gospel, which is composed in Greek as classic as any which the New Testament presents, and the narrative in chapters i. and ii. suggests at once a Hebrew or Aramaic original for the narrative.[114] Luke may not have been acquainted with either of these languages,[115] but the documents could be readily rendered into Greek. That the peculiar cast of these chapters, which move in the sphere of Old Testament

[111] Luke ii. 51.
[112] Acts xxi. 17.
[113] Acts xxi. 17, 18.
[114] *Comm.* of Godet and Plummer; Machen, *Princeton Theol. Rev.*, 1906, pp. 47 ff.; Robertson, *Grammar Greek N. T.*, pp. 106 ff. Orr, *Virgin Birth*, p. 78.
[115] Zahn, *Int. N. T.*, III, pp. 14, 27.

thought and clothe themselves in Old Testament forms of speech, was due to conscious imitation of the style of the Old Testament by Luke, is highly improbable. For Luke was a Gentile, and his Gospel was written when the old covenant had been superseded by the new. It is hardly credible that under such conditions he should have been able to reproduce, or should have cared to reproduce, with such fidelity the thoughts and aspirations of pious Jews, and should have confined himself within the limits of Old Testament teaching. It is far more reasonable to suppose that this intensely Jewish story was drawn by the Gentile evangelist from Jewish sources.

How thoroughly Jewish it is, even a cursory glance will disclose. Apart from the words of Simeon, which will be examined hereafter, nowhere is a distinctively Christian note struck except in the recognition of the fact that the promised Christ has come. In every other respect the thought is bounded by Old Testament conceptions, and the universality characteristic of the Third Gospel nowhere appears, except in the words of Simeon. A similar difference, it may be noted, appears in the Acts, where the Hebrew character of the opening chapters is conspicuous.[116] The hymns contained in these opening chapters are thoroughly Jewish in style and spirit, and are couched largely in the language of the Old Testament, as a glance at Burton and Goodspeed's *Harmony of the Synoptic Gospels* will show. The Canticles of Mary and Zacharias indeed are in form and substance Old Testament Psalms, and might readily take their place in the Psalter, to which in fact they are appended in the *Codex Alexandrinus*.[117] When the song of Mary and the song of Hannah are set side by side in parallel

[116] Meyer on Acts. Introd., Sec. II; *HBD.*, I, 34, 2.
[117] Swete, *LXX Int.*, 253, II, VIII. See Warfield, "Messianic Psalms of N. T." *Expositor*, 3rd Series, II, pp. 301, 321; Machen, *Princeton Theol. Rev.*, 1912, p. 1.

columns, as in Plummer's *Commentary,* the resemblance indicates how thoroughly Mary was imbued with the conceptions and the language of the Old Scripture. As her spirit was profoundly moved, her emotions clothed themselves in the familiar garb of Old Testament speech.

A fuller discussion of the relation of the gospel narratives to the earlier revelation is reserved for the following chapter. We are concerned with it here only as it may throw light upon the sources from which Luke drew his information. It is probable that he made use of documents which enshrined the memories of Mary, and were written in her mother tongue. We may believe that to the mother of Jesus we owe this exquisite story of such delicacy and grace, even as we may believe that through her communion with the beloved disciple she bore a part in weaving the Fourth Gospel. Who but a mother would have remarked that the coat of Jesus was without seam, woven from the top throughout (John xix. 23)—the mother who had woven the garment with her own hands?

CHAPTER III

THE VIRGIN BIRTH—II.

With this preliminary discussion we are prepared to enter upon a detailed study of the narratives. While our immediate concern is with the operation of the Holy Spirit, the story is so closely woven that his work cannot be even partially understood without the knowledge of the circumstances and conditions of his activity. And if the Gospels are not trustworthy in their history how can we accept their witness in the realm of the supernatural? If they have told us earthly things, and we believe not, how shall we believe if they tell us of heavenly things? But if it may be shown that they are accurate in all matters in which we can put them to the test, we may be prepared to believe them when they testify of events which lie beyond the range of our experience.

We shall set the narratives together and note the points of resemblance and difference which they present. A glance at the Harmony discloses how widely they differ. Nowhere are they parallel, except in the genealogies, and there, too, points of divergence are more striking than the points of agreement. The records must be woven together before the picture is complete, for each supplies much that is lacking in the other.

This will appear most plainly if we set side by side the order of events in the Gospels.

Matthew	*Luke*
1—the betrothal	1—the annunciation to Zacharias
2—the conception	2—Elisabeth's conception
3—the purpose of Joseph	3—the annunciation to Mary
4—the message of the angel	4—Mary's visit to Elisabeth
5—the marriage	5—the magnificat
6—the birth in Bethlehem	6—the birth of John
7—the visit of the wise men	7—the benedictus
8—the conduct of Herod	8—the decree of Caesar
9—the flight into Egypt	9—the journey to Bethlehem
10—the slaughter of the children	10—the birth of Jesus
11—the return from Egypt	11—the message of the angel to the shepherds
12—the home in Nazareth	12—the song of the angels
	13—the visit of the shepherds
	14—the circumcision of Jesus
	15—the presentation in the temple
	16—the return to Nazareth

When the narratives are combined, this is the order of events as they are arranged in Burton & Goodspeed's *Harmony,* an order in which scholars generally occur:

1—the genealogy
2—the birth of John promised
3—the annunciation to Mary
4—the annunciation to Joseph
5—Mary's visit to Elisabeth
6—the birth of John the Baptist
7—the birth of Jesus
8—the angels and the shepherds
9—the circumcision
10—the presentation in the temple
11—the wise men from the east
12—the flight into Egypt, and the home in Nazareth.

The points noted by Matthew and not by Luke are these:

1—Joseph's knowledge of Mary's condition and his purpose to put her away secretly
2—the visit of the angel to Joseph
3—the journey of the wise men
4—the trouble of Herod and Jerusalem
5—the assembling of the chief priests and scribes
6—Herod's question and the answer
7—Herod's interview with the wise men
8—the adoration of the wise men

    9—their return to their own country
    10—the flight into Egypt
    11—the slaughter of the children
    12—the return from Egypt

These are the points noted by Luke and not by
Matthew:

    1—the birth of John the Baptist, which is related in great
        detail
    2—the home of Joseph and Mary in Nazareth
    3—the annunciation to Mary
    4—Mary's visit to Elisabeth
    5—the decree of Caesar Augustus
    6—the journey of Joseph and Mary to Bethlehem
    7—the circumstances of the birth of Jesus
    8—the appearance of the angel to the shepherds
    9—the song of the angel host
    10—the visit of the shepherds
    11—the circumcision
    12—the presentation in the temple.

The story of the virgin birth itself is told with great
modesty and reserve. Matthew does not, properly
speaking, relate the birth at all. He anticipates it,
refers to it, he does not relate it. Contrast the meagre-
ness of his narrative with the particularity of Luke.
He conducts us to Bethlehem indeed, but says nothing of the inn and the manger. He places the birth
in the days of Herod, the king, but tells us nothing
of Caesar Augustus, and the decree that all the world
should be enrolled. In time and place and circumstance his story is meagre in the extreme, and the
greatest event in history is disposed of with scarcely
an intimation of how it came to pass.

Certain characteristic features of the narratives are
brought to light by this review.

1—Luke's account is far more copious and detailed.
Apart from the genealogies Matthew's narrative comprises thirty-one verses and Luke's one hundred and
fifteen. Matthew tells us nothing of the birth of John,
but introduces him abruptly as Elijah appeared to
Ahab; while Luke devotes to him a long chapter.

Luke sets the story in the framework of Roman history. He is indeed pre-eminently the historian of the New Testament, making use of all available sources of information, as he affirms in the preface to the Gospel, and using his material with rare accuracy and skill. Modern scholarship which long looked upon him with suspicion and distrust is coming to recognize his gifts as a historian of the first rank—accurate, vivid, systematic, with firm grasp of details and the ability to marshal facts in the most striking and impressive fashion.

The most surprising feature of Matthew's Gospel is, as we have seen, that it contains in fact no account of the birth of Jesus, which is rather assumed than related. He seems indeed to promise a full account of it—"Now the birth of Jesus Christ was on this wise;" [1] but when we turn to the narrative this is all we find: Joseph "knew her not till she had brought forth a son; and he called his name Jesus"; [2] "Now when Jesus was born in Bethlehem in the days of Herod the king." [3] He points forward to the birth, he looks back to it as an accomplished fact; but he does not relate it. How striking is the contrast between these meagre references and the copious account of Luke. Evidently the third evangelist had ampler sources at his command and drew upon the memories of a mother.

2—Not only does Luke far surpass Matthew in the breadth and fulness of his narrative, but the accounts move in different spheres. The essential facts are the same, but they are presented in different settings and from different points of view. It is evident that Matthew derived his information ultimately from Joseph, and Luke from Mary. Joseph holds the place of pre-eminence in the First Gospel and Mary in the Third. This appears immediately in the genealogies, if we

[1] Matt. i. 18.   [2] Matt. i. 25.   [3] Matt. ii. 1.

may refer the second to Mary. It must be said, however, that the matter remains in doubt in spite of all the learning and labour that have been expended on it. The wording of Luke seems to point rather to Joseph than to Mary; and if Matthew could introduce into his list of names Tamar and Ruth and Bathsheba no reason appears why Luke should not have named Mary, if indeed he was tracing the line of descent through her. And why should the name of Mary appear in the genealogy of Joseph given by Matthew, while it is not found in her own recorded by Luke?

Apart from this, however, the place accorded to Joseph by Matthew and to Mary by Luke is clearly marked. In Matthew the angel announces the approaching birth to Joseph, in Luke to Mary; in Matthew the name of Jesus is given by the father, in Luke by the mother: in one Gospel it is the thoughts and feelings of Joseph that are disclosed, his knowledge of Mary's condition, his purpose to put her away secretly; in the other Gospel the emotions of the virgin mother are portrayed. In Matthew the divine visions and revelations are all granted to Joseph,[4] to vindicate Mary, to send him to Egypt, to bid him return to the land of Israel, to warn him to withdraw into Galilee. It is the experience, the conduct of Joseph with which the First Gospel is mainly concerned. The single instance in which Mary assumes greater prominence is in the account of the visit of the wise men who "came into the house and saw the young child with Mary his mother,"[5] where Joseph is not named.

In Matthew Joseph is named seven times and Mary four; while in Luke the name of Mary occurs thirteen

[4] See art. "Dreams," by B. B. Warfield, in *HDCGs.*, which shows with abundant illustrations how large a part dreams have played in history and experience.
[5] Matt. ii. 11.

times and that of Joseph only three. Joseph plays no independent part in Luke's account. When the shepherds visit the holy family the order is "Mary and Joseph, and the babe lying in the manger." It is the emotions, the experiences, the conduct of Mary with which Luke is concerned, and Joseph is barely mentioned and only when the course of events requires it. This difference lies upon the face of the narrative, and needs no further illustration. Evidently the ultimate source of Matthew's narrative was Joseph, while Luke drew upon the memories of Mary.

3—Luke's narrative is radiant with light and joy, while Matthew's is overshadowed by sorrow and danger. Matthew alone relates the suspicions of Joseph, and his purpose to put Mary away. The child Jesus is beset with perils from his birth, and the shadow of the cross falls upon the manger. The attempt of Herod to kill him, the slaughter of the children, the mourning of the mothers of Bethlehem, the flight into Egypt, the fear of Archelaus which drove them to Galilee: it is a gloomy picture which Matthew paints, relieved only by the visit of the wise men and their adoration of the new-born child. These Gentiles accorded him the only welcome that he received, while his own received him not, and their king sought to destroy him.

When we turn to Luke, we enter a new world. It is an idyllic scene that he depicts. The voice of joy and praise is heard on every side. Elisabeth and Zacharias rejoice in the promise of a son; the unborn babe leaps for joy; Elisabeth and Mary and Zacharias lift to God the song of praise; the angel brings to the shepherds good tidings of great joy; the multitude of the heavenly host raise the strain of rapturous adoration, Glory to God and peace on earth; the shepherds return from the manger glorifying and praising God for all the things that they have heard and seen, and

as they tell the story the people hear with wonder.
The child is welcomed by Simeon in the temple as
the promised Christ. And when the requirements of
the law have been fulfilled the family return to Nazareth in peace. We are no longer under the shadow
of the cross, but in the full sunshine of the divine grace
which abode upon him who grew in favour with God
and men. If we had only Luke to guide us here, we
might readily infer that his own people were prepared
to receive him with gladness as their Saviour and
Lord.

In this chorus of joy and praise a single discordant
note is heard; one small cloud appears in the bright-
ness of the sky that bends above the infant Jesus.
Simeon foresees that "this child is set for the falling
and the rising of many in Israel; and for a sign which
is spoken against," and the heart of his mother shall
be pierced with sorrow.[6]

The calmness, the peace, the beauty, the holy joy of
Luke's narrative furnish a striking contrast to Matthew's dark and troubled tale. Jesus is acknowledged
by all to whom he is made known. Matthew's picture
is dark, relieved by a single ray of light; Luke's is
radiant, darkened by a single cloud.

Thus the strangely contrary aspects of Jesus' life
are thrown into bold relief at his birth. He is a man
of sorrows, he is the King of Glory; and this double
representation of the opening scenes of his life fore-
shadows the character and work of him who was to
be both sufferer and saviour.

4—The narrative of Luke the Gentile is more thoroughly Jewish in form and spirit than the story of
Matthew the Jew. It moves wholly within the sphere
of Palestinian Judaism. Not only is the scene laid
in Nazareth and Bethlehem and Jerusalem, but the
world of thought and feeling to which we are intro-

[6] Luke ii. 34, 35.

duced is the world of the Old Scripture. David would have felt at home here. The only Gentiles who appear upon the scene are Augustus and Quirinius, and they are named simply because the course of history required it. The birth of the forerunner of the Christ is related at length. Zacharias, Elisabeth, Mary, Joseph, the shepherds, Simeon, Anna, all are Jews, devout Jews, who breathe the air of the Old Testament, cherish the hope of the Christ, look for the redemption of Israel, and express their emotions in the language of Psalmist and Prophet. It is Luke who conducts us to the temple, where Zacharias ministers, and Simeon prays, and Anna worships. He alone records the observance of the law of Moses, the circumcision of Jesus, the purification of Mary, the presentation in the Temple, the offering of the sacrifice. Thus they "accomplished all things that were according to the law of the Lord." [7]

Of all this Matthew has nothing. Instead of the shepherds he tells us of the wise men from the east. Herod the Idurnean King is a conspicuous figure. John the Baptist does not appear until Jesus was almost thirty years of age. In place of the visit to the temple he relates the flight into Egypt. And while direct citations from the Scripture are more frequent in his narrative, it is not saturated like Luke's with the thought and language of the Old Testament. Evidently the early documents or traditions upon which Luke relies laid stress upon the keeping of the law, and he follows them with scrupulous fidelity; while Matthew's chief interest is in the fulfilment of the predictions regarding the Christ. [8]

The copious use of the Scripture in Luke is not due to the evangelist but to the sources from which his

[7] Luke ii. 39.
[8] On the familiarity with Jewish laws and customs which Luke's narrative displays see Machen, *Princeton Theol. Rev.*, 1912, pp. 258 ff.

account is drawn. With the single exception of the reference to the law in ii. 23, we are indebted for this rich store of Old Testament citations to the pious Jews, Mary and Zacharias and Simeon, and not to the Gentile historian. In Matthew, on the other hand, every reference to the Old Testament is due to the evangelist himself, with the single exception of the answer of the chief priests and scribes to Herod's question where the Christ should be born.[9]

Moreover references to Scripture in Luke are general, while those in Matthew are specific. There is no direct quotation from the Old Testament in Luke except the reference to the law of Moses in ii. 23; and the only direct allusion to the prophets is couched in general terms by Zacharias—"Blessed be the Lord, the God of Israel; for he hath visited and wrought redemption for his people, and hath raised up a horn of salvation for us in the house of his servant David; as he spake by the mouth of his holy prophets that have been of old."[10] There seems to be no good reason to regard the last verse as a parenthesis, though it is so treated in the Revised Versions, both American and English. Matthew, on the other hand, cites four specific prophecies which were fulfilled in the circumstances of Jesus' birth, and records another which was quoted by the chief priests and scribes in answer to the question of Herod regarding the birthplace of the Christ.

The prophecies cited by Matthew are:

1—Isaiah vii. 14: "Behold, the virgin shall be with child, and shall bring forth a son, and they shall call his name Immanuel."[11] Matthew's use of the prophecy raises two questions—(a) What was the original meaning of the prophecy, and how may it be applied to Jesus? It is evident that the primary reference of the prediction was to an event in the immediate

[9] Matt. ii. 5, 6.   [10] Luke i. 68-70.   [11] Matt. i. 23.

future.[12] The Old Testament points unmistakably to a contemporary event; the New Testament with equal clearness refers the prediction to the birth of Jesus. Obviously the words are regarded as having a double meaning, foretelling at once a near and a remote event, which are so related that one is the type and prophecy of the other. The principle of double reference is amply illustrated throughout the whole course of Messianic prophecy, which presents various foreshadowings of the Christ, as in Melchisedec and Moses and David and Israel and the high priests, each of whom represents some feature of the life and character of the Christ. What was true of them in certain particulars is true in immeasurably higher degree of him. The reference of this passage to the Messiah was not apprehended by the Jews, perhaps not even by the prophet; but lay in the mind of the Spirit, and in the fulness of time was brought to light in the Gospel. Now the question arises, Is the Hebrew *Almah* properly rendered by παρθένος, virgin? The word occurs nine times in the Old Testament: Gen. xxiv. 43; Exod. ii. 8; Psalms lxviii. 25; Prov. xx. 19; Song of Sol. i. 3, vi. 8; Isa. vii. 14; and the plural occurs twice in musical notation—I Chron. xv. 20; Ps. xlvi. 1. The American Revision reads *virgins* in Song of Sol. and *virgin* in Isa. vii. 14; with *maiden* or *maidens* in the margin; *maiden* in Genesis, Exodus and Proverbs; *damsels* in Psalm lxviii. 25. The English Revisers agree with the American in translating the word by *virgin* or *virgins* only in the three passages noted above, and in placing *maiden* or *maidens* in the margin. The LXX renders by παρθένος only in Genesis and Isaiah. The word signifies properly a maiden of marriageable age but not yet married. In every instance of its use in the Old Testament this is the natural meaning of the

---

[12] For the history of the interpretation of the passage see Gray, *Int. Crit. Com.*, on Isaiah, *in loc.*

term. There is another Hebrew word, bethulah, which apparently always denotes a virgin, even in Joel i. 8—"Lament like a virgin clothed with sack cloth for the husband of her youth"—where by *husband* is probably meant betrothed.[13] In Genesis xxiv. 16 the word is further defined: "a virgin, neither had any man known her."

The evangelist uses the word, therefore, in its ordinary significance when he renders it by virgin. But this difference appears: in Isaiah the word denotes a woman who was a virgin when the promise was given; in its application to Mary it denotes a woman who was a virgin when the promise was fulfilled. The sign promised Ahaz was not the miraculous birth of the promised child, but his character and fortune. The New Testament, according to its custom, takes up the prophecy and translates it to a higher sphere.[14] In a similar way the name Immanuel, which occurs in the New Testament only here, is used in a lower and a higher sense. In the mouth of the prophet it signified, God is with us: in the mouth of the evangelist, God with us.

2—Micah v. 2: "And thou Bethlehem, land of Judah, Art in no wise least among the princes of Judah: For out of thee shall come forth a governor. Who shall be shepherd of my people Israel."[15] The quotation follows neither the Hebrew nor the LXX exactly, and the last clause of the original is omitted—"Whose goings forth are from of old, from everlasting." These differences do not concern us here, and it is sufficient to note that the passage was commonly interpreted of the Messiah by the Jews.

3—Hosea xi. 1: "When Israel was a child, then I

[13] See *Intern. Crit. Comm., in loc.*
[14] On the interpretation of this verse see Johnson, *Quotations of N. T. from O. T.,* p. 276; Forbes, *Pres. Rev. 7,* p. 700. *Comm., in loc.*
[15] Matt. ii. 6.

2 4767

loved him, and called my son out of Egypt." [16] Matthew cites the last clause of the verse, and applies it to the return of the child Jesus from Egypt to his own country. Various textual and exegetical difficulties of the passage are treated by Prof. Harper in his Commentary. Some of them are purely gratuitous: as when doubt is cast upon the text because elsewhere Hosea always speaks of God as the husband and not the father of Israel. Yet in the immediate context, as Prof. Harper observes, God is represented as teaching Israel to walk, taking him in his arms. If he is depicted as performing the offices of a father, why may he not be called father? Isaiah calls him the father,[17] the mother,[18] and the husband [19] of his people. The LXX reads, "Out of Egypt I called my children" where the plural conveys the collective sense of the term son. Israel is the son of God in the Old Testament, Christ is the Son of God in the New; and what is said of Israel as the object of God's love and care is preeminently true of him. In a similar fashion the title Servant of Jehovah is applied by Isaiah first to the Jewish people, then to the Messiah in whom the covenant and promises are fulfilled. Here again there is no reason to suppose that this application of the word was in the mind of Hosea, for the Spirit often spoke by the mouth of the prophets words far beyond their reach or their understanding. As Egypt was to Israel a place of safety in the infancy of the race, so was it a refuge to the infant Jesus: and like Israel he must leave Egypt to find in Canaan a home.

4—Jeremiah xxxi. 15: "A voice was heard in Ramah, weeping and great mourning, Rachel weeping for her children: and she would not be comforted, because they are not." [20] The captives of Judah and Jerusalem were assembled by Nebuzarada, captain of the guard

[16] Matt. ii. 15.   [17] Isa. lxiii. 16.   [18] Isa. lxvi. 13.
[19] Isa. lxv. 5.   [20] Matt. ii. 18.

of King Nebuchadrezzar, at Ramah,[21] and Rachel is represented as the mother of the chosen people mourning for her children about to be carried into exile. In like manner there was mourning in Bethlehem when the children were slaughtered by Herod. And the comparison is particularly apt and striking because Rachel died and was buried near Bethlehem.[22] Thus again the fortunes of Israel are seen to prefigure the life of the Christ.

5—When Joseph returned from Egypt after the death of Herod, he "came and dewlt in a city called Nazareth: that it might be fulfilled that was spoken through the prophets, that he should be called a Nazarene." [23] The phrase *through the prophets* indicates that the evangelist has no specific prediction in mind, but rather the general trend of prophecy. Precisely what he had in view cannot be determined, for the words occur nowhere in the Old Scripture. The various explanations which have been proposed are set forth in the Commentaries of Meyer and Broadus and Allen. The most plausible are these: (1) Matthew refers to Isaiah xi. 1—"And there shall come forth a shoot out of the stock of Jesse, and a branch out of his roots shall bear fruit." *Branch* is in the Hebrew *netzer*, and from this Nazareth is perhaps derived. Similar prophecies are found in Isa. iv. 2; Jer. xxiii. 5, xxxiii. 15; Zech. iii. 8, vi. 12; though in all these cases the Hebrew term is a different word of kindred signification. (2) Nazarene is taken as a term of contempt, and denotes the lowly and despised condition of the Messiah, as foretold in Isa. liii. That Galilean and Nazarene were used in this sense is evident from the Gospels and the Acts.[24]

The attempt to connect the word Nazarene with Nazirite has nothing to recommend it, for Jesus was

[21] Jer. xl. 1.
[22] Gen. xxxv. 19.
[23] Matt. ii. 23.
[24] John i. 46; vii. 41; Acts xxiv. 5.

not a Nazirite, nor is there reason to believe that the name was ever applied to him.

No interpretation of the passage has won general assent, and it presents one of the unsolved problems of New Testament exegesis.

In citations 1, 3 and 5 it is affirmed that the correspondence between the prophecy and the event was not a mere coincidence, but was ordained of God. The Old Testament is regarded as in its essential nature a preparation for the coming of the Christ; and not only the general course of his life but particular incidents of it are foreshadowed by divine direction in the unfolding of the history of Israel and the predictions of the prophets. Bacon says that every work treating of the history of prophecy should be of such a nature

> that every prophecy of the Scripture be sorted with the event fulfilling the same, throughout the ages of the world; both for the better confirmation of faith, and for the better illumination of the church, touching those parts of prophecies which are yet unfulfilled; allowing nevertheless that latitude which is agreeable and familiar unto divine prophecies; being of the nature of their author, with whom a thousand years are but as one day; and therefore are not fulfilled punctually at once, but have springing and germinant accomplishment throughout many ages, though the height or fulness of them may refer to some one age.[25]

We turn from the prophecies of Matthew to the canticles of Luke.

(1) The song of Elisabeth.[26] There is no apparent reason why the passage should not be treated as poetry, and thrown into metrical form, though it is not so

---

[25] *Advancement of Learning,* Book II.   [26] Luke i. 42-45.

given in our English versions. In Plummer's *Commentary* the Greek is arranged in two strophes of four lines each. Prof. Warfield affirms that the salutation of Elisabeth

> is unmistakably verse, even elaborately and artistically verse. Beginning with short lines of three beats of the accent each, the first strophe closes with a longer line of four, while the second strophe continues with this longer line, to close, itself, with a still longer line of five tones.[27]

He is speaking of the English translation, and presents it in the form of poetry.

Elisabeth pronounces a blessing upon Mary and her unborn child; expresses her sense of unworthiness in receiving a visit from the mother of her Lord; tells of the joy of the babe in her womb; and again pronounces Mary blessed because of her faith.

(2) The Magnificat.[28] This is ascribed to Elisabeth by Harnack and others.[29] The textual argument may be briefly stated. All Greek manuscripts read Mary, and the great preponderance of patristic testimony is in accord with them, from the days of Tertullian[30] and Irenaeus.[31] Origen intimates that some codices referred the words to Mary and others to Elisabeth,[32] but it is doubtful whether the passage should be ascribed to Origen or to his translator, Jerome. Three Latin manuscripts of the fourth, fifth and seventh centuries read Elisabeth.[33] The external evidence is

[27] "Messianic Psalms of the N. T.," *Expositor*, 3rd Series, Vol. II, p. 303.
[28] Luke i. 46-55.
[29] So Moffatt, *Int. Lit. N. T.*, p. 271.
[30] *On the Soul*, 26.
[31] *Her.* 3, 10, 2. In 4, 7, 1 some mss. read Elisabeth, but in view of the other passage cited this should be regarded as an error of the translator or scribe.
[32] 5th Hom. on Luke v.
[33] *HDC & Gs.*, Vol. II, p. 101.

thus overwhelmingly in favour of Mary, and Elisabeth
may be rejected without hesitation.

The alternative remains, however, which is accepted
by many scholars, that the original text read simply
εἶπεν, without specifying the subject.[34]   Then we
are compelled to determine the speaker from the
nature of the speech. If we accept this suggestion
Mary is to be preferred on the evidence which the
words themselves present. That immediately after
addressing the mother of her Lord and pronouncing a
blessing upon her in such glowing terms, Elisabeth
should have proceeded to say of herself, "Behold, from
henceforth all generations shall call me blessed" is
hardly credible, while the words fall naturally from
the lips of Mary. The *low estate* of verse 48 is not
the barrenness from which Elisabeth had been delivered, but a natural expression of humility on the part
of one who had been chosen to be the mother of the
Christ. The *handmaid* of verse 48 recalls Mary's use
of the word in verse 38. Elisabeth pronounced her
blessed, and she takes up the word and recognizes
that through God's grace she shall be blessed in the
eyes of all coming generations.[35]

The correspondence between the Magnificat and
the Song of Hannah [36] is very close and intimate.[37]
In Plummer's *Commentary* the Greek text of the LXX
and of Luke are set in parallel columns, and the likeness between them is strikingly apparent. It should
also be observed that Mary makes large use of the
Psalms and the Prophets. The mother of Jesus, like
every pious Jew, was acquainted with the thoughts,
the imagery, the language of the Scripture. When

[34] Moffatt, *Int. Lit. N. T.*, p. 271.
[35] See "Hymns of first two Chapters of Luke" by J. G. Machen,
Princeton Theol. Rev., 1912.
[36] I Sam. ii.
[37] The parallel passages are noted in Burton & Goodspeed's *Harmony of the Synoptic Gospels; HDC. and Gs.* Vol. II, p. 102.

her feelings were deeply moved, they clothed themselves in the familiar forms of Old Testament speech. The Song is a mosaic of Old Testament passages. Of the one hundred and two words which it contains fifty-four are marked as quotations in Burton & Goodspeed's Harmony. Even where there is no direct citation the thought moves entirely within the sphere of the Old Scripture. The only conspicuous difference between the Songs of Mary and Hannah is that Mary recognizes the greater blessing that is hers. Hannah praises God that the reproach of her barrenness is taken away; Mary praises him for the honour which shall win for her the benediction of all coming generations. When this is said, she turns at once to praise him in general terms for his goodness to his people. There is no direct allusion to the approaching birth, though it is presupposed in verse 48. Mary did not yet fully comprehend the greatness of her child who should be born of her, or she shrank from putting into words a conception so sublime. There is nothing indeed in the Magnificat, except verse 48, that might not be put with equal propriety in the mouth of Hannah. In form it displays the characteristic features of Hebrew poetry; it is God's mercy to his people that is celebrated; and his covenant is with Israel alone. Nowhere does the thought of Mary stray beyond the Old Scripture, except in the implication of verse 48 that the redemption long promised is at hand.

(3) The Benedictus of Zacharias [38] is also drawn from the Scripture. Of the one hundred thirty-seven words which it contains forty-eight are marked by Burton & Goodspeed as direct citations, while the thought moves throughout in the realm of Old Testament conceptions. This is shown by the use of parallel columns in Plummer's *Commentary*. But again it is plainly declared that the salvation long foretold by

[38] Luke i. 68-79.

the prophets is about to be revealed. His own son John he recognizes as the immediate forerunner of the Christ. Here too the work of the Messiah is limited to Israel. The phrase "Them that sit in darkness and the shadow of death" [39] is borrowed from Isaiah, and is used in the same sense, to designate the northern part of the promised land, as is suggested by *us* and *our* in the immediate context. In none of these songs does the thought travel beyond the bounds of Israel.

The divinity of the Messiah is acknowledged by Elisabeth and Zacharias in the use of the term Lord; but appears only by remote implication in the Song of Mary. Both Mary and Zacharias follow that line of Old Testament teaching which appears to associate the coming and the triumph of the Christ as if one followed directly upon the other. There is no conception of the suffering which he must endure, of the conflict between good and evil, prolonged for centuries before the victory is won.

The word *redemption* λύτρωσιν in the Benedictus —"Blessed be the Lord God of Israel; for he hath visited and redeemed (literally, made redemption for) his people" [40] should not be pressed to its specific New Testament sense, as involving a purchase price, and therefore implying a sacrifice by which God's people shall be delivered. Alike in the LXX and the New Testament the thought of a ransom is often forgotten, and the word is used in the general sense of release; and the same is true of the corresponding term in Hebrew. Thus the word is employed to represent the deliverance from Egypt, [41] so that Moses is called by Stephen a redeemer (λυτρωτὴν); [42] the release from Babylon; [43] and the escape of individuals

[39] vs. 79.   [40] vs. 68.
[41] Exod. vi. 6; Deut. ix. 6; Neh. i. 10; Ps. lxxvii. 15, 16; Isa. l. 2.
[42] Acts vii. 35.
[43] Isa. li. 11; Jer. l. 33, 34; Lam. v. 8.

from the hands of their enemies or from their afflictions.[44] [45] There is no reason to attribute to Zacharias the thought of redemption by the death of the Christ, a truth clearly taught indeed in the Old Scripture, but foreign to the thought of the Jews when Jesus was born. They were looking for a conquering king, not a suffering saviour; for release from the dominion of Rome rather than from the bondage of sin.

(4) The Nunc Dimittis of Simeon [46] is of the same character. Of the thirty-six words which it contains fifteen are enclosed in quotation marks by Burton & Goodspeed. In two respects, however, this song taken in connexion with the words that follow represents a marked advance: (1) in placing the Gentiles side by side with the Jews—"A light for revelation to the Gentiles, And the glory of thy people Israel." Here for the first time in the narrative the breadth of the Messiah's mission is disclosed. (2) To Simeon alone is granted the vision of the sufferings of the Messiah. To Mary he said, "This child is set for the falling and the rising of many in Israel; and for a sign which is spoken against; yea, and a sword shall pierce through thine own soul." [47] And the conception is the more remarkable because it found no place in the current Jewish thought of the time,[48] though it was taught with the utmost clearness by Isaiah. In his representation of the calling of the Gentiles and of the suffering Christ Simeon goes far beyond the thought of his day; and shows how firmly and clearly he had grasped those fundamental teachings of the prophets which were apprehended neither by the Jews, nor by Jesus' disciples until they were interpreted by

[44] I Sam. xiv. 45; II Sam. iv. 9; Ps. cxliv. 10.
[45] See Westcott on Hebrews, add. note on ix. 5, and especially the thorough discussion of the term by Warfield, *Princeton Theol. Rev.*, 1917.
[46] Luke ii. 29-32.   [47] vs. 34.   [48] Schürer, *HJP.* II, 2, 184-7.

his resurrection. Three times in the brief story of Simeon the Holy Spirit appears, "The Holy Spirit was upon him"; "It had been revealed unto him by the Holy Spirit, that he should not see death before he had seen the Lord's Christ"; "He came in the Spirit into the temple." His life was ruled by the Spirit, his thoughts were inspired by the Spirit.

If these canticles were found by Luke in documents which he has incorporated with his narrative, they form the earliest literature of the Christian church, and show how it sprang from the bosom of Judaism.

The work of the Holy Spirit is more fully brought to light in Luke. Twice only is he named in Matthew's account of the birth, as we have seen. We do not read of him again until John declares that the Christ "shall baptize you in the Holy Spirit and in fire." [49] In Luke, on the other hand, the operation of the Spirit is conspicuous throughout the whole course of the narrative. Zacharias is told by the angel that the son promised him shall be filled with the Holy Spirit. To Mary the angel declares "The Holy Spirit shall come upon thee." Elisabeth was filled with the Holy Spirit when Mary came to her, and so was Zacharias. The Spirit came upon Simeon, and revealed to him not only the coming of the Christ but his world-wide ministry, and the suffering that lay before him.

The angels fill a large place in Scripture as the messengers and ministers of God. Their number is vast [50] so that Bildad may well inquire, "Is there any number of his armies?" [51] Their power is great.[52] They bore a part in giving the law to Israel.[53] They execute

[49] Matt. iii. 11.
[50] Dan. vii. 10; Heb. xii. 23; Rev. 5. 11.
[51] Job xxv. 3.
[52] Ps. ciii. 22.
[53] Acts vii. 53, 38; Gal. iii. 19; Heb. ii. 2.

God's judgments upon the wicked, and comfort and strengthen the righteous.[54]

In the consciousness of the Protestant world today they find scanty recognition, for the abuses of angel worship have provoked a strong reaction. And as Jesus taught so clearly the fatherly care and goodness of God, and brought men into such immediate relation to him, that there seems to remain no room for the intermediate ministry of angels. In days when God seemed remote and inaccessible, and his face was hid from men, the guardian care exercised by the angels was a cherished truth; but now that we have seen God face to face in his Son, what need have we of other ministry than that of Christ and the Holy Spirit? The interest in angels among Protestants today is almost entirely historical or dogmatic, and we do not feel that they concern us nearly. And though the doctrine of angels is essential to a complete theology, it cannot be said that there has been material loss in virtually eliminating them from Christian experience. We believe in them, we are no longer conscious of their presence or their power.

Of this innumerable host two only are named in Scripture, Gabriel and Michael. Michael is represented in Dan. x. 13 and xii. 1 as the champion of the people of God. "In the days of tribulation which shall come upon Israel shall Michael stand up, the great prince who standeth for the children of thy people." He executes the same office in the New Testament; for Jude pictures him defending the body of Moses against Satan,[55] and in the Apocalypse he appears as the captain of the army of God which wages war in heaven against the apostate and rebellious angels.[56] He alone bears the title of archangel,[57]

[54] Matt. xiii. 41; xviii. 10; Heb. i. 14.   [56] Rev. xii. 7.
[55] Jude vs. 9.   [57] Jude ix.

and we naturally infer that it is his voice which shall summon the dead to rise from their graves and present themselves before the judgment seat of God.[58] The common belief that Gabriel is meant has no warrant in Scripture, though it is in accord with Jewish tradition.

Gabriel too is sent to Daniel, but he comes not like Michael to battle, but to interpret the visions that perplex the prophet.[59] He is the angel of revelation as Michael is the angel of judgement. The distinction is plainly drawn both in the Old Testament and in the New. It is Gabriel who announces to Zacharias the birth of John, and to Mary the birth of Jesus; it is he also, we presume, though he is not named, who appears three times in a dream to Joseph, and who brought the shepherds good tidings of great joy on the plains of Bethlehem. In Matthew he appears always in a dream, never in Luke.

Angels often ministered to Jesus during his earthly life. Continually they ascended and descended upon him;[60] they waited upon him in the wilderness after his temptation.[61] And if the verse which affirms that an angel from heaven strengthened him in Gethsemane has no place in the original text of Luke xxii. 43, yet we may believe that it preserves an early and trustworthy tradition. Westcott and Hort reject verses 43 and 44, but affirm that "These verses and the first sentence of xxiii. 34;[62] may be safely called the most precious among the remains of this evangelic tradition, which were rescued from oblivion by the scribes of the second century."[63] An angel rolled away the stone from the door of Joseph's sepulchre; within

[58] I Thess. iv. 16.
[59] Dan. viii. 16; ix. 21.
[60] John i. 51; Matt. xxvi. 53.
[61] Matt. iv. 11.
[62] "And Jesus said, Father, forgive them; for they know not what they do."
[63] *Notes on Sel. Readings,* p. 67.

the tomb the women and a little later Mary Magdalene had a vision of angels.[64]

Three times Scripture speaks of the joy of the angels: When the work of creation was finished, "the morning stars sang together, and all the sons of God shouted for joy";[65] when Jesus was born in Bethlehem the choir of angels raised the chorus of exultant praise; when a penitent sinner turns to God "there is joy in the presence of the angels of God." [66]

Gabriel thus performs a preliminary and preparatory work in connexion with the birth of Jesus, announcing it to Mary and to Joseph, and proclaiming it when it has taken place.

The actual conception was the work of the Holy Spirit alone without human or celestial agent. The birth of Isaac, of John the Baptist, were supernatural in that they transcended the ordinary course of nature; the birth of Jesus was divine, for he was begotten by the immediate operation of the Spirit of God. Although the Spirit assumed the place of the earthly father, the Scripture never calls him the father of Jesus, for the eternal generation of the Son is always kept in view. Turrettin says that the Spirit was not the Father of Jesus because he was not generated of the substance of the Spirit, but by his creative power; nor did the Spirit impart to him a nature like his own.[67]

The *Gospel of the Hebrews,* dating from the second century, reports Jesus as saying, "Just now, my mother, the Holy Spirit, took me by one of my hairs and bore me away to the great mountain, Thabor." This singular tradition is apparently of Hebrew origin, for Spirit, *ruach,* is feminine in Hebrew. Origen's explanation is as curious as the passage itself: "If he who does the will of the Father in heaven is Christ's mother and sister and brother, and if the name of

[64] Matt. xxviii. 2; John xx. 11. [66] Luke xv. 10.
[65] Job xxxviii. 7.   [67] *Theol. Loc.* XIII Qn. 11, 4, 5.

brother of Christ may be applied, not only to the race of men, but to beings of diviner rank than they, then there is nothing absurd in the Holy Spirit's being his mother, every one being his mother who does the will of the Father in heaven." [68]   The same *Gospel* referring to the baptism of Jesus tells us that "When the Lord had come up out of the water the Holy Spirit with full stream came down and rested upon him, and said to him, My son, in all the prophets I was waiting for thee, that thou shouldest come, and I might rest in thee. For thou art my rest; thou art my first-born son, who reignest forever." [69]

The birth of Ishmael [70] and of Samson [71] was foretold by an angel, and the birth of Isaac was announced to Abraham by God himself; in what way we are not told. [72]   Gabriel foretells the birth of John and of Jesus. In Matthew he speaks to Joseph only, affirming that Mary's conception was by the Holy Spirit, and that the son whom she is about to bear shall be called Jesus, because he shall save his people from their sins. Matthew sees in the promise the fulfilment of Isaiah's prophecy, and applies to Jesus the name Immanuel. God alone is the saviour of his people, and he only may be called Jesus who is also called Immanuel.

Luke records the annunciation to Mary. She was amazed and troubled, yet the words were gracious: "Hail, thou that are highly favoured, the Lord is with thee." For *highly favoured* the margin of the Revised Version reads, *endued with grace!* But the words that follow, "Thou hast found favour with God," and the whole tone of the passage are decisive in favour of the reading of the text. It is not Mary's worthiness but God's grace that is magnified. "The Lord is with

[68] *Com. on John,* Bk. II, 6.
[69] Quoted in Westcott *Int. Study Gs.,* p. 456. See Turrettin, *Theol. Locus* XIII Qn 11.
[70] Gen. xvi. 10.   [71] Judg. xiii. 3.   [72] Gen. xvii. 15.

thee," that was Mary's Immanuel. She was troubled,
for she knew that the angel's visit portended some new
and strange experience of which she might deem herself incapable or unworthy. All those whom God calls
in extraordinary ways to extraordinary service are dis-
turbed and alarmed. As Mary was perturbed by the
news of Jesus' birth, so was another Mary by the
tidings of his resurrection.[73] Man is never at ease in
presence of the supernatural, the divine. Her agita-
tion and perplexity were heightened by the words that
followed: "Fear not, Mary, for thou hast found favour
with God. And behold thou shalt conceive in thy
womb and bring forth a son." The name that the
child shall bear, Jesus, is given, but it is not interpreted as in Matthew. For he is not now represented
as a saviour but as a king: "He shall be great, and
shall be called the Son of the Most High: and the
Lord God shall give unto him the throne of his father
David: and he shall reign over the house of Jacob
forever; and of his kingdom there shall be no end."
The promise is confined to Israel, and again it is manifest how thoroughly Jewish are the authorities upon
which Luke depends. The prediction is based upon
God's covenant with David,[74] but the promise then
given to the house of David here becomes personal—
he shall reign. For he shall be not only a king, but a
divine king, the Son of the Most High. This title is
frequently ascribed to God in the Old Testament,
especially in the Psalms and Daniel, but is rarely employed in the New. In the Gospels it is confined to
Luke [75] with the exception of the cry of the demoniac
in Mark v. 7. Jesus uses it only once—"Ye shall be
sons of the Most High."[76] Beyond the Gospels it is
found only in the Acts,[77] and in Heb. vii. 1.

[73] Matt. xviii. 5, 8.
[74] II Sam. vii. 13-16.
[75] Luke i. 32, 35, 76; vi. 35.
[76] Luke vi. 35.
[77] Acts vii. 48; xvi. 17.

Mary's first thought was not of the honour that was about to befall her, nor of the greatness of the son whom she should bear; but in sheer bewilderment she asks, "How shall this be?" For she saw that this child should not be born in the ordinary course of wedlock. Abraham was incredulous when Isaac was promised, and Zacharias when the birth of John was foretold. The question of Mary sprang not from unbelief or distrust, but from pure perplexity, as Nicodemus inquired about the new birth. How could she understand without further revelation? To this birth there was no parallel in all the history of mankind. As soon as the manner of the conception was made known to her, she replied in humility and faith, "Be it unto me according to thy word." [78]

The mode of the conception is disclosed as clearly as it could be expressed in human speech. "The Holy Spirit shall come upon thee, and the power of the Most High shall overshadow thee." The Holy Spirit revealed in the Old Scripture as the creative energy of God shall accomplish in her the mystery of the incarnation. This is the way in which the Word became flesh, by the immediate operation of the Spirit of God. "The Holy Spirit shall come upon thee"— the phrase is drawn from the Old Testament, where it is often used. The Spirit came upon judges and kings and prophets, taking possession of them, endowing them with supernatural gifts of wisdom and strength, and working through them his own gracious purposes. God put his Spirit upon men.[79] In a striking figure the Spirit is said to have clothed himself with Gideon.[80] According to the Hebrew and the LXX the Spirit leaped upon Samson [81] and upon Saul.[82] The word expresses the forcible, even violent,

[78] Luke i. 38.
[79] Num. xi. 25.
[80] Judg. vi. 34.

[81] Judg. xiv. 6, 19; xiv. 14.
[82] I Sam. x. 10.

overpowering and taking possession of men. Isaiah prophesied that the Spirit should rest upon the Christ.[83] The Spirit entered into Ezekiel,[84] fell upon him;[85] Joel foretold that the Spirit should be poured out on all the people of Israel.[86] The coming of the Spirit is always significant of some new and extraordinary experience and endowment.

After the Hebrew manner this clause is followed by another which serves to define it: "The power of the Most High shall overshadow thee." The term *overshadow* suggests the luminous cloud, representing the divine glory, which lead the children of Israel through the wilderness;[87] and abode upon Mt. Sinai, where Moses communed with God[88] and upon the tabernacle.[89] This the rabbis named the Shekinah, the visible and glorious manifestation of the presence of Jehovah with his people.[90] Upon Jesus the divine glory rested throughout his earthly life. "The Word became flesh and tabernacled among us, and we beheld his glory."[91] His body was a temple,[92] and wherever God establishes his temple there his glory abides. When Jesus was transfigured a bright cloud overshadowed him.[93] When he parted from his disciples on Mount Olivet, "A cloud received him out of their sight."[94]

As the conception is of God the child is divine. The Spirit is the power of the Most High by whom the Son of the Most High shall be begotten. The Authorized Version followed substantially by the American Revisers, reads, "That holy thing which

---

[83] Isa. xi. 2.
[84] Ezek. iii. 24.
[85] Ezek. xi. 5.
[86] Joel ii. 29; *cf.* Isa. xliv. 3.
[87] Exod. xiii. 21, 22; vi. 10.
[88] Exod. xxiv. 16.
[89] Exod. xl. 34, 38; Num. ix. 15, 16.
[90] See Sanday & Headlam on Rom. iii. 23 and ix. 4. Art. "Shekinah," *HBD*.
[91] John i. 14.
[92] John ii. 21.
[93] Matt. xvii. 5.
[94] Acts i. 9.

promises are fulfilled.[107] "Jehovah said unto me, Thou art my son; this day have I begotten thee." [108] [109] The assurance given to David of an eternal kingdom requires for its fulfilment a king ever-living and divine.

In the New Testament also the word is used in different senses.

(a) Adam is termed the son of God,[110] since he was created by God in his own image. There is a sense in which all men are by nature, like Adam, sons of God, because he has imparted to them a nature kindred to his own, which is the essential note of fatherhood. Paul cites and approves the words of the heathen poet, "For we are also his offspring." [111] This is the truth which underlies the incarnation and inspires the appeal which the Gospel makes to men, and is vividly illustrated in the parable of the Prodigal Son.[112]

But though this natural relation is recognized in the New Testament, it is so completely overshadowed by the gracious relation into which God enters with men through Christ that after the fall no man is termed directly a son of God unless he has been renewed by the Spirit of God. Augustine in a striking passage shows how the name may at the same time be granted and denied to men, as the Jews were and were not the children of Abraham.[113] [114] They are children of God by origin, but not by character; have the nature but not the spirit of sons.

[107] Dalmann, *Words of Jesus*, 268, ff; Westcott, *Eps. of John*, 27-34; Sanday & Headlam on *Rom.* i. 4.
[108] Ps. ii. 7, 12.
[109] Briggs, *in loc*.
[110] Luke iii. 38.
[111] Acts xvii. 28.
[112] Salmond, "Homiletic Aspects Fatherhood of God," *Pres. & Ref. Rev.*, Vol. 4. Burton on *Gal.* p. 390. *Cf.* my *Teaching of the Gospel of John*, p. 70.
[113] John viii. 37, 39.
[114] *Tract. on John.* xlii. 10-15.

(b) Jesus is called pre-eminently the Son of God.[115] Like Adam, he was a son because he entered human life through the immediate act of the Almighty;[116] but he did not derive his sonship from the incarnation. His birth was simply the manifestation of the Eternal Son.

In the Synoptic Gospels the title is ordinarily equivalent to the Messiah, the head and representative of the people to whom the name was first given; and the term *first born* which belongs to Israel in the earlier Scripture is transferred to Jesus. But the word sometimes conveys a profounder meaning, and designates him as the Son of God in a sense transcendent and unique, which distinguishes him from mankind, gives him a place beside the Most High. Between these senses of the term it is at times difficult to distinguish; and when the term is evidently employed in a Messianic significance, we must inquire whether the speaker or writer conceived of the Messiah as divine.

The title was given to Jesus by evil spirits.[117] In Mark i. 34 and Luke iv. 41 Son of God and Christ are convertible terms; by his disciples when he calmed the storm;[118] by the centurion who stood beside the cross [119] where Luke has "a righteous man." [120] Either the centurion used both phrases, or Luke regarded the terms as equivalent. In none of these instances does the thought appear to go beyond the conception of the Messiah which prevailed among the Jews. They seem to have commonly thought of him as a descend-

[115] List of passages in Westcott, *Introd. to Study of Gospels*, 145, note 4. Warfield, *Lord of Glory*: Synoptic use of the term, p. 137, ff. John's use of term, p. 195, ff. Dalmann, *Words of Jesus*, p. 268-89. Schürer, *HJP*. II, 2, p. 159, ff.

[116] Luke i. 35.

[117] Matt. viii. 29; Mark iii. 11, v. 7; Luke viii. 28.

[118] Matt. xiv. 33.

[119] Matt. xxvii. 54; Mark xv. 39.

[120] Luke xxiii. 47.

ant of David who should establish an earthly kingdom of surpassing power and glory. He was not divine, but enjoyed the special favour of God, and was endowed with supernatural powers.[121]

There are other instances in which the higher sense of the title is probable, is even required. Gabriel tells Mary that Jesus shall be called the Son of the Most High, the Son of God, and also the Son of David. Thus the contrast is drawn before his birth which Paul presents in Rom. i. 3, 4: "born of the seed of David according to the flesh, who was declared to be the Son of God with power, according to the spirit of holiness, by the resurrection from the dead." Both Luke and Paul attest at once the human and the divine nature of Jesus, though Luke refers the title Son of God to his miraculous birth and Paul to his resurrection.

At his baptism a voice from heaven declared, "This is my beloved son"[122] or "Thou art my beloved Son."[123] Satan caught up the word when he tempted Jesus in the wilderness.[124] Again the heavenly voice was heard when Jesus was transfigured; "This is my beloved Son,"[125] or as Luke reads, "My Son, my chosen."[126]

> There are three moments to each of which are applied with variations the words of Psalm ii. 7, "Thou art my Son: this day have I begotten thee." They are: (1) the Baptism;[127] (2) the Transfiguration;[128] (3) the Resurrection.[129] . . . The moments in question are so many steps in the passage through an earthly life of One who came forth from God and returned to God, not

[121] Machen, *Origin Paul's Religion*, 181 ff.
[122] Matt. iii. 17.
[123] Mark i. 11; Luke iii. 21.
[124] Matt. iv. 3, 6; Luke iv. 3, 9.
[125] Matt. xvii. 5; Mark ix. 7.
[126] Luke ix. 35.
[127] Mark i. 11.
[128] Mark ix. 7.
[129] Acts xiii. 33.

stages in the gradual deification of one who began his career as ψιλὸς ἄνθρωπος.[130]

In the light of what has just been said we may prefix to this list of moments another, the incarnation.

The Revised Version renders Mark i. 1, "The beginning of the gospel of Jesus Christ, the Son of God," but the text is uncertain, and, as is indicated in a marginal note, some ancient authorities omit the final clause. So evenly balanced is the evidence that Westcott and Hort, while they incline to regard the words as an early interpolation, yet add that neither reading can be safely rejected.[131] If the words are retained the whole character of the Gospel will not only warrant but constrain us to interpret them in the highest sense.

We cannot determine precisely the bounds of Peter's thought when he made his great confession at Caesarea Philippi: "Thou art the Christ, the Son of the living God;"[132] where Mark has simply the Christ,[133] and Luke reads the Christ of God.[134] It is true that Jesus discovers in his words a special revelation from God: "Flesh and blood hath not revealed it unto thee, but my Father who is in heaven"; and that this is not the first occasion on which his Messiahship had been acknowledged by his disciples.[135] But his manner of life and his teaching had so contravened their conceptions of the Messianic king that they might easily begin, like John the Baptist in his prison, to waver in their minds, and question whether he were indeed the Christ; so that a divine revelation was required to confirm and establish their faith. The utmost that we may affirm is that while Peter's words in themselves are capable of a higher meaning, yet in view

[130] Sanday & Headlam on *Rom.* i. 4.
[131] *Notes on Selected Readings,* p. 23.
[132] Matt. xvi. 16.   [134] Luke ix. 21.
[133] Mark viii. 30.   [135] John i. 41, 49; Matt. xiv. 43.

of the form in which they are recorded by Mark and Luke, it is probable that his thought did not extend beyond the Messianic significance of the term.[136]

When we turn to the Gospel of John we find the same distinction in the meaning of the phrase. On the lips of Nathaniel: "Rabbi, thou art the Son of God; thou art the king of Israel," [137] and of Martha: "I have believed that thou art the Christ, the Son of God," [138] it seems to be used in the ordinary Messianic sense. John the Baptist evidently gives to it the highest possible significance, for he ascribes to Jesus divine attributes, pre-existence, the taking away of sin, and baptizing with the Holy Spirit.[139] The evangelist himself expressly distinguishes Jesus from men, as the only begotten Son.[140] [141] The reading *only begotten God* in i. 18 is too precarious to sustain an argument If *only begotten Son* is retained, the transcendental sense of the term again appears.[142] The Gospel was written "that ye may believe that Jesus is Christ, the son of God; and that believing ye may have life in his name." [143] He is thus presented as the object of faith and the source of eternal life. In Peter's confession [144] the better reading is "The Holy One of God."

It is apparent from this review that the statement of Dalman that "Jesus was not called the Son of God by any contemporary" (*Words of Jesus,* p. 275) cannot be maintained without doing violence to the text of the Gospels.

Jesus rarely applied the title to himself, never in

[136] See the judicious note of Broadus on *Matt.* xvi. 16.
[137] John i. 49.
[138] John xi. 27.
[139] John i. 29, 30, 33, 34.
[140] John i. 14, *cf.* I John iv. 9.
[141] See Westcott, *Eps. of John,* p. 162.
[142] For the reading θεὸς see *W. & H. Notes on Select Readings;* Hort, *Two Dissertations;* Warfield, *Textual Criticism, N. T.,* p. 189. For υἱὸς see Godet *in loc.,* and arts. by Ezra Abbot there cited.
[143] John xx. 32, *cf.* I John v. 1 and iv. 15.
[144] Peter vi. 69.

the Synoptic Gospels. But he spoke of the Father and the Son in a manner which is precisely equivalent, representing himself in the clearest and most unequivocal manner as the Son of God, even though he does not use the exact term. "All things have been delivered unto me of my Father: and no one knoweth the Son save the Father; neither doth any know the Father save the Son, and he to whomsoever the Son willeth to reveal him." [145] Here he claims virtual equality in knowledge and in power with the Father, whom he had just addressed as Lord of heaven and earth. Speaking of his final coming he says, "But of that day or that hour knoweth no one, not even the angels in heaven, neither the Son, but the Father." [146] There is some doubt whether the words *neither the Son* are properly retained in the parallel passage, Matt. xxiv. 36, but Westcott and Hort hold that "the documentary evidence in their favor is overwhelming" (*Notes on Select Readings*, p. 18). Here Jesus exalts himself as the Son above men and angels; and as the angels are uniformly represented in Scripture as the highest of all creatures he exalts himself above the whole creation, even while in this particular he confesses his inferiority to his Father. To the question how he is at once above the created universe yet lower than God, the only answer is furnished by the union of the divine and human natures in the person of the incarnate Son. In the parable of the wicked husbandman [147] he represents himself in distinction from the servants as the Son, the only and beloved Son of the owner of the vineyard. The vineyard is Israel, the owner is God, and the Son is sharply distinguished from lawgivers, rulers and prophets, as in Heb. i. 1, 2. In the baptismal formula he associates Father, Son and Spirit, and in connexion with it

[145] Matt. xi. 27; Luke x. 22.
[146] Mark xiii. 32.
[147] Matt. xxi. 33-35; Mark xii. 1-12; Luke xx. 9-19.

asserts that all authority hath been given unto him in heaven and on earth, and that he will be with his disciples always, even unto the end of the world, the consummation of the age.[148] There is no reason to doubt that these are the words of Jesus, for they contain nothing essentially new, but simply bring together various elements of his previous teaching. The doctrine of the Trinity which here finds clear expression underlies his whole representation of the divine nature.

Moreover, while he nowhere in the Synoptic Gospels directly appropriates the title Son of God, yet he accepted it from others. When the high priest adjured him by the living God "that thou tell us whether thou be the Christ, the Son of God," [149] or as Mark has it, "Art thou the Christ, the Son of the Blessed?" [150] he answered, "Thou hast said," or as Mark reads, "I am." And when in the course of his trial before the Sanhedrin they all said, "Art thou then the Son of God?", he replied, "Ye say that I am." This they understood to be an affirmative answer to their question, for they cried, "What further need have we of witness? For we ourselves have heard from his own mouth." [151] As he hung upon the cross they that passed by railed on him, crying, "If thou art the Son of God, come down from the cross." And the rulers mocked him, saying, "He trusteth on God; let him deliver him now, if he desireth him; for he said, I am the Son of God." [152]

It must also be observed that Jesus always distinguishes himself from other men in his relation to God. He taught his disciples to say "Our Father," but he always said "My Father." To Mary Magdelene he said, "I ascend unto my Father and your Father, and my God and your God." [153] God is not his Father in the same sense that he is the Father of men. He

[148] Matt. xxviii. 18, 20.
[149] Matt. xxvi. 63.
[150] Mark xiv. 61.
[151] Luke xii. 70, 71.
[152] Matt. xxvii. 40, 43.
[153] John xx. 17.

is Son of God by nature, they become sons of God by grace through him. And though he taught his disciples to pray Our Father who art in heaven, he never addressed God in that way, so far as the record indicates; for the added clause suggests the thought of elevation and remoteness which is not appropriate upon the lips of him who is always in the bosom of the Father.[154]

In the Fourth Gospel Jesus several times called himself the Son of God. To Nicodemus he spoke of himself as the only begotten Son.[155] There is no sufficient reason to ascribe these words to the evangelist, for the flow of thought is unbroken, and the arguments adduced by Westcott in favour of such reference are drawn mainly from certain peculiarities of expression which may be otherwise explained, as Godet has well shown. In the picture of the general resurrection in v. 25-29 he declares that the dead shall hear the voice of the Son of God; and they that hear shall live. The question that he addressed to the blind man whom he had healed,[156] which reads in the Authorized and Revised Versions, "Dost thou believe on the Son of God?" should rather be rendered in accordance with the decided weight of manuscript authority as in the margin of the Revised Version, "Dost thou believe on the Son of man?" When the Jews charged him with blasphemy because he said, "I, and the Father are one," and thereby being a man made himself God, he answered them in the words of Ps. lxxxii. 6: "I said, ye are gods." If this name is given to earthly rulers as representatives of the Almighty, how can it be denied to him whom the Father hath sanctified and sent into the world?[157] The sequence of the words does not of itself imply that his sanctification or consecration was exceptional, for

[154] John i. 18.
[155] John iii. 16.
[156] John ix. 35.
[157] John x. 34-36.

Jeremiah too was sanctified before his birth,[158] and so was John the Baptist [159] and Paul.[160] The consecration indeed must always precede the sending. But in view of the uniform teaching of the Gospel regarding his pre-existence there is no reason to doubt that he has in mind here his consecration in the counsels of eternity. In xi. 4 he tells his disciples that the sickness of Lazarus "Is not unto death, but for the glory of God that the Son of God may be glorified thereby." The glory of the Father and the glory of the Son are one.

Thus it appears that only in four instances, which are recorded in John alone, did Jesus apply to himself directly the title Son of God. But constantly throughout the Fourth Gospel he speaks of himself as the Son and of God as his Father. The Jews recognized that by this mode of speech he claimed equality with God, and accused him therefore of blasphemy.[161] To Pilate they said, "We have a law, and by that law he ought to die, because he made himself the Son of God." [162] It is evident that in the Gospel of John the term Son, or Son of God, upon the lips of Jesus bears not merely a Messianic sense, but expresses a relation of intimacy and affection, a community of nature which he had with the Father before the world was.[163] He was not the Son because he was the Messiah, he was the Messiah because he was the Son. Ordinarily it is the personal and not the official relation that he has in mind.

The question arises here whether Son of God was commonly regarded by the Jews in the time of Jesus as a Messianic title. Extra-canonical literature throws little light upon the matter, and the only trustworthy evidence that we possess is derived from the New

[158] Jer. i. 5.
[159] Luke i. 15.
[160] Gal. i. 15.

[161] John v. 25.
[162] John xix. 7.
[163] John xvii. 5.

Testament. The natural conclusion to be drawn from the passages cited is that the title was recognized as a designation of the Messiah when it was employed by Jesus, but was not in common use at the time. This would naturally follow from the strict monotheism of the Jews. The Messiah seems to have been regarded as a man supernaturally endowed for his high mission, but in no sense divine.[164]

(d) The term is applied to those who through faith in Christ are born again of the Spirit;[165] imitate the character and conduct of God.[166] "Be ye therefore imitators of God, as beloved children" and do the will of God.[167] John reserves υἱός for Jesus alone, and calls men τέκνα, while Paul applies both terms to men.

Thus the Holy Spirit prepares the way for the coming of Christ through the ministry of John the Baptist, who was filled with the Spirit even from his mother's womb; conceived him in the womb of the virgin Mary, and equipped him for the ministry to which he was appointed of God. It is not said of him indeed, as of John the Baptist, that he was filled with the Spirit, nor is the Spirit said to have descended upon him until his baptism. Upon Elisabeth and Zacharias, upon Simeon and Anna, the Spirit came; upon Jesus the Spirit always abode according to the prophecy of Isaiah,[168] as is implied in the statement that the grace of God was upon him.[169]

The question remains whether the representation of the Holy Spirit in the story of the infancy goes beyond the teaching of the Old Testament. Do Matthew and Luke throw new light upon the personality of the Spirit? The term Spirit as employed by Matthew may signify simply the creative power of God,

[164] Schürer, HJP. II, 2, p. 160 ff. Edersheim, Life of Christ I p. 171.
[165] John i. 13; iii. 3.
[166] Matt. v. 9, 44, 45; cf. Ephes. v. 1.
[167] Mark iii. 35.   [168] Isa. xi. 2; lxi. 1.   [169] Luke ii. 40.

as in the Old Testament, and in this sense no doubt Joseph understood it. Every phrase that Luke employs to denote the work of the Spirit is used in a similar sense in the Old Scripture. Elisabeth and Zacharias and John the Baptist were filled with the Spirit;[170] so was Bezalel.[171] The Spirit came upon Mary and Simeon; he came upon judges and kings and prophets under the old economy.[172] The Spirit disclosed to Simeon the coming of the Christ; to Balaam he unveiled the future and gave him to see the star that shall come out of Jacob, and the sceptre that shall rise out of Israel.[173] In the Spirit Simeon came into the Temple; by the Spirit Ezekiel was brought into the Temple,[174] into the inner court of the Temple.[175] Point by point the New Testament representation of the Spirit answers to the Old. There is nothing of course in the early record which corresponds to the work of the Spirit in the conception of Jesus, but in Luke i. 35 "the Holy Spirit shall come upon thee" is parallel with "the power of the Most High shall overshadow thee." The Holy Spirit and the power of the Most High, if no further light were given us, would readily be taken as equivalent terms. In the same way we read that John the Baptist was filled with the Holy Spirit and that the hand of the Lord was with him.

It cannot be said therefore that the Gospel narratives of the birth when taken alone lead us beyond the sphere of Old Testament thought. The personality of the Spirit was not yet clearly revealed, and was probably not apprehended by those in whom he wrought. The truth trembles upon the verge of disclosure, but is not plainly declared. Nothing is ascribed to him that may not be referred simply to the power of God.

[170] On this phrase see Plummer on *Luke* i. 15.
[171] Exod. xxxi. 3; xxxv. 31.
[172] Judg. vi. 31; I Sam. xi. 6; Ezek. xi. 5.
[173] Num. xxiv. 17.   [174] Ezek. xi. 1.   [175] Ezek. xliii. 5.

Luke is true to the traditions from which his narrative is drawn, and records the facts as they appeared to those by whom they were attested. When the personality of the Spirit is disclosed by Jesus it is seen to be in harmony with all earlier representations whether in the Old Scripture or the New. As it is the peculiar office of the Spirit under the new dispensation to reveal and apply to men the atoning work of the Son, he was not given in the full sense of the term, was not fully imparted or fully made known to men, until Jesus was glorified.[176] Throughout the Scripture the revelation of the Spirit follows the revelation of the Son.

[176] John vii. 39.

CHAPTER IV

THE HOLY SPIRIT IN THE LIFE OF JESUS

The Holy Spirit in the life of Jesus and the Holy Spirit in the teaching of Jesus are themes which though closely related are yet distinct, and require separate consideration. And a distinction must also be drawn between the record of the Synoptic Gospels and the record of the Fourth Gospel; not because the Fourth Gospel is less trustworthy and authoritative, but because of the peculiar form in which the narrative is cast. We have no hesitation in accepting it as the work of John the son of Zebedee, bosom friend of Jesus,[1] and we believe that the style of mingled majesty and grace which marks this Gospel was caught from the lips of the Master. The earlier evangelists report, John interprets; and we may call the Gospel an interpretation of the life and teaching of Jesus in the light of more than half a century of Christian history and experience. Matthew, Mark, and Luke present no such exposition of the words and even the thoughts of Jesus as is contained in John ii. 21, 23-25; vii. 39; xii. 33, except in Mark vii. 19, which will presently engage our attention.

The theme of the present chapter is the place of the Holy Spirit in the life of Jesus according to the Synoptic Gospels, and the chapter following will treat of the place of the Spirit in the life of Jesus according to John.

[1] The reasons for this judgement are given in my articles on "The Authorship of the Fourth Gospel," *Princeton Theol. Rev.*, July, 1912, and Jan., 1913.

References to the place and work of the Spirit in the life of Jesus are not numerous in the earlier Gospels, and are all examined below, except those relating to his birth, which have already been considered.[2]

I. THE WITNESS OF JOHN THE BAPTIST

I indeed baptize you in water unto repentance; but he that cometh after me is mightier than I, whose shoes I am not worthy to bear: he shall baptize you in the Holy Spirit and in fire.

Matt. iii. 11.

And he preached, saying, There cometh after me he that is mightier than I, the latchet of whose shoes I am not worthy to stoop down and unloose. I baptized you in water; but he shall baptize you in the Holy Spirit.

Mark i. 7, 8.

And as the people were in expectation, and all men reasoned in their hearts concerning John, whether haply he were the Christ; John answered saying unto them all, I indeed baptize you with water; but there cometh he that is mightier than I, the latchet of whose shoes I am not worthy to unloose: he shall baptize you in the Holy Spirit and in fire: whose fan is in his hand, thoroughly to cleanse his threshing-floor, and to gather the wheat into the garner; but the chaff he will burn up with unquenchable fire.

Luke iii. 15-17.

It may be noted at the beginning of our study that no distinction can be drawn between the use of the term Holy Spirit with and without the article. Upon Mark i. 8 Swete remarks that "πνεῦμα ἅγιον is the Holy Spirit in his operations; contrast τὸ πν. τὸ ἅγ.,[3] the Holy Spirit regarded as a Divine Person." But obviously Holy Spirit in the Greek as in the English is a proper name, and may be used indifferently with or without the article, like θεός and Κύριος and Χριστός.[4] Meyer says correctly that in the New Testament "πνεῦμα ἅγιον with and without the article is

---

[2] On the New Testament use of πνεῦμα see Burton on *Galatians*, pp. 486-92, and literature there cited.

[3] Mark vs. 29.

[4] Robertson's *Grammar Greek N. T.*, p. 761, 794-5. Ellicott on *Gal.* v. 5. Meyer on *Gal.* v. 16. Swete, *Holy Spirit in N. T.*, note P.

ever the Holy Spirit in the ordinary Biblical dogmatic sense." [5]

John contrasts his baptism with the baptism which Jesus shall administer. One symbolizes the cleansing and renewing of the heart, which is accomplished by the other. The Spirit effects what the water represents. "I baptize you," ἐν ὕδατι,[6] or ὕδατι.[7] The dative with or without the preposition may have either a local or an instrumental sense—*in* or *with*.[8]

There is no reason here to forsake the ordinary local sense of the word. John baptized *in* water, probably by immersion, as we naturally infer from the phrase; Jesus was baptized *into* (εἰς) the Jordan by John.[9] The American Revisers in Matthew and Mark read *in* water, and place *with* in the margin; while in Luke they render *with* water, and give no alternative reading. Why this distinction is made between Mark and Luke, both of whom use the simple dative, does not appear.[10] The English Revisers read *with* in every case, with *in* as a marginal reading in Matthew and Mark. Water may obviously be regarded either as the element or the instrument of baptism.

The immediate occasion of John's witness according to Luke [11] was the questioning that arose among the people whether haply he were the Christ. So great was the interest excited by his preaching that "the Jews sent unto him from Jerusalem priests and Levites to ask him, Who art thou? And he confessed, and denied not; and he confessed, I am not the

[5] *Com. on John* xx. 22.   [6] Matt.   [7] Mark and Luke.
[8] On the use of ἐν in the N. T. see Moulton, *Gram N. T. Grk.* 1, 61. Plummer on *Luke* iii. 16. Charles on *Rev.* i., p. cxxx. Robertson, *Gram. Grk. N. T.*, pp. 520, 525, 568 ff. He goes too far in affirming that "all the N. T. examples of ἐν can be explained from the point of view of the locative" (p. 590). Elsewhere he remarks "as a practical matter this use of ἐν with the locative was nearly equivalent to the instrumental case" (*Id.*, p. 524).
[9] Mark i. 9.
[10] Some mss. read ἐν ὕδατι in Mark, but the decisive weight of authority is in favour of the simple dative.
[11] Luke iii. 15.

Christ," [12] and turned the thoughts of men from himself to the Christ who shall soon appear.

The origin of John's baptism is sought in various directions. [13]

(a) As outward defilement is cleansed by water, it is the natural means of ceremonial purification, and has been so employed among all races of men. [14] The law of Moses gave a large place to ceremonial washings, which symbolized the cleansing of the heart. [15] So Pilate washed his hands before the multitude, saying, "I am innocent of the blood of this righteous man; see ye to it." [16]

(b) The initiation of proselytes into the fold of Judaism was accomplished by a threefold ceremony; circumcision, washing, sacrifice. Meyer [17] and Broadus [18] maintain that the baptism of proselytes was not in use so early as the time of Christ, but the weight of evidence appears to be on the other side.

> Strange to say, with regard to one of the things here in question, namely, the baptism or washing with water, the view has prevailed among Christian scholars since the beginning of the eighteenth century, that it was not observed as yet in our Lord's time. Originally it was for dogmatic reasons that this was maintained, while in modern times nothing but an imperfect acquaintance with the facts of the case can account for the way in which the once dominant prejudice has been allowed to linger on. Surely everyone in the least acquainted with Pharisaic Judaism must know

[12] John i. 19.
[13] See art. "Baptism" in *HBD*.
[14] See for example the use of water in the Eleusinian mysteries, Machen, *Origin of Paul's Religion*, p. 218.
[15] Oehler, *O. T. Theol.*, sec. 142. Art. "Water" in *HBD*. For refinements of later Judaism in the time of Christ see Schürer, *HJP*. II, 2, pp. 106 ff.
[16] Matt. xxvii. 24.
[17] Matt. iii. 5.
[18] Matt. iii. 6.

how frequently a native Jew was compelled in accordance with the enactments of Lev. xi.-xv. and Num. xix. to take a bath with a view to Levitical purification. . . . But a Gentile, not being in the habit of observing those regulations with regard to Levitical purity, would as such be unclean and that as a simple matter of course. In that case how was it possible that he could be admitted into Jewish communion without his having first of all subjected himself to a טְבִילָה (a Levitical bath of purification)? This general consideration is of itself so conclusive that it is needless to lay much stress upon individual testimonies.

References follow to the Mishua, Arrian, and the Sibylline oracles.[19] [20].

Both of these washings are distinguished from the baptism of John in that they were merely ceremonial. They accomplished the purifying of the flesh and fulfilled the requirements of the ceremonial law, while his baptism not only represented but required the cleansing of the heart. He administered baptism as a rite acceptable to God, "supposing still," as Josephus says, "that the soul was thoroughly purified beforehand by righteousness" (*Ant.* XVII, 5, 2).[21]

And further, this difference in the form of the ordinance appears: in general the Jew who was unclean according to the Levitical law and the proselyte who was admitted to the fold of Judaism applied the water to himself; while John baptized those who came to him. So distinctive and peculiar was the office which he exercised that it gave him the title of the Baptist.

Again his baptism differed from the washing of the proselyte because it was required of Jews as well as

[19] Schürer, *HJP.* II, 2, pp. 321 ff.
[20] See also *HDCGs.* 1, p. 863. Edersheim, *Life of Christ,* App. 12. App. 12.
[21] See Schürer, *HJP.* II, 2, p. 324, note 308.

Gentiles. The Jews are not birthright members of the kingdom of God—"think not to say within yourselves, We have Abraham to our father for I say unto you that God is able of these stones to raise up children unto Abraham";[22] but must enter the kingdom by the narrow gate of repentance. Thus Jesus said to Nicodemus, Ye, ye Jews too, must be born again.

(c) Much nearer in spirit to the baptism of John are the references of Psalmist and Prophet to the cleansing of the heart under the figure of washing with water. "Wash me thoroughly from mine iniquity, and cleanse me from my sin. . . . Wash me and I shall be whiter than snow."[23] "Wash you, make you clean."[24] "O Jerusalem, wash thy heart from wickedness, that thou mayest be saved."[25] "And I will sprinkle clean water upon you, and ye shall be clean: from all your filthiness, and from all your idols, will I cleanse you."[26] "In that day there shall be a fountain opened to the house of David and to the inhabitants of Jerusalem, for sin and for uncleanness."[27] With the teaching of the Old Scripture John was familiar, and his baptism was according to the form of the law and the spirit of the prophets. It is closely related to these high conceptions in that it was not ceremonial but moral and spiritual in purpose; it is distinguished from them in that it is brought into immediate relation to the coming of the kingdom. "The kingdom of heaven is at hand." What they foretold is near, and this gives weight and power to his message; the case is urgent. To these figurative expressions of the Old Scripture he gives concrete reality in his ministry.

The spiritual significance of John's baptism appears in the phrases that are employed to describe it. "John

[22] Matt. iii. 9.
[23] Ps. li. 2, 7.
[24] Isa. i. 16.
[25] Jer. iv. 14.
[26] Ezek. xxxiii. 25.
[27] Zech. xiii. 1.

came, who baptized in the wilderness, and preached
the baptism of repentance unto remission of sins." [28]
"I indeed baptize you in water unto repentance." [29]
"They were baptized of him in the river Jordan, confessing their sins." [30]   Repentance, confession, baptism is the divine order; and only those who professed
repentance and acknowledged their sins were baptized.
Baptism did not effect an inward cleansing; it attested
that the inward cleansing had already been accomplished. It was the sign and seal of repentance, the
outward and visible sign of an inward and spiritual
purification.

John's baptism thus marks a great advance over the
washings prescribed by the Levitical law, for it presupposed and required a change of heart in those who
received it. It falls below Christian baptism because
it was not administered in the name of Christ, and did
not involve the distinct recognition of the Holy Spirit
nor the gift in full measure of his gracious power. [31]
John's whole ministry was preparatory to the coming
of Christ, and he sharply distinguishes his baptism
from the baptism of Jesus. "I baptized you in water,
but he shall baptize you in the Holy Spirit." [32]   John
speaks of his ministry as finished when Christ appears.
In the Holy Spirit answers to the phrase *in water*. As
water is the element of John's baptism, the element in
which men are immersed, so the Holy Spirit is the
sphere of Jesus' baptism, the new life element of the
believer. Those whom Jesus baptizes are in the
Spirit, [33] and must walk in the Spirit as the sphere of
the new life in Christ. [34] It is better, therefore, to
read *in* the Holy Spirit than *with* the Holy Spirit,
giving to the phrase the largest, richest sense that words

[28] Mark i. 4.
[29] Matt. iii. 11.
[30] Matt. iii. 6.
[31] Acts xix. 1-6.

[32] Mark i. 8.
[33] Rom. viii. 9.
[34] Gal. v. 10.

may convey. A striking instance of the use of the phrase is found in I Cor. xii. 3: "Wherefore I make known unto you, that no man speaking in the Spirit of God saith, Jesus is anathema; and no man can say, Jesus is Lord, but in the Holy Spirit." In both clauses the English and American Revisers read correctly, *in the (Holy) Spirit;* while the Authorized Version reads *by the (Holy) Spirit.* The term *in the Spirit* is obviously similar to the phrases frequently employed in the New Testament, in God, in Christ, in the Lord. They all convey the thought that in Him, alike in the natural and spiritual sphere, we live and move and have our being.

The outpouring of the Spirit was foretold as a characteristic feature of the days of the Messiah. "For I will pour water upon him that is thirsty, and streams upon the dry ground; I will pour my Spirit upon thy seed." [35] "I will put my Spirit within you." [36] "And it shall come to pass afterward, that I will pour out my Spirit upon all flesh." [37] The phrase *baptize in the Spirit* is found only twice in the New Testament, beside the witness of John the Baptist here and in John i. 33: in Acts i. 5 Jesus said to his disciples, "John indeed baptized with water, but ye shall be baptized in the Holy Spirit not many days hence"; and Peter cites this word of the Lord in Acts xi. 16. The term is evidently peculiar to John the Baptist, from whom Jesus derived it, and was suggested by his peculiar office. Baptism is the form which the outpouring of the Spirit naturally takes in his mind.

Though the gift of the Spirit is characteristic of the Messianic Kingdom, in the Old Testament it is never referred to the Messiah. It is God who pours forth the Spirit, and he alone. The Messiah receives the Spirit from God, "I have put my Spirit upon him," [38] cited in Matt. xii. 18. It is also true that

[35] Isa. xliv. 3.
[36] Ezek. xxxvi. 25-27.
[37] Joel ii. 28.
[38] Isa. xlii. 1.

nowhere else in the Synoptic Gospels is Jesus said to bestow the Spirit upon men, and he himself ascribes the gift of the Spirit to the Father. "But when they deliver you up, be not anxious how or what ye shall speak; for it shall be given you in that hour what ye shall speak. For it is not ye that speak, but the Spirit of your Father that speaketh in you." [39] "If ye then, being evil, know how to give good gifts unto your children, how much more shall your heavenly Father give the Holy Spirit to them that ask him?" [40] In one instance, however, we find if not a direct claim, yet a suggestion on the part of Jesus that he too imparts the Spirit. Mark xiii. 11 reads: "And when they lead you to judgment, and deliver you up, be not anxious beforehand what ye shall speak; but whatsoever shall be given you in that hour. that speak ye; for it is not ye that speak, but the Holy Spirit"; while the parallel passage in Luke xxi. 14, 15 reads: "Settle it therefore in your hearts, not to meditate beforehand how to answer; for I will give you a mouth and wisdom, which all your adversaries shall not be able to withstand or to gainsay." If the Holy Spirit speaks in the disciples, and the wisdom with which they answer their adversaries is given them by Jesus, there is an evident implication that the Spirit is imparted by him.

In the Fourth Gospel he explicitly associates himself with the Father in the gift of the Spirit. "I will pray the Father, and he shall give you another Comforter, that he may be with you forever, even the Spirit of truth"; [41] "the Comforter, even the Holy Spirit, whom the Father will send in my name"; [42] "When the Comforter is come, whom I will send unto you from the Father"; [43] "If I go not away, the Comforter will not come unto you; but if I go, I will send him unto you." [44] These passages will receive further consideration when we enter upon the study of Jesus'

[39] Matt. x. 19, 20.
[40] Luke xi. 13.
[41] John xiv. 16.
[42] John xiv. 26.
[43] John xv. 26.
[44] John xvi. 7.

teaching. It is sufficient here to observe how the Fourth Gospel in this matter, as in so many others, brings out into clear light what is implicit but obscure in the earlier Gospels.

Jesus himself did not baptize in water, as John is careful to inform us, correcting the rumours that had reached the Pharisees. "Jesus himself baptized not, but his disciples." [45] Paul affirmed, "Christ sent me not to baptize, but to preach the Gospel." [46] Peter *commanded* Cornelius and those who were with him to be baptized. [47] The prophets of the Old Testament constantly and vehemently insisted that rites and forms, even though enjoined by the law of God, have no value in themselves, apart from the spirit of the worshipper. "To obey is better than sacrifice, and to hearken than the fat of rams," [48] is the first principle of their teaching. Ceremonies and sacrifices as the expression of righteousness are accepted, as the substitute for righteousness are condemned. "The sacrifice of the wicked is an abomination to Jehovah." [49] The immeasurable superiority of the moral and spiritual to the external and formal is fundamental in Old Testament doctrine. [50] David exclaims, "Thou delightest not in sacrifice; else would I give it: Thou hast no pleasure in burnt offering. The sacrifices of God are a broken spirit." [51] By the mouth of Jeremiah God declares, "I spake not unto your fathers, nor commanded them in the day that I brought them up out of the land of Egypt, concerning burnt offerings or sacrifices: but this thing I commanded them, saying, Hearken unto my voice." [52] Compared with obedience the law of sacrifice counts for nothing.

The same principle prevails in the New Testament. Here the outward and formal is always subordinate to the inward and spiritual. Rites and forms have

[45] John iv. 1, 2.
[46] I Cor. ii. 17.
[47] Acts x. 48.
[48] I Sam. xv. 22.
[49] Prov. xv. 8; xxi. 27.
[50] Isa. i. 10; Amos v. 21-24; Micah vi, 6-8.
[51] Ps. li. 16, 17.
[52] Jer. vii. 22, 23.

value only as the offering of a holy heart. While therefore baptism as a divine ordinance is to be observed, like the prescriptions of the ceremonial law of Israel, like them, too, it is of value only as the sign and seal of the covenant relation between God and his people. If the change of heart which it is appointed to attest is wanting, the ceremony becomes an empty show. Jesus committed baptism in water to his disciples; he alone may baptize in the Holy Spirit. Only when men have been baptized in the Spirit does the baptism in water avail; for the water is the outward sign of the inward cleansing of the Spirit.

To baptize in the Spirit is to confer upon men the gift of the Spirit in his saving and sanctifying power.

To the witness of John, "He shall baptize you in the Holy Spirit," Matthew and Luke add, "and fire" (καὶ πυρί) which Mark omits. The question is much debated whether the fire signifies purification or destruction. Does it represent one aspect of the work of the Spirit, or something entirely distinct from it? That it signifies sanctification is said to be required by the intimate association of fire with the Spirit which is indicated by the omission of ἐν before πυρί. We read not ἐν πνεύματι καὶ ἐν πυρί as two distinct and contrasted elements, but ἐν πνεύματι καὶ πυρί, as two aspects of the same work. The position is well taken. The rule is clearly laid down by Winer[53]:

> When two or more substantives dependent on the same preposition immediately follow one another joined together by a copula, the preposition is most naturally repeated, if the substantives in question denote things which are to be conceived as distinct and independent . . . ; but not repeated if the substantives fall under a single category, or (if proper names) under one common class . . . if the substantives are connected dis-

[53] *Thayer's ed. Gr. N. T.,* p. 419.

junctively or antithetically, the preposition is in
the former case usually, and in the latter case
always repeated. . . . In general, there is a greater
tendency to repeat the preposition in the New
Testament than in Greek prose.

Robertson speaks to the same effect [54]: "With the
antithesis the repetition is the rule," but he recognizes in the same paragraph that the rule is not without exception. It must be admitted that the gram-
matical construction here strongly favours the view
which regards fire as a symbol of the sanctifying power
of the Spirit. In both Matthew and Luke the English
Revisers insert *with* and the American Revisers *in*
before fire, both in italics of course; but the addition
is an interpretation of the text. It is better to read
simply, as the original has it, in the Holy Spirit and
fire. Additional support for this view is sought by
some scholars in the tongues of fire which rested upon
the heads of the disciples at Pentecost,[55] but they were
the symbols not of sanctification, but of a particular
gift of the Spirit which was then imparted, a χάρισμα
the gift of prophetic inspiration, of speaking with other
tongues. The arguments in favour of this interpretation are presented by Godet and Plummer on Luke
iii. 16.

On the other hand, the context, as most expositors
recognize, imperatively requires the penal sense of
the term. Fire is used with this significance in the
verse preceding in Matthew: "And even now the axe
lieth at the root of the trees: every tree therefore that
bringeth not forth good fruit is hewn down, and cast
into the fire" [56] and in the verse following: "Whose
fan is in his hand, and he will thoroughly cleanse his
threshing floor; and he will gather his wheat into the
garner, but the chaff he will burn up with unquench-

[54] *Gram. Grk. N. T.,* p. 566.   [56] Matt. iii. 10; *cf.* Luke iii. 9.
[55] Acts ii. 3.

able fire." [57]   Here are three successive verses treating
of the ministry of Christ. Is it credible that *fire* should
have one meaning in the first and third verses, and an
entirely different meaning in the second?   Moreover
John's whole representation of the work of Christ in
the Synoptic Gospels is dominated by the thought of
judgment; for John came in the spirit and power
of Elijah, the bold reformer and judge of Israel, and
he drew his conception of the Messiah from the Old
Testament where judgment constantly appears as the
purpose of his ministry. In Isaiah iv. 4 he shall cleanse
Jerusalem "by the spirit of justice, and by the spirit
of burning." "He shall smite the earth with the rod
of his mouth; and with the breath of his lips shall he
slay the wicked." [58] "He is like the refiner's fire, and
like fullers' soap." [59]   Fire is the natural symbol and
minister of judgment,[60] and is frequently employed
in the Gospels to represent the torments of hell;[61] as
well as elsewhere in the New Testament.[62]   The Lord
Jesus shall return from heaven "with the angels of his
power in flaming fire, rendering vengeance to them that
know not God, and to them that obey not the gospel
of our Lord Jesus." [63]   Jesus declared that he came to
judge as well as to save, "For judgment came I into
this world." [64]   Elsewhere he said, "God sent not the
Son into the world to judge the world, but that the
world should be saved through him";[65] "I came not

[57] Matt. iii. 12; *cf.* Luke iii. 17.
[58] Isa. xi. 4.
[59] Mal. iii. 2.
[60] Gen. xix. 24; Exod. ix. 23, 24; Deut. xxxvii. 22; Ps. xxi. 9;
1. 3; xcvii. 3; Isa. xxix. 6; xxx. 27; Jer. iv. 4; v. 14; Ezek. xxi. 31;
Amos vii. 4; Neh. i. 6; iii. 15; Zech. ix. 4; Mal. iv. 1.   The list
might be prolonged indefinitely.
[61] Matt. v. 22; xiii. 30, 40, 42, 56; xviii. 9; xxiii. 41; Mark ix. 44,
48; Luke xvi. 24.
[62] Heb. xv. 27; II Peter iii. 7; Jude vii.; Rev. xiv. 10; xix. 20;
xx. 10, 14, 15; xxi. 8.
[63] II Thess. i. 7, 8.
[64] John ix. 30.
[65] John iii. 17.

to judge the world, but to save the world." [66] In one case he speaks of the purpose, in the other of the result of his mission; as in Matt. x. 14: "I came not to send peace, but a sword." The purpose of his coming is to save, but judgment is forced upon him by the unbelief and disobedience of men.

There are two passages in Jesus' teaching which call for careful consideration here. The first is Luke xii. 49, 50: "I came to cast fire on the earth; and what do I desire, if it is already kindled? But I have a baptism to be baptized with; and how am I straitened till it be accomplished?" Here too baptism and fire are joined, but the baptism relates to his own personal experience, the fire to his ministry among men. The nature of the fire is precisely indicated in the verses following: "Think ye that I am come to give peace in the earth? I tell you, Nay; but rather division: for there shall be from henceforth five in one house divided; three against two, and two against three. They shall be divided, father against son, and son against father; mother against daughter, and daughter against her mother; mother-in-law against her daughter-in-law, and daughter-in-law against her mother-in-law." In a passage of similar import, though drawn from a different occasion, Matthew has the sword instead of fire as the minister of judgment. [67] In both instances the reference is to the divisions which attended the coming of Christ, and which everywhere accompany the preaching of the gospel. Now this part of his work has been accomplished: the fire has been kindled, the line of division has been drawn. What remains? To what does he look forward? What more does he desire? His baptism, the sacrificial sufferings and death which shall fulfil his earthly mission, his atoning work, so that he may say with dying breath, It is finished. With that baptism his disciples also

[66] John xii. 47.   [67] Matt. x. 34.

shall be baptized; [68] not of course that they shall have a part in that atonement which it is his alone to make, but that the Kingdom which is established by the service and sacrifice of the Son of God must be continued and extended by the service and sacrifice of his disciples; so that every believer may say in this sense with Paul, "I fill up on my part that which is lacking of the afflictions of Christ in my flesh for his body's sake, which is the church." [69]   The disciple must be baptized, must be crucified, with his Lord.

Mark ix. 49 is one of the most obscure and difficult passages in the New Testament. Taking the words with the context we read, "And if thine eye cause thee to stumble, cast it out: it is good for thee to enter into the kingdom of God with one eye, rather than having two eyes to be cast into hell; where their worm dieth not, and the fire is not quenched. For every one shall be salted with fire. Salt is good: but if the salt have lost its saltness, wherewith will ye season it? Have salt in yourselves, and be at peace one with another." Meyer notes and rejects fourteen interpretations of the phrase, salted with fire. His own exposition assumes the genuineness of the clause, "and every sacrifice shall be salted with salt," which the best critical authorities reject.

The first question that confronts the expositor is the extent of the term *every one* ($\pi\tilde{\alpha}\varsigma$); does it mean every man or every disciple? The reference to the fire of hell in the immediate context renders it impossible to confine the word to believers; while the description of salt as good, and the injunction, "Have salt in yourselves," forbid the exclusive reference of the term to the wicked. Evidently both the righteous and the wicked are included. Every man shall be salted with fire. But the phrase, *salted with fire*, seems to involve a contradiction in terms. Salt preserves, fire destroys;

[68] Mark x. 38.   [69] Col. i. 24.

what is it then to be salted with fire? To be at once preserved and destroyed? How may these conceptions be harmonized? How can fire perform the office of salt? These are questions hard to answer, and no interpretation of the words has commanded general assent. The most satisfactory explanation appears to be that salting with fire includes both purification and destruction. The fire both purifies and destroys, and in both cases the salt indicates the enduring effect of the fire. The sanctification of the righteous and the punishment of the wicked are alike eternal. The verse preceding tells of the fire that consumes the wicked, and the verse following speaks of the salt that shall preserve the righteous. This verse unites the two conceptions, and blends them in a single phrase—"Every one shall be salted with fire." This interpretation is not free from difficulties, but no better has been suggested.

Thus the double office of fire is indicated, which Paul has portrayed with such clearness and force in the picture of the judgment.[70]

The sanctifying power of the Spirit of necessity involves destruction. The individual is purified by the casting out of evil, the people are purified by the destruction of the wicked, as precious metal is purged of its dross.[71] The double work of fire in purifying and destroying answers to the double office of the Spirit. Jesus distinguished sharply between the work of the Spirit in the disciples—guiding them into all the truth as it is in him; and his work in the world—convicting in respect of sin, and of righteousness, and of judgment.[72] "The word of God is living, and active, and sharper than any two-edged sword, and piercing even to the dividing of soul and spirit, of both joints and marrow, and quick to discern the

[70] I Cor. iii. 12-15.
[71] Ps. cxix. 119; Prov. xxv. 4; Isa. i. 25; Ezek. xxii. 18, 19.
[72] John xvi. 8, 13.

thoughts and intents of the heart";[73] and this word
of God is the sword of the Spirit,[74] who searcheth all
things, yea the deep things of God." [75]   In Joel ii. 28,
30 the promised outpouring of the Spirit upon all
Israel is attended by "wonders in the heavens and in
the earth: blood, and fire, and pillars of smoke."   And
the thought finds its highest expression in Heb. xii. 29
—"for our God is a consuming fire."   The phrase *our
God* designates him as the God of the New Testament,
revealed in Christ, and the whole tenor of the passage
makes it evident that the writer had in mind the attitude of God both toward the righteous, whom as fire
he purifies, and toward the wicked, whom as fire he
destroys.

Spirit and fire are not therefore antithetical and
mutually exclusive conceptions, but fire expresses one
feature of the Spirit's work, one aspect of his holy ministry.   "He shall baptize you in the Holy Spirit," and
in particular in that discriminating and separating and
sanctifying element of the Spirit's work which is
signified by fire.

Objection is taken to this view of the double office
of the Spirit because *you* (ὑμᾶς) refers to a single
definite group, who could not be at once sanctified and
destroyed.   But the objection has little weight.   Those
to whom John spoke were a motley company—Pharisees and Sadducees,[76] publicans and soldiers,[77]
multitudes from all the regions round about.[78]
Surely the Spirit did not perform the same work
in every one to whom John preached.   Moreover
you is here to be understood in a generic sense—not
simply *you who are here,* but *you men,* or at least *you
men of Israel.*   According to the better interpretation
you has the same generic force in Luke xvii. 21.   To
the rendering, the kingdom of God is within you

[73] Heb. iv. 17.   [76] Matt. iii. 7.
[74] Ephes. vi. 17.   [77] Luke iii. 12, 14.
[75] I Cor. ii. 10.   [78] Luke iii. 7, 10.

(ἐντὸς ὑμῶν), which is given in the Authorized Version and in the English and American Revised Versions, objection is made that this was not true of the Pharisees to whom Jesus spoke. We must therefore render, as in the margin of the Revised Versions, *in the midst of you.*[79] But *within you,* though apparently rejected by most modern expositors, accords better with the context: "The kingdom of God cometh not with observation"; and *you* means not you Pharisees but you men. This rendering is maintained by Godet, *in loc.;* Robertson, *Grammar of the Greek New Testament,* p. 641; Dalman, *Words of Jesus,* p. 145. Plummer is uncertain. If the thought is that the kingdom was actually present among them in the Person of Jesus, what is the meaning of the words, "Neither shall they say, Lo, here, or there"? That is exactly what would be said and must be said in such a case. The truth which Jesus has in mind is that which George Eliot has finely expressed in Romola: "Who shall put his finger on justice, and say 'It is here'? Justice is like the Kingdom of God—it is not without us as a fact, it is within us as a great yearning." That is not the whole truth, of course, but it is a highly important aspect of the truth; which finds a place alike in the Old Testament and in the New. The kingdom which is righteousness and peace and joy in the Holy Spirit [80] must set up its throne in the individual heart before it can be established in the world.

There is thus abundant warrant both in the context and in the general tenor of Scripture teaching, alike in the Old Testament and the New, to interpret fire as signifying judgment, the discriminating judgment which purifies the good and destroys the evil. Spirit and fire are not mutually exclusive terms, but fire is the apt and striking symbol of the Spirit's work among men. The Spirit and fire are associated here as the

[79] See Briggs, *Messiah of the Gospels,* p. 245.   [80] Rom. xiv. 17.

Spirit and water are associated in John iii. 5. There, too, the preposition is not repeated (ἐξ ὕδατος καὶ πνεύματος). Water and fire both express aspects of the Spirit's ministry; in one case his cleansing power, and in the other, both cleansing and destruction are signified. The Spirit is both dove and fire; as Jesus is both lion and lamb.

II. The Baptism of Jesus

Then cometh Jesus from Galilee to the Jordan unto John, to be baptized of him. But John would have hindered him, saying, I have need to be baptized of thee, and comest thou to me? But Jesus answering said unto him, Suffer it now: for thus it becometh us to fulfil all righteousness. Then he suffered him. And Jesus, when he was baptized, went up straightway from the water: and lo, the heavens were opened, and he saw the Spirit of God descending as a dove, and coming upon him; and lo, a voice out of the heavens, saying, This is my beloved Son, in whom I am well pleased.

Matt. iii. 13-17.

And it came to pass in those days, that Jesus came from Nazareth of Galilee, and was baptized of John in the Jordan. And straightway coming up out of the water, he saw the heavens rent asunder, and the Spirit as a dove descending upon him: and a voice came out of the heavens, Thou art my beloved Son, in thee I am well pleased.

Mark i. 9-11.

Now it came to pass, when all the people were baptized, that, Jesus also having been baptized, and praying, the heaven was opened, and the Holy Spirit descended in a bodily form, as a dove, upon him, and a voice came out of heaven, Thou art my beloved Son; in thee I am well pleased.

Luke iii. 21, 22.

"Then cometh Jesus from Galilee to the Jordan unto John, to be baptized of him." [81] Mark says specifically that Jesus came from Nazareth of Galilee. The scene of the baptism cannot be precisely fixed. John was "in the wilderness of Judea," [82] the region adjoining the western shore of the Dead Sea, and of the lower

[82] Matt. iii. 1.   [81] Matt. iii. 13.

Jordan.[83] Tradition places the baptism of Jesus near Jericho, but the tradition is late, and no great weight may be attached to it. A little later, according to the Fourth Gospel, John was baptizing at Bethany, not Bethaharah,[84] as in the Authorized Version. But the site of Bethany is unknown, and we are not told whether Jesus was baptized there. Prof. B. B. Warfield,[85] following Caspari, affirms that "it is capable of something very like demonstration that Bethany was situated in the region about Et-Tell, north of the lake of Galilee. It has been already pointed out that the nationality of the crowds which surrounded John had changed to a more northern complexion. That he was now baptizing, not near Jericho but some three days' journey north of it, follows again from the length of time consumed by Jesus' journey from this place to the Olivet Bethany." Further argument is drawn from a comparison of the Synoptic Gospels with John, and from John's account of Jesus' movements after his baptism; and the conclusion is reached that "by the time our Lord came to his baptism, John had traversed the whole length of Palestine, preaching repentance . . . and the king delayed his coming until the preparation was complete." We may hold that it is at least probable that Bethany lay to the north of the Sea of Galilee. Whether Jesus was baptized there remains uncertain, but we may reasonably suppose that his baptism took place somewhere in the region to which Bethany belonged. Matthew alone relates that when Jesus presented himself to be baptized John would have hindered him, saying, "I have need to be baptised of thee, and comest thou to me?" "I have need of the baptism of the Holy Spirit which thou only canst impart." He recognizes both the personal

[83] Luke iii. 3.   [85] *Expositor,* 3rd series, vol. i, p. 267.
[84] See Origen on *John,* Bk. vi. 24.

and the official priority of Jesus; and in the record of
the Fourth Gospel he states distinctly the ground on
which it rested: "This was he of whom I said, He
that cometh after me is become before me: for he was
before me."[86]   The humility of John is answered by
the greater humility of Jesus: "Suffer it now: for thus
it becometh us to fulfil all righteousness." "Suffer it
now": this is the immediate duty of the hour.

Why did Jesus submit to be baptized of John? Baptism was not to him as to other men, a symbol of cleansing from sin, as John recognized. The precise purport
of the act has given rise to much discussion. Meyer
enumerates various explanations.[87]   He was baptized
as the bearer of the guilt of others; because as a member of an unclean people he was unclean according to
the Levitical law; because he regarded the collective
guilt of the nation as resting upon him; because he
would separate himself inwardly from the sins of the
nation; because he would honour the baptism of John
by his example; because he would bind himself to the
observance of the law. Other explanations are added,
but these may suffice; for Jesus himself has stated
his purpose in terms which are not obscure. "Thus it
becometh us to fulfil all righteousness." It becometh
us—you and me. We have each a duty to perform,
and that duty is to fulfil all righteousness, to obey the
divine law, the law which I am not come to destroy,
but to fulfil. Jesus recognizes that the office of John
was of divine appointment. It was he whom Malachi
foretold, who came in the spirit and power of Elijah,
and his baptism was from heaven.[88]   Jesus as a pious
Jew submitted to every ordinance of the law, and thus
he set an example of obedience. Though he had no

[86] John i. 15.
[87] Matt. iii. 13.
[88] Matt. xxi. 25; Mark xi. 30; Luke xx. 4; *cf.* Matt. xi. 11-14.

personal need of baptism, by refusing or neglecting it he would have cast discredit upon the work of John, and thrown a stumbling-block in the way of others. In the same spirit though he might claim exemption from the half-shekel tax as the Son of God, yet he bade Peter pay it, "lest we cause them to stumble." [89]

Moreover, though we may not speak precisely of the baptism as his ordination to the office of Messiah, since baptism never appears in Scripture as a rite of ordination; yet as it was accompanied by the descent of the Spirit, the divine anointing,[90] and marked the opening of his public ministry, it was in effect an act of consecration and ordination. Then he emerged from the obscurity of thirty years, was recognized by John as the Christ of God, and entered upon that career which has made him the foremost man in the history of the world. He did not then begin to be conscious of his Messianic office and divine Sonship; for when he was twelve years of age, Mary found him in the Temple, sitting in the midst of the teachers, hearing them, and asking them questions; and when she gently rebuked him—"Son, why hast thou thus dealt with us? Behold thy father and I sought thee sorrowing?"—he replied, "Why did you seek me? Why look elsewhere? Knew ye not that I must be in my Father's house?" She said, Thy father Joseph; he answered, My Father God." [91] [92]

Thus by his baptism Jesus at the same time fulfilled the law and inaugurated the gospel. John yields to him, and he assumes the place of prominence and power which his forerunner had held; and though John continued to preach and baptize for a considerable time, his prediction was fulfilled, "He must increase, but I must decrease." [93]

[89] Matt. xvii. 24-27.
[90] Isa. lxi. 1.
[91] Luke ii. 47-49.
[92] See art. "Consciousness" in *HDCGs*.
[93] John iii. 30.

When Jesus was baptized, he prayed.[94]   The nature of that prayer is not disclosed, but the whole tenor of his life assures us that he besought his Father to prepare him for the ministry which was opening before him.   The prayer was answered by the gift of the Holy Spirit, who "descended in a bodily form (σωματικῷ εἴδει). as a dove, upon him." [95] [96]   It was not merely a vision, an apparition; the Spirit assumed the form of a dove, and came visibly upon him.   Jesus saw the Spirit,[97] and John saw him.[98]   Whether others saw him we are not told.   It may be that the dove and the voice from heaven were seen and heard only by those whose eyes were illumined by the Spirit, and whose ears were attuned to the speech of heaven.   At a later time when God spoke from heaven the multitude that stood by, and heard it, said that it had thundered: others said, an angel hath spoken to him.[99]   In the account of Saul's conversion in Acts ix. it is recorded that "the men that journeyed with him stood speechless, hearing the voice, but beholding no man";[100] and in his account of the matter Paul says that "they that were with me beheld indeed the light, but they heard not the voice of him that spake to me." [101]   The apparent discrepancy is removed by the obvious supposition that his companions heard the sound of the voice but did not distinguish the words.   The divine presence was recognized by all, for they "were all fallen to the earth"; [102] the message was for Saul alone.

In his baptism the Spirit is associated with Jesus in the Gospel records for the first time since his birth. In Gen. i. 2, when the earth was waste and void, the

[94] Luke iii. 21.
[95] Luke iii. 22.
[96] See Swete on *Mark* i. 10.
[97] Matt. iii. 16; Mark i. 10.
[98] John i. 32.
[99] John xii. 29.
[100] Acts ix. 7.
[101] Acts xxii. 9.
[102] Acts xxvi. 14.

Spirit of God is seen brooding upon the face of the waters, as a bird upon its nest. At the inauguration of the Messianic Kingdom the Spirit appears in a similar form. Without him nothing was accomplished in the sphere of nature or of grace.

The dove is the symbol of purity and gentleness. Jesus commanded the twelve, when he sent them forth as sheep in the midst of wolves, to be "wise as serpents, and harmless as doves." [103] The word rendered *harmless* by the Authorized and Revised Versions (ἀκέραιοι), with *simple* in the margin of the Revised Versions, is by some derived from κέρας, a horn, signifying therefore without horns, harmless. But it is properly derived from κεράννυμι, to mix, and means therefore unmixed, pure; and in the moral sphere *without guile*. Elsewhere in the New Testament the word is found only in Phil. ii. 15, where again it is rendered *harmless* by the Revised Versions, without marginal note; and in Rom. xvi. 19, where it is rendered, *simple*. Simple is better than harmless, but because it is used in Scripture at times in an unfavourable sense equivalent to foolish, it would be well to read *guileless* or *pure*. Augustine aptly remarks that "there are those who are said to be simple who are only indolent. They are called simple, but they are only slow." [104] [105] The word is used of wine unmingled with water, of metals free from alloy, and fitly describes the simplicity which should characterize the Christian life, the absence of all that is inconsistent with the purity which should mark the children of God. [106]

[103] Matt. x. 16.

[104] *Tract on John* vi. 3.

[105] On the symbolism of the dove see Lightfoot, *Apost. Fas.* II, p. 974. Smith and Cheatham, *Dict. Chr. Aut.*, Art. "Dove." Swete, *Holy Spirit in N. T.*, note A. Philo sees in the dove the symbol of the wisdom of God. *Quis Rer. Div. Her.*, sec. 25.

[106] On the derivation and meaning of the term see Ellicott on *Phil.* ii. 15; Trench, *Syn. N. T.*, LVI.

Possessing such qualities the dove appears in the Old Testament as a term of affection;[107] and the eyes of the beloved are compared to doves.[108] Because of its innocence and gentleness the dove, like the lamb, was frequently offered in sacrifice: in the burnt offering;[109] in the trespass offering;[110] in the cleansing of the leper,[111] and upon other occasions. Of special interest is the command that after child birth, when the days of her purifying are fulfilled, the mother shall offer a lamb for a burnt offering, and a young pigeon, or a turtle dove, for a sin offering: "And if her means suffice not for a lamb, she shall take two turtle doves, or two young pigeons." [112]   Joseph and Mary took advantage of this provision of the law and offered according to their poverty.[113]   The only birds allowed in sacrifice according to the law of Moses were the pigeon and the dove. They were offered for sale in the courts of the Temple at the passover; and Jesus drove out those who sold them in the beginning [114] and again at the close of his ministry.[115]   No reason can be shown why Jesus should not have performed this natural and significant act upon both occasions. Like every wise teacher he frequently repeated his instruction. The assertion is often made when sayings are found in different connexions in the different evangelists that the various reports cannot all be correct. And the argument often proceeds upon the wholly unwarranted assumption that Jesus never repeated himself. On the contrary it is incredible that he did not repeat himself often, for repetition is the primary law of education. And

---

[107] Ps. lxxiv. 19; Song of Sol. ii. 14; v. 2; vi. 9.
[108] Song of Sol. i. 15; iv. 1; v. 12.
[109] Lev. i. 14.
[110] Lev. v. 7, 11.
[111] Lev. xiv. 22, 30.
[112] Lev. xii. 6-8.
[113] Luke ii. 24.
[114] John ii. 14-16.
[115] Matt. xxi. 12.

if he taught the same lessons upon various occasions, why might he not perform for a second time an act at once so natural and so significant of the nature of his ministry? Arguments drawn in particular instances from the improbability that such teaching would have been given under such circumstances deserve careful attention, but arguments which assume that Jesus could never have spoken the same words or performed the same act upon different occasions are entitled to little consideration.

The comment of Augustine upon this passage furnishes a curious example of those strange conceits which so often disfigure the pages of this great expositor.

> Now if the dove's note is a moaning, as we all know it to be, and doves moan in love, hear what the apostle says, and wonder not that the Holy Ghost willed to be manifested in the form of a dove: "for what we should pray for as we ought, says he, we know not; but the Spirit Himself intercedes for us with groanings which cannot be uttered." . . . . It is not then in Himself . . . that the Holy Spirit groans; but in us He groans because He makes us to groan.[116]

After the baptism came the descent of the Spirit, after the descent of the Spirit the voice of God. Thus Father, Son, and Spirit are associated at the beginning as at the end of Jesus' earthly ministry, and in both instances in connection with baptism: when he is baptized and when he commands his disciples to baptize all the nations into the name of the Father and the Son and the Holy Spirit.[117] Nowhere else in the Synoptic record are the Persons of the Trinity thus brought together. The baptism

[116] *Tract on John* vii. 2.   [117] Matt. xxviii. 19.

designates Jesus as a man, made under the law; the anointing of the Spirit proclaims him the Messiah; the voice from heaven declares him to be the Son of God.

> For in the name of Christ is implied, He that anoints, He that is anointed, and the unction itself with which He is anointed. And it is the Father who anoints, but the Son who is anointed by the Spirit, who is the unction, as the Word declared by Isaiah, "The Spirit of the Lord is upon me, because he hath anointed me"— pointing out both the anointing Father, the anointed Son, and the unction, which is the Spirit.[118]

The dove descends and abides upon the Lamb. The same personal qualities and sacrificial value belong to each of them. The purity and gentleness of the human nature of Jesus spring from the indwelling of the Spirit of God, the source of all holiness in the life of man.

Various symbols are employed in the Gospels to represent the Holy Spirit, each of them setting forth some aspect of his character and work. In the birth of Jesus he is signified by the cloud that over-shadows the virgin mother,[119] the cloud which is the symbol of the divine presence and here specifically of the presence of the Spirit; at the baptism of Jesus he assumes the form of a dove; in his purifying and sanctifying ministry he appears as fire; in Jesus' words to Nicodemus he is figured by the wind in his free self-determination; by water[120] in his refreshing and life-giving power. As he is a dove he may be grieved;[121] as he is fire, he may be quenched.[122]

III. The Temptation

Then was Jesus led up of the Spirit into the wilderness to be tempted of the devil. And when he had fasted forty days and forty nights, he afterward hungered. And the tempter came and said unto him, If thou art the Son of God, command that these stones become bread. But he answered and said, It is written, Man shall not live by bread alone, but by every word that proceedeth out of the mouth of God. Then the devil taketh him into the holy city; and he set him on the pinnacle of the temple, and saith unto him, If thou art the Son of God, cast thyself down: for it is written, He shall give his angels charge concerning thee: and, On their hands they shall bear thee up, Lest haply thou dash thy foot against a stone. Jesus said unto him, Again it is written, Thou shalt not make trial of the Lord thy God. Again, the devil taketh him into an exceeding high mountain, and showeth him all the kingdoms of the world, and the glory of them; and he said unto him, All these things will I give thee, if thou wilt fall down and worship me. Then saith Jesus unto him, Get thee hence, Satan: for it is written, Thou shalt worship the Lord thy God, and him only shalt thou serve. Then the devil leaveth him; and behold, angels came and ministered unto him.

Matt. iv. 1-11.

And straightway the Spirit driveth him forth into the wilderness. And he was in the wilderness forty days tempted of Satan; and he was with the wild beasts; and the angels ministered unto him.

Mark i. 12, 13.

And Jesus, full of the Holy Spirit, returned from the Jordan, and was led in the Spirit in the wilderness during forty days, being tempted of the devil. And he did eat nothing in those days: and when they were completed, he hungered. And the devil said unto him, If thou art the Son of God, command this stone that it become bread. And Jesus answered unto him, It is written, Man shall not live by bread alone. And he led him up, and showed him all the kingdoms of the world in a moment of time. And the devil said unto him, To thee will I give all of this authority, and the glory of them: for it hath been delivered unto me; and to whomsoever I will I give it. If thou therefore wilt worship before me, it shall be thine. And Jesus answered and said unto him, It is written, Thou shalt worship the Lord thy God, and him only shalt thou serve.

And he led him to Jerusalem, and set him on the pinnacle of the temple, and said unto him, If thou art the Son of God, cast thyself down from hence: for it is written. He shall give his angels charge concerning thee, to guard thee: and, On their hands they shall bear thee up, lest haply thou dash thy foot against a stone. And Jesus answering said unto him, It is said, Thou shalt not make trial of the Lord thy God. And when the devil had completed every temptation, he departed from him for a season.

Luke iv. 1-13.

The Spirit began at once to direct and impel the life of Jesus, and the first step is indicated by Matthew in a striking sentence: "Then was Jesus led up of the Spirit into the wilderness to be tempted of the devil." [123] It is a strange combination: "led up of the Spirit to be tempted of the devil." Satan too is God's servant; and though for an appointed time and in a limited degree he is permitted to exercise power over men, yet his authority is narrowly confined, and he cannot lay a finger upon God's children until God gives him leave. That is one of the great lessons of the Book of Job, which carries us behind the experience of the sufferer, and exhibits to us at once the malice of Satan and the controlling and restraining hand of God. Temptation has two aspects: in the purpose of Satan it is designed to seduce and destroy, in the purpose of God it is designed to purify and strengthen. Temptation is opportunity. These two aspects of temptation often blend in a single act, a single experience: as Paul's thorn in the flesh was at once a messenger of Satan to buffet him, and a means of grace through which the power of Christ was conveyed to him. In the very endeavour to thwart the purpose of God Satan is made the agent of the divine will.

Luke records that "Jesus, full of the Holy Spirit, returned from the Jordan, and was led in the Spirit in the wilderness," [124] portraying thus both the local

[123] Matt. iv. 1.   [124] Luke iv. 1.

and the spiritual sphere of the temptation, and indicating that he was directed by the Spirit throughout the whole period of the forty days. Mark according to his custom adds to the narrative several graphic touches. *"Straightway"*; immediately upon his baptism followed the temptation. Contrast the glory of the scene at the Jordan, the open heavens, the anointing of the Spirit, the voice from heaven, with the dreary solitude and fierce conflict of the wilderness. In similar fashion the glory of the transfiguration mount gave place to the scene of demoniac possession. "The Spirit *driveth* him forth into the wilderness." The word expresses strong compulsion; and though it is sometimes used in a weakened sense in the New Testament, yet here there is no reason to forsake the ordinary meaning of the term. The Spirit took control of him and impelled him to the wilderness. Is there in the word a suggestion of the shrinking of Jesus from the trial that awaited him? We may not presume to answer a question that penetrates so deeply into the mystery of his Person; but upon other occasions it is recorded that he did thus recoil from the suffering that lay before him. When his death drew near he cried, "Now is my soul troubled; and what shall I say? Father save me from this hour.[125] But for this cause came I unto this hour. Father, glorify thy name."[126] Thus nobly does the Spirit triumph over the weakness of the flesh. In Gethsemane with strong crying and tears, with groans and bloody sweat he prayed that the appointed cup might pass from him, yet surrendered himself with implicit obedience to the Father's will.[127]

Mark adds also that he was with the wild beasts, depicting the loneliness of the wilderness in which he

[125] Whether this sentence be regarded as a petition or a question does not materially affect the sense of the passage.

[126] John xii. 27, 28.

[127] Luke xxii, 42-44; Heb. v, 7.

encountered Satan, like the loneliness of the Garden and the cross.

The purpose for which the Spirit led him to be tempted is clearly indicated in the Scripture, though the Gospels, as their manner is, relate the story without remark or comment.

1—Temptation is an essential part of the discipline of human life, and Jesus as a true man must be tried as other men are tried. That is the truth plainly and repeatedly declared in the Epistle to the Hebrews. "It became him, for whom are all things, and through whom are all things, in bringing many sons unto glory, to make the author of their salvation perfect through sufferings." [128] "Who in the days of his flesh, having offered up prayers and supplications with strong crying and tears unto him that was able to save him from death, and having been heard for his godly fear, though he was a son, yet learned obedience by the things which he suffered, and having been made perfect, he became unto all them that obey him the author of eternal salvation." [129]

2—He left us an example, that we should follow his steps.[130] It is noteworthy that when Jesus is commended to us as an example in the apostolic writings, it is always his sufferings that the writer has in mind.

3—Through his temptations he learned to sympathize with men in their temptations. This too the author of the Hebrews insists upon again and again. "Wherefore it behooved him in all things to be made like his brethren, that he might become a merciful and faithful high priest in things pertaining to God, to make propitiation for the sins of the people. For in that he himself hath suffered being tempted, he is able to suffer them that are tempted." [131] "For we

[128] Heb. ii. 10.
[129] Heb. v. 7-9.
[130] I Peter ii. 21.
[131] Heb. ii. 17, 18.

have not a high priest that cannot be touched with the feeling of our infirmities; but one that hath been in all points tempted like as we are, yet without sin." [132] Here are set forth the range of our Lord's temptation—"in all points"; the reality—"like as we are"; and the result—"yet without sin." "Let us therefore draw near with boldness unto the throne of grace, that we may receive mercy, and my find grace to help in time of need."

4—As he came to destroy the devil,[133] it was incumbent upon him to meet the adversary face to face.

The Spirit impelled him to the conflict, the Spirit gave him the victory. For the weapon with which he repulsed the assaults of the enemy and drove him beaten from the field was the sword of the Spirit, which is the Word of God.

The period of temptation was forty days. The three temptations recorded by Matthew and Luke represent each the climax of a long continued effort on the part of Satan, bidding higher or tempting more adroitly with each refusal of Jesus to give ear to his seductions; or they gather up in few words the substance of temptations which were represented in many forms. The battle with Satan which began in the wilderness raged without ceasing throughout the whole life of Jesus. Luke records "the devil departed from him for a season." [134] Appeal was made continually to every motive of hope and fear; and he was tried by foes and tempted by friends; Peter the rock becomes a stumbling-block. A rock in place is a foundation, a rock out of place is a stumbling-block. His life was one long conflict with the powers of evil. Satan put forth the utmost of his power to seduce him in the wilderness; and when he could not lead him astray he sought to destroy him. He appears most active at the beginning of our Lord's ministry, and again at its close,

[132] Heb. iv. 15-16.   [133] Heb. ii. 14.   [134] Luke iv. 13.

when he instigated Judas to betray him,[135] and the Jews to seek his life.[136]   When he cannot pervert, he endeavours to destroy.   If he cannot turn Jesus from the way of the cross, he will crush him by the cross, not merely putting an end to his life but loading him with the shame and ignominy of a felon's death.

IV. JESUS RETURNED IN THE POWER OF THE SPIRIT TO GALILEE

"And Jesus returned in the power of the Spirit to Galilee; and a fame went out concerning him through all the region round about." [137]   Luke assigns no reason for the return to Galilee, but Matthew and Mark connect it with the imprisonment of John the Baptist. "Now when he heard that John was delivered up, he withdrew into Galilee; and leaving Nazareth, he came and dwelt in Capernaum." [138]   "Now after John was delivered up, Jesus came into Galilee, preaching the Gospel of God." [139]   John assigns a different reason. "When therefore the Lord knew that the Pharisees had heard that Jesus was making and baptizing more disciples than John (although Jesus himself baptized not, but his disciples), he left Judea, and departed again into Galilee." [140]   There is no contradiction here between John and the earlier Gospels, for the imprisonment of the Baptist and the jealousy of the Pharisees are closely related.   Josephus tells us that "When many came in crowds about him, for they were greatly moved by hearing his words, Herod, who feared lest the great influence John had over the people might put it into his power and inclination to raise a rebellion (for they seemed ready to do anything he should advise), thought best, by putting him to death, to prevent any mischief

[135] Luke xxii. 3; John xiii. 27.
[136] John viii. 39-44.
[137] Luke iv. 14.
[138] Matt. iv. 12, 13.
[139] Mark i. 14.
[140] John iv. 1-3.

he might cause, and not bring himself into difficulty by sparing a man who might make him repent of it when it should be too late." [141] The motives of a man are ordinarily complex, and fear of John's influence with the people might readily combine with personal resentment for his bold rebuke to lead Herod to deal with him as he did. And the Pharisees in like manner might well be moved by envy of the popularity of Jesus and fear of the political consequences which that popularity might entail: "If we let him thus alone, all men will believe on him; and the Romans will come and take away both our place and nation." [142]

It was not to escape from Herod that Jesus withdrew into Galilee, for Galilee too was under his rule, but to avoid the jealous hatred of the Pharisees. The Gospel narratives indicate that Judea, and especially Jerusalem, was his chosen field of labour, which he visited as often and as long as he could, turning to Galilee only when he was driven out by his enemies. [143] "O Jerusalem, Jerusalem . . . how often would I have gathered thy children together." [144] The term *withdrew* (ἀνεχώρησεν) which Matthew uses, ordinarily carries with it in the New Testament the thought of avoiding difficulty or danger. The imprisonment of John turned the minds of the people and the fears and jealousies of the Pharisees to his yet more popular and dangerous successor. John had at first drawn all eyes to himself; then he had divided the allegiance of the people with Jesus: but now Jesus stands alone, a shining mark for the envy and malice of the rulers.

But there were yet other and profounder influences at work than the plots of the enemies of Jesus. He withdrew into Galilee, says Matthew, [145] "that it might

[141] Ant. XVIII, 5, 2.
[142] John xi. 48.
[143] See my *Teaching of the Gospel of John*, pp. 25, 26.
[144] Luke xiii. 33, 34.
[145] Matt. iv. 14.

be fulfilled which was spoken through Isaiah the
prophet, saying,

"The land of Zebulun and the land of Naphtali,
Toward the sea, beyond the Jordan,
Galilee of the Gentiles,
The people that sat in darkness
Saw a great light
And to them that sat in the region and shadow of death
To them did light spring up." [146]

It was according to the divine purpose that he preached
the gospel in Galilee of the Gentiles.   And this is
indicated also by the words of Luke that "he returned
in the power of the Spirit into Galilee."   Even when
his conduct was determined by obvious reasons it
was still directed by the Spirit.   Beneath all the im-
pulses and motives that swayed his life was the
inspiring and controlling operation of the Spirit of
God.

But more than that is conveyed by the phrase.   Not
only under the impulse and guidance of the Spirit but
clothed with the power of the Spirit he came into
Galilee.   That power was manifest in his teaching.
"He taught in their synagogues, being glorified of
all." [147]   When he spoke to his neighbours in the
synagogue of Nazareth, "all bare him witness, and
wondered at the words of grace which proceeded out
of his mouth." [148]   Always he taught "as one having
authority, and not as their scribes." [149]   And the power
of the Spirit appeared also in his miracles, especially
in the casting out of evil spirits.   The first miracle that
he performed on this visit to Galilee was the healing
of a man with a spirit of an unclean demon in the
synagogue of Capernaum; [150] and this cure was followed

[146] Isa. ix. 1, 2.
[147] Luke iv. 14.
[148] Luke iv. 22.

[149] Matt. vii. 29.
[150] Mark i. 23; Luke iv. 33.

on the same day by many others of the same kind.[151]
It is significant that Jesus refers this form of miracle,
and this only, to the power of the Spirit. "If I by the
Spirit of God cast out demons, then is the kingdom of
God come upon you." [152] In the parallel passage Luke
reads, "By the *finger* of God," [153] indicating probably
the impersonal way in which the disciples at the time
conceived of the Holy Spirit as a manifestation or
operation of the divine power. In the same way Ezekiel speaks: "The hand of Jehovah was upon me, and
he brought me out in the Spirit of Jehovah." [154] Demoniac possession was the most conspicuous and striking manifestation of the power of the kingdom of
darkness, and the casting out of demons the supreme
exhibition of the sovereignty of God over the forces
of unrighteousness. Jesus therefore ascribes it directly
to the Spirit of God. Only by the Spirit of God can
the spirits of evil be expelled.

That Jesus believed in evil spirits and in their power
over men is too obvious to be questioned. There are
those who recognize the fact but hold that he was
mistaken; and there are those who maintain that he
knew better but accommodated his teaching to the
prejudices and superstitions of his hearers. Then we
must believe that by word of mouth and by his acts he
deliberately encouraged and fostered a false opinion,
liable to fearful abuse. From such a course no possible
advantage could accrue to truth or to the kingdom of
God; and that Jesus followed it is simply incredible. If
we were forced to choose, it would be better to hold him
ignorant of the truth than careless of the truth. But
no such alternative is thrust upon us. He taught the
reality of demoniac possession simply because it was
a fact. That evil spirits inhabit men is the visible
evidence of the power of sin and in the casting out of

[151] Matt. viii. 16, 17; Mark i. 32-34; Luke xiv. 40, 41.
[152] Matt. xii. 28.   [153] Luke xi. 20.   [154] Ezek. xxxvii. 1.

evil spirits he recognized the token and prophecy of the overthrow of the kingdom of Satan.[155]

V. Jesus Rejoiced in the Holy Spirit

"In that same hour he rejoiced in the Holy Spirit, and said, I thank thee, O Father, Lord of heaven and earth, that thou didst hide these things from the wise and understanding, and didst reveal them unto babes: yea, Father, for so it was well pleasing in thy sight." [156]

The passage in which these words occur is found only in Luke, for it falls within the so-called Perean section of the Third Gospel, with which Matthew and Mark have few points of contact.[157] Jesus "appointed seventy others"—in addition to the twelve—[158] "and sent them two and two before his face into every city and place, whither he himself was about to come." [159] When they returned, they were filled with joy, exclaiming, "Lord, even the demons are subject unto us in thy name." He did not rebuke their joy, but rejoiced with them: "I beheld Satan as lightning fall from heaven." The change of *fall* to *falling* in the English Revised Version and to *fallen* in the American Version is in neither case an improvement. "I watched him fall." [160] At the same time he reminds them of a higher and purer joy that is theirs, that their names are written in heaven. The thought of a book of life in which God inscribes the names of his people was familiar to the Jews.[161] There are those who teach that concern for our personal salvation is purely selfish, and unworthy of a disciple of Christ; we should forget ourselves in care for others. However we may

[155] Luke x. 17, 18.
[156] Luke x. 21.
[157] Luke ix. 51—xviii. 14.
[158] Luke ix. 1.
[159] Luke x. 1.
[160] Moulton, *Gram. N. T. Greek,* p. 134.
[161] Exod. xxxii. 32; Ps. lxix. 28; Dan. xii. 11; Mal. iii. 16.

reason about the matter, that is evidently not the teaching of Christ or of the New Testament generally. The Scripture constantly presses upon men the motives of hope and fear, holds out to them the promise of reward and the threat of penalty as incentives to holy living. The life of a man is not his own; it belongs to God: and he is bound to care for it, and train it, enrich it, for the glory of God. The first concern of every man is to see that he is himself right with God. Why should he be careful of the souls of others, and careless of his own? Is his soul less precious in the sight of God than his neighbour's? Nor is the life equipped for service merely by serving. The roots must be nourished that the fruit may abound, and he who does not give heed to the development of his own spiritual life, his own salvation in the largest sense of the term, will have little strength or grace with which he may minister to God or man. Because the individual soul is of itself unspeakably precious before God, and that it may be rendered effective and fruitful in the service of the kingdom, every man is required to look to himself, to make sure of his place among the children of God.

This is the only occasion recorded in any of the Gospels upon which Jesus is said to have rejoiced. Much is told of his emotional life, of the passions and affections that stirred his heart. Thrice it is related that he wept: when from the height of Olivet he looked down upon Jerusalem, and thought of the sin of the chosen people, and the judgment that awaited them;[162] when he mingled his tears with those of the sisters of Lazarus;[163] and in Gethsemane, where he offered up "prayers and supplications with strong crying and tears unto him that was able to save him from death." [164] Four times it is recorded that he loved:

[162] Luke xix. 41.   [163] John xi. 35.   [164] Heb. v. 7.

he loved the rich young ruler;[165] Martha and Mary and Lazarus;[166] and the company of his disciples, the twelve;[167] and John is distinguished as the disciple whom Jesus loved. Twice he marvelled: at the faith of the centurion;[168] and at the unbelief of the men of Nazareth.[169] He was often moved with compassion by the sorrows and miseries of men. His soul was troubled in view of the suffering that threatened him.[170] On one occasion he was moved to mingled grief and anger by the hardness of men's hearts.[171]

Only here is it said that he rejoiced. That is not to say that his life was spent in darkness and sorrow. The prophet calls him a man of sorrows, and that is true, but it presents only one aspect of his life. Sorrow played upon his life and sometimes penetrated to the depths of his spirit,[172] but the dominant note of his experience was joy. "My meat is to do the will of him that sent me."[173] The writer of the Epistle to the Hebrews puts into the mouth of Christ the words of Ps. xl. 8, which read in the original, I delight to do thy will, O my God. In his last discourse to his disciples beneath the shadow of the cross he spoke of his joy.[174] But this is the only instance in which the joy that filled his heart is given a definite place in the record of his life. See paper, "The Emotional Life of Our Lord," by Prof. B. B. Warfield, in *Biblical and Theological Studies* by the Faculty of Princeton Seminary.

What was the immediate occasion of his rejoicing? Luke associates it with the return of the seventy and the report which they gave to him of their ministry. "In that same hour he rejoiced." The words that

[165] Mark x. 27.
[166] John xi. 5.
[167] John xiii. 1; xv. 5.
[168] Matt. viii. 10.
[169] Mark vi. 6.
[170] John xii. 27; Matt. xxvi. 37.
[171] Mark iii. 5.
[172] John xii. 27; Mark xiii. 34.
[173] John iv. 34.
[174] Heb. xii. 2.

follow, "I thank thee, O Father," are reported by
Matthew in a different connexion, following the woes
that Jesus pronounced upon the cities that had not
repented though they beheld his mighty works, and
the invitation, "Come unto me, all ye that labour and
are heavy laden." [175] But his note of time is not so
precise as Luke's—"At that season";[176] while Luke
reads, "In that same hour." We may presume that
the words were twice spoken, or note that while Matthew's point of time is indefinite, Luke has fixed the
very hour. That Matthew uses the phrase *at that
season* in an indeterminate sense elsewhere is plain.[177]

The ground of his rejoicing is "that thou didst hide
these things from the wise and understanding, and
reveal them unto babes." The question at once arises,
What is meant by *these things?* Jesus does not say,
but obviously he has in mind the mysteries of the
kingdom of heaven which he had revealed unto his
disciples, and had commissioned them to proclaim.[178]
These are the things which God hides from some and
discloses to others among men.

There are those who would find the ground of Jesus'
thanksgiving simply in the revelation of these things
to babes, and read "though, or whereas, thou didst hide
these things from the wise and prudent." But the
difficulty is not removed by this rendering. In any
case Jesus recognizes that God hides the mysteries of
the kingdom from some and reveals them to others.
The fact indeed is written broadly across the face of
history. Nor is the rendering warranted. Rom. vi. 17
is not parallel. The literal rendering of that verse is:
"But thanks be to God that ye were bondservants of
sin, but obeyed from the heart." Here the adversative,
but (δέ) justifies the rendering of the Revised Version: "But thanks be to God, that whereas ye were

[175] Matt. xi. 25.
[176] Matt. xi. 25.
[177] Matt. xii. 1; xiv. 1.
[178] Luke viii. 10; Matt. xiii. 11.

servants of sin." Here, however, the clauses are joined
by *and* (καὶ), and must be taken as together furnish-
ing the reason for his thanksgiving. It is in harmony
with all Scripture teaching, and especially with the
teaching of Jesus, to regard the hiding and the reveal-
ing as alike moving him to thanksgiving, because both
are comprehended in the purpose of God as principles
of the divine administration, and because taken together they promote the highest ends. The wise and
prudent are the worldly wise, those who are wise in
their own conceits, who rely upon their own understanding, and will not submit to be taught of God;
the babes are the humble, the docile. Paul enjoins the
Corinthians, "Brethren, be not children in mind: yet
in malice be ye babes, but in mind be men." [179] Jesus
rejoices that the truth is hidden from one class and
made known to the other, because God is thus glorified
as the source of all true wisdom. Only they are wise
who learn of him. The condition of entrance into the
kingdom of heaven is not intellectual superiority or
abundant learning, nothing that is confined of necessity to a limited class; it is the meek and teachable
spirit; the gates of eternal life are thrown open to all
those who suffer God to be their guide.

The law here recognized prevails not only in the
realm of religious truth, but in every sphere of thought.
Lord Bacon tells us that "The access also to this work"
—man's acquisition of power over nature—"hath been
by that port or passage, which the divine Majesty
(who is unchangeable in his ways) doth infallibly
continue and observe; that is the felicity wherewith
he hath blessed an humility of mind, such as rather
laboureth to spell and so by degrees to read in the
volumes of his creatures, than to solicit and urge and
as it were to invocate a man's own spirit to divine
and give oracles unto him. For as in the inquiry of

[179] I Cor. xiv. 20.

divine truth, the pride of man hath ever inclined to leave the oracles of God's word and to vanish in the mixture of their own inventions; so in the selfsame manner, in inquisition of nature they have ever left the oracles of God's works, and adored the deceiving and deformed imagery which the unequal mirrors of their own minds have represented unto them. Nay, it is a point fit and necessary in the front and beginning of this work without hesitation or reservation to be professed, that it is no less true in the human kingdom of knowledge than in God's kingdom of heaven that no man shall enter into it *except he become first as a little child.*" [180]

Paul has repeatedly set forth the same truth. "Professing themselves to be wise, they became fools." [181] "Hath not God made foolish the wisdom of the world? For seeing that in the wisdom of God, the world through its wisdom knew not God, it was God's good pleasure through the foolishness of the preaching to save them that believed." And the reason assigned is "that no flesh should glory before God." [182]   Jesus rejoices that men do not enter the kingdom of heaven through their own wisdom, but through humility and faith; for thus the kingdom is thrown open to every sincere and earnest soul, and to God is given all the glory of their salvation.

The nature as well as the ground of his rejoicing is indicated. He rejoiced in the Holy Spirit. The phrase does not occur again in the New Testament. Certain manuscripts omit *Holy,* and some scholars of the first rank, therefore, as Meyer and Godet, read, he rejoiced in spirit. Similar expressions are found elsewhere: he perceived in his spirit; [183] he sighed deeply in his heart; [184] he groaned in the spirit; [185] he

[180] *On the Interpretation of Nature,* ch. i.   [183] Mark ii. 5.
[181] Rom. i. 22.   [184] Mark viii. 12.
[182] I Cor. i. 20-30.   [185] John xi. 33.

was troubled in the spirit.[186]   But the weight of
authority is in favour of the reading, *Holy;* and
though the phrase is unique, the thought is familiar.
"The kingdom of God is not eating and drinking, but
righteousness and peace and joy in the Holy Spirit." [187]
"The fruit of the Spirit is love, joy." [188]   The joy
that thrilled the heart of Jesus was the joy of the
Holy Spirit,[189] the joy begotten by the Spirit in the
hearts of the children of God.   From him all righteousness and peace and joy proceed.   To him is
properly referred every pure emotion and holy passion and experience that stirs within the hearts of
men.

The passage shows that not only was the conduct
of Jesus, his outward activity, directed and controlled
by the Holy Spirit, but the Spirit inspired the very
thoughts and feelings of his heart. He walked not
after the flesh but after the Spirit, and he lived in the
Spirit, as the very source and spring of his life. The
joy that filled his heart he imparts to his disciples,[190]
and Paul bids believers, Rejoice in the Lord.[191] We
cannot fail to note that while as a man Jesus receives
from the Holy Spirit the gifts of peace and joy, as
Son of God he bestows these gifts on men.[192] All
that is good in men is the gift of the Father through
the mediation of the Son by the operation of the Holy
Spirit.

From our study it is plain that references to the
Holy Spirit in the life of Jesus are not numerous in
the Synoptic Gospels. There are indeed only six,
beside those contained in the narrative of his birth.
(1) the words of John the Baptist "He shall baptize
you with the Holy Spirit." [193] (2) The Spirit de-

[186] John xiii. 21.
[187] Rom. xiv. 7.
[188] Gal. v. 22.
[192] John xiv. 27; xv. 11.
[193] Matt. iii. 11; Mark i. 8; Luke iii. 16.

[189] I Thess. i. 6.
[190] John xv. 11.
[191] Phil. iv. 4.

scended upon him at his baptism.[194]   (3) He was led
by the Spirit into the wilderness to be tempted of
the devil.[195]   (4) He returned in the power of the
Spirit into Galilee.[196]   (5) "I will put my Spirit upon
him." [197]   (6) He rejoiced in the Holy Spirit.[198]   Four
of these passages are found in Matthew, three in Mark,
and five in Luke. (5) is peculiar to Matthew, (4) and
(6) are peculiar to Luke.

But while these references are few, they are of great
importance, because they occur at critical points in
the history, as in his conception, his baptism, his
temptation, and because they imply the continuous
operation of the Spirit in his life. What is told us
of his acts and experiences upon these exceptional and
extraordinary occasions may fairly be taken to indicate that the Spirit who then controlled and inspired
him was his constant guide and comforter, to whom
he committed all his ways and from whom he derived
unfailing supplies of strength and wisdom and grace.
That indeed is plainly declared by Matthew who
applies to Jesus the prophecy of Isaiah:

Behold, my servant whom I have chosen;
My beloved in whom my soul is well pleased;
I will put my Spirit upon him,
And he shall declare judgment to the Gentiles.
He shall not strive nor cry aloud;
Neither shall anyone hear his voice in the streets.
A bruised reed shall he not break,
And smoking flax shall he not quench,
Till he send forth judgment unto victory.
And in his name shall the Gentiles hope.[199]

His character and his ministry are the fruit of the
Spirit of God.

[194] Matt. iii. 16; Mark i. 10; Luke iv. 1.   [197] Matt. xii. 18.
[195] Matt. iv. 1; Mark i. 12; Luke iv. 1.   [198] Luke x. 21.
[196] Luke iv. 14.   [199] Matt. xii. 18-21.

CHAPTER V

THE HOLY SPIRIT IN THE LIFE
OF JESUS—II.

Each of the four Gospels presents Jesus as God manifest in the flesh. He is not simply man in Matthew, Mark, and Luke, and God in John: in all of them alike he is God-man. This union of the divine and human natures in one Person gives rise to startling contrasts. He was thirsty by Jacob's well and asked a woman of Samaria for a drink of water; to her he gave the water of life eternal. He was asleep in a boat, wearied with the labour of the day; he calmed the storm with a word. He had nowhere to lay his head; and all things were delivered unto him of the Father. He wept beside the tomb of Lazarus; he called the dead to life. He was a man of sorrows; he bequeathed to his disciples his peace, his joy. Knowing that the Father had given all things into his hands, with those same hands he washed the feet of the disciples, setting the power of God to perform the office of a slave. Dying on the cross, to the penitent robber he opened the gates of Paradise.

The earlier Gospels do not represent Jesus as man becoming God, while John represents him as God become man. The same Jesus appears in all of them, the Word made flesh. But while this truth of the twofold nature of Jesus is written broadly across the face of every Gospel, it is also true that his divinity shines most conspicuously in John, because the beloved disciple penetrated most deeply into the mystery of his Person. The divine nature is not thrown into relief by concealing his humanity, but rather by setting the words and deeds of the Son of God side by side with the physical infirmities and sorrows of the Son of man. Nowhere else is Jesus at once so evidently human and so conspicuously divine, as in the Fourth Gospel. John does not depict the transfiguration scene, but the transfigured Christ appears on every page. This is especially evident in Jesus' witness to himself. In the earlier Gospels his chosen theme, is the kingdom of heaven, of God; and his characteristic phrase, The kingdom is like: in John he is himself the central theme, and the characteristic phrase, I am. Much, therefore, that is merely implied or suggested in the Synoptic Gospels is fully disclosed here. Jesus is no more truly divine but he is more evidently and radiantly divine in John.

We have seen that the Synoptic Gospels contain only six references to the place and work of the Holy Spirit in the life of Jesus; the Fourth Gospel contains only, two, which we may now proceed to consider in order.

1—The witness of John the Baptist.

The Fourth Gospel does not relate the baptism of Jesus, as the others do, but gives John the Baptist's account of the descent of the Spirit, which accompanied it. Of the baptism itself neither the evangelist nor the Baptist speaks, and we learn of it only from the Synoptic record.

> On the morrow he seeth Jesus coming unto him, and saith, Behold, the Lamb of God, that taketh away the sin of the world. This is he of whom I said, After me cometh a man who is become before me: for he was before me. And I knew him not; but that he should be made manifest to Israel, for this cause came I baptizing in water. And John bare witness, saying, I have

beheld the Spirit descending as a dove out of heaven; and it abode upon him. And I knew him not: but he that sent me to baptize in water, he said unto me, Upon whomsoever thou shalt see the Spirit descending, and abiding upon him, the same is he that baptizeth in the Holy Spirit. And I have seen, and have borne witness that this is the Son of God.[1]

The repeated phrase, I knew him not, evidently means, I knew him not until I saw the Spirit descending upon him; that is, I did not recognize him as the Christ. But this appears to imply that John had no personal acquaintance with Jesus. It is hardly credible that John should not have known of the birth and office of Jesus from Elisabeth his mother, who in the unborn babe in Mary's womb recognized *my Lord*.[2] Even if his father and mother, already advanced in years at his birth, were dead before he was old enough to receive the story from their lips, it is highly improbable that the tradition from which Luke derived his narrative was unknown to him whom it so nearly concerned. And it is no more credible that John should have wholly lost sight of him whose forerunner he knew himself to be. To say therefore, I knew him not as the Christ implies, I did not know that it was Jesus of Nazareth who came to me to be baptized. They were kinsmen, yet there is in the record no indication that they had ever met before. John was in the deserts, the wilderness of Judea, till the day of his showing unto Israel;[3] while Jesus was brought up in Nazareth of Galilee, and the Gospels give no indication that he ever visited Judea from the time that he was twelve years old until he entered upon his public ministry.

That John might know the Christ when he ap-

[1] John i. 29-34.   [2] Luke i. 43.   [3] Luke i. 80.

peared a sign was promised. The star made him
known to the wise men, the angel to the shepherds;
the Spirit declared him to John. It was the characteristic and distinguishing mark of the Messiah as foretold by the prophets that the Spirit of Jehovah should
rest upon him; and in the sight of John the prophecy
was fulfilled in Jesus. It might be said of John confessing Christ as of Peter, "Flesh and blood hath not
revealed it unto thee, but my Father who is in
heaven." [4]

At this point there is an apparent discrepancy between the Fourth Gospel and the First. Here John
the Baptist affirms that he did not know Jesus until
he saw the Spirit descending upon him, and this occurred, as the other Gospel informs us, when he had
been baptized. But Matthew says that when Jesus
came to John to be baptized, John would have hindered him, saying, "I have need to be baptized of thee,
and comest thou to me?" [5] How can these statements
be reconciled? If John "knew him not," what is the
meaning of the words that Matthew records? Why
should John seek to hinder Jesus from receiving baptism at his hands, unless he recognized in him the
Christ? It is not enough to say in answer to the
difficulty that John was impressed by the character
of Jesus, that he had ascertained the purity and holiness of his life, through personal intercourse with him
before he presented himself for baptism. The words
obviously convey a higher meaning. For John as a
prophet of God could recognize in the discharge of his
office no superior except the Christ. No mere man,
however exalted his character or holy his life, could
John regard as beyond the need of baptism and repentance. But if he recognized in Jesus the Christ
before his baptism, how could he say, I knew him not

[4] Matt. xvi. 17.   [5] Matt. iii. 14.

until the Spirit came upon him after his baptism?
The only adequate solution of the difficulty is that according to Matthew John had a premonition or anticipation of the truth which came to full assurance only
when the promised sign was given. John believed that
Jesus was the Christ when he came to him to be baptized, and he learned who he was; but he had no
authoritative and official knowledge of the fact until
he saw the Spirit rest upon him. Since the promise
had been given that the Christ should be indicated by
the descent of the Spirit upon him, for that sign John
must wait. The witness of John must follow the witness of the Spirit. However fully he might be persuaded in his own mind, he could not proclaim Jesus
as the Christ until the prophecies of the Old Testament and the promise of God had been fulfilled in
him. The prophet must speak by revelation, and not
run before he is sent.

Here as in the earlier Gospels John contrasts his
baptism with the baptism of Jesus. "He that sent me
to baptize in water, he said unto me, Upon whomsoever
thou shalt see the Spirit descending, and abiding upon
him, the same is he that baptizeth in the Holy Spirit."
To the Synoptic record John adds, "And it abode upon
him." *It* may here be justified as expressing John's
point of view, for there is no reason to suppose that
he apprehended the Personality of the Spirit; or as
referring to the visible manifestation of the Spirit in
the form of a dove, since the subject of the verb *abode*
is not expressed in the Greek. The abiding of the
Spirit upon Jesus distinguishes him from the rulers
and prophets to whom the Spirit was given on a particular occasion for a special purpose and a limited
time.

The other Gospels relate that Jesus saw the descent
of the Spirit in the form of a dove, which marked his

entrance upon his Messianic work; the Fourth Gospel records that John also beheld it, and it was to him the promised sign of the Christ.

Jesus receives the Spirit that he may impart the Spirit to men. He on whom the Spirit descends and abides is he who baptizes with the Spirit. As in baptism the body is immersed in water, so the soul is immersed in the Spirit, affected in every part by his cleansing power.

John omits *and fire,* which is found in Matthew and Luke, and the omission points to a striking difference between the two representations of Jesus. In Matthew and Luke John presents him predominantly, almost exclusively, as a judge. The axe, the winnowing fan, the fire, are the instruments of justice. The destruction of the wicked is the conspicuous feature of his ministry. But in the Fourth Gospel John presents him as the Saviour, and the note of judgment is wanting. How striking is the contrast between him who wields the axe, baptizes with fire, burns the chaff with unquenchable fire, and the Lamb of God who taketh away the sin of the world! There is nothing in the record of the Fourth Gospel that answers to the axe and the fire; there is nothing in the Synoptic account that answers to the Lamb bearing the sins of men. The Baptist was charged with a twofold message, of which the first part is recorded by the Synoptic Gospels only, and the second part only by the Fourth Gospel. Before Jesus came to him, he cried, "Repent ye; for the kingdom of heaven is at hand." After Jesus came to him he cried, "Behold, the Lamb of God." Repentance and faith formed the burden of his preaching; repentance that prepares the way for the coming of the Saviour; faith that lays hold upon him when he comes. John's representation of Jesus is in harmony with the purpose which dominates the Fourth Gospel throughout, and is expressed in

xx. 31: "These are written that ye may believe that
Jesus is the Christ, the Son of God; and that believing
ye may have life in his name." Faith is the dominant
note of John's Gospel, as love is the dominant note
of his Epistle. Here, as often elsewhere, we must combine the records of the various Gospels to reach the
full measure of the truth as it is in Jesus.

2—The Spirit given without measure.

> He that cometh from above is above all: he
> that is of the earth is of the earth, and of the earth
> he speaketh: he that cometh from heaven is above
> all. What he hath seen and heard, of that he
> beareth witness; and no man receiveth his witness.
> He that hath received his witness hath set his seal
> to this, that God is true. For he whom God hath
> sent speaketh the words of God; for he giveth
> not the Spirit by measure. The Father loveth the
> Son, and hath given all things into his hand. He
> that believeth on the Son hath eternal life; but
> he that obeyeth not the Son shall not see life, but
> the wrath of God abideth on him.[6]

Two preliminary questions must be considered before we undertake to ascertain the meaning of the reference to the Spirit.

(1) Are these the words of John the Baptist, who has
just been speaking, or of the evangelist? It cannot be
shown that the thought of the passage is too advanced
for John the Baptist, for it contains nothing that is
not virtually contained in his witness to Jesus.[7] In
i. 33, 34 the several Persons of the Trinity already appear, though John could not have apprehended the full
mystery of the Godhead as it is brought to light in the
New Testament. "He that sent me," the Father; he on
whom the Spirit rests, the Son. There is nothing in
this passage which is not implicitly contained or ex-

[6] John iii. 31-36.   [7] Godet, in loc.

plicitly declared in John's witness in the first chapter of the Gospel.

It is often affirmed that the passage cannot be referred to the Baptist because "no man receiveth his witness" is inconsistent with vs. 29—"He that hath the bride is the bridegroom; but the friend of the bridegroom, that standeth and heareth him, rejoiceth greatly because of the bridegroom's voice: This my joy therefore is made full." How could he rejoice if no man receiveth Christ's witness? But the argument is not weighty. John's joy in Christ was not measured or determined by the faith of men. He could rejoice in hearing the bridegroom's voice if there were none to share his joy. Nor must the sorrowful words, "No man receiveth his witness" be too literally understood; for immediately he adds, "He that hath received his witness." Here as in John i. 11, 12—"He came unto his own, and they that were his own received him not, But as many as received him"—the general truth is noted, and then the proper exception made. In the heart of John joy and sorrow were blended, as in the heart of Jesus. The present tenses of the passage also point to John, and while the question cannot be absolutely determined, the balance of probability is decided in favour of the view that these are the words of John the Baptist.[8]

(2) The construction of the sentence is in doubt. What is the subject of the verb? The Authorized Version reads, "God giveth not the Spirit by measure *unto him*," but both *God* and *unto him* are properly omitted in the Revised Version. The Greek reads simply, οὐ γὰρ ἐκ μέτρου δίδωσιν τὸ πνεῦμα, and the subject must be supplied. It is possible that either Father, Son, or Spirit may be the subject. The Father gives the Spirit,

---

[8] So Godet and Meyer, though Meyer adds that the passage was "elaborated in its whole style and coloring by John" (the evangelist). For the view that it is the evangelist who speaks, see Westcott, *in loc.*

the Son gives the Spirit, or the Spirit gives, with the object not specified. The third alternative may be dismissed with little hesitation, for throughout the Gospels the Spirit ordinarily does not give, but is given, and there is no reason to forsake the common usage here. It is not so easy to determine between the Father and the Son, both of whom appear in the preceding clause. But here again the predominant usage of the Gospels is in favour of regarding the Father as the subject. Usually it is the Father who gives. This passage presents the Father as sending the Son, and giving all things into his hand. He who sends the Son gives the Spirit; and in the *all things* which he gives the Spirit is embraced. We may therefore with little hesitation read, "God giveth not the Spirit by measure." [9] And this is in evident accord with the whole tenor of the passage. The Father sends the Son, and the Son speaks the words of the Father, because the Father gives the Spirit without measure.

Having thus cleared the way, we may proceed to the interpretation of the text. It is unlimited in form, and declares a general truth—"God giveth not the Spirit by measure." The law prevails alike in nature and in grace; and the affluence of the divine bounty and goodness is a theme on which the sacred writers delight to dwell both in the Old Testament and in the New.[10] It is in accordance with the uniform teaching of Scripture, therefore, that God is said to give the Spirit without measure. He gives the Spirit to every man as fully as he is able to receive him. As earth and sky are flooded with light, and the eye receives of its radiance all that it is capable of receiving; as the atmosphere envelops the earth, and the lungs receive of it all that they are able to contain; so the Spirit is

[9] For the view that the Son is the subject see Westcott, *in loc.*
[10] Ps. xxxi. 1, xxxiii. 5, lxv. 11, lxxxi. 10, lxxxiv. 11; Matt. vi. 33, vii. 11; I Cor. iii. 21-23; Ephes. iii. 19-21; Phil. iv. 19; Jas. i. 5.

poured out without measure and makes the hearts of
men his temples. It is recorded of many of the saints
of God that they were filled with the Spirit. The first
to whom that honour is ascribed in the Old Testament
record was not Abraham or Moses or David, not war-
rior or sage or king or prophet; but Bezalel, whose
office it was "to devise skilful works, to work in gold,
and in silver, and in brass, and in cutting of stones
for setting, and in carving wood, to work in all manner
of workmanship." [11] Thus early in the history of the
race did God set high honour on that manual toil
which centuries later was glorified by the Son at the
carpenter's bench in Nazareth.

There are many instances of the limitless gift of the
Holy Spirit in the New Testament, especially in the
writings of Luke, who alone of New Testament writers
uses the terms full of the Spirit, filled with the Spirit;[12]
unless Ephes. v. 18 should be deemed an exception—
πληροῦσθε ἐν πνεύματι—where the thought is the same
though the construction is different. Some scholars
render, with the margin of the American Revision,
in spirit. But ἐν is evidently instrumental. The
contrast requires *with the Spirit;* and *filled in spirit*
standing alone conveys no intelligible meaning. The
phrase *full of* or *filled with the Spirit* in Luke has
always the simple genitive, though in ii. 40 he has
πληρούμενον σοφίᾳ.

Jesus taught this truth by a familiar figure—"If ye
then, being evil, know how to give good gifts unto
your children, how much more shall your heavenly
Father give the Holy Spirit to them that ask him?" [13]

This general law of the divine administration alike
in nature and in grace finds its supreme exhibition in
the Son. Men are limited partly by necessity, as

[11] Exod. xxxi. 2-5.
[12] Luke i. 15, 41, 67; iv. 1; Acts ii. 4; iv. 8, 31; vi. 3; vii. 55; ix. 17;
xi. 24; xiii. 9, 52.
[13] Luke xi. 13.

creatures, partly by their own moral nature, as sinners. They are straitened in themselves.   There is no limit to God's will and power to give, there is a limit to their capacity to receive.   In Christ alone is lodged the capacity that answers to the largeness of the gift.   He alone is able to receive as God is able to give; for in him is no hindrance of sin, no withholding or resistance, no creature infirmity that may impair the free exercise and operation of the power of the Spirit.   He alone can receive without measure the gift of the Spirit of God in whom dwelleth the fulness of the Godhead bodily.

PART THREE

THE HOLY SPIRIT IN THE TEACHING
OF JESUS

A—IN THE SYNOPTIC GOSPELS

CHAPTER VI

THE HOLY SPIRIT IN THE TEACHING
OF JESUS—I.

The Jewish apocryphal writings add nothing to the
Old Testament representation of the Spirit, nor do they
appreciably affect the teaching of the New Testament upon this theme. This is clearly shown by
Swete.[1] The doctrine of the New Testament is developed directly from the Old. So close is the correspondence between the old revelation and the new, so
carefully does the earlier teaching prepare the way
for the truth of the Personality of the Spirit, that the
transition to the doctrine of Jesus and of Paul was
made without a trace of antagonism or even of dissent
on the part of the disciples or of the Jews. The new
teaching was seen to be simply the logical sequence
of the old.

The earlier exangelists use the terms Spirit, Holy
Spirit, and Spirit of God [2] where Mark has *the Spirit,*
and Luke *the Holy Spirit.* They represent Jesus as
speaking of the Spirit, the Holy Spirit, the Spirit of
God,[3] where Luke has *finger of God,* probably indicating the sense in which *Spirit of God* was understood
by the hearers, Spirit of your Father.[4] In the Author-

[1] *Holy Spirit in New Testament,* pp. 4, 398.
[2] Matt. iii. 16.
[3] Matt. xii. 28.
[4] Matt. x. 21.

ized Version Ghost is frequently used instead of Spirit. Hastings says. "Wherever πνεῦμα is accompanied with ἅγιον it is translated in A. V. after all the previous versions 'Holy Ghost' (in 1611 always written 'Holy Ghost,' which is the more surprising that Rhem. New Testament has almost always 'Holy Ghost'). When πνεῦμα occurs without ἅγιον, and the reference is to the Holy Ghost, it is translated 'spirit' or 'Spirit'." [5] The rule is correctly stated, but there are a few exceptions. In Luke xi. 13; Ephes. i. 13; iv. 30; I Thess. iv. 8, πνεῦμα ἅγιον is rendered Holy Spirit. The English Revisors in some instances retain Holy Ghost and in others substitute Holy Spirit, as is indicated in the appendix of the American Revision. In seventy-three instances Holy Ghost is retained, upon what grounds does not appear. When the phrase *Holy Ghost* first appears, in Matt. i. 18, it is accompanied by a marginal note, "Or, Holy Spirit, and so throughout this book," and a similar note is added wherever the phrase occurs throughout the New Testament. The American Revisers have taken a wiser course and read uniformly *Holy Spirit*. This is the better way not only because it is in harmony with modern usage, but because it preserves the term which is enshrined in the earlier revelation. Why should we speak of the Holy Spirit in the Old Testament and of the Holy Ghost in the New Testament?

Here we must inquire, What is the precise significance of the term Holy Spirit? God is holy, God is a Spirit; why then is the Third Person of the Trinity specifically designated as the Holy Spirit? Augustine's answer to the question is interesting, if not adequate. His treatise *On the Trinity*, upon which he laboured for nearly thirty years, is the ripe fruit of the most original and powerful intellect that the church has known since the days of the Apostles. In Book V, Ch.

[5] *HBD.*, II, 165, art. "Ghost."

xi. of this great work after remarking that the Trinity cannot be called either the Father or the Son, he adds,

> But it can be called in its entirety, the Holy Spirit, according to that which is written, "God is a Spirit"; because both the Father is a spirit and the Son is a spirit, and the Father is holy and the Son is holy. Therefore since the Father, the Son and the Holy Spirit are one God, and certainly God is Holy, and God is a Spirit, the Trinity can be called also the Holy Spirit. But yet that Holy Spirit who is not the Trinity, but is understood as in the Trinity, is spoken of in his proper name, of the Holy Spirit relatively, since he is referred both to the Father and to the Son, because the Holy Spirit is the Spirit both of the Father and of the Son. But the relation is not itself apparent in that name, but it is apparent when he is called the gift of God; for he is the gift of the Father and of the Son, because "he proceeds from the Father," as the Lord says; and because that which the apostle says, "Now, if any man have not the Spirit of Christ, he is none of his;" he says certainly of the Holy Spirit himself. . . . Therefore the Holy Spirit is a certain unutterable communion of the Father and the Son; and on that account, perhaps, he is so called, because the same name is suitable to both the Father and the Son. For He Himself is called specially that which they are called in common; because both the Father is a spirit and the Son is a spirit, both the Father is holy and the Son holy. In order, therefore, that the communion of both may be signified from a name which is suitable to both, the Holy Spirit is called the gift of both.

In commenting on these words in the third volume

of the Nicene and Post-Nicene Fathers, Dr. Shedd remarks:

> The reason which Augustine here assigns, why the name Holy Spirit is given to the third person —namely, because spirituality is a characteristic of both the Father and Son, from both of whom he proceeds—is not that assigned in the more developed trinitarianism. The explanation in the latter is, That the third person is denominated the Spirit because of the peculiar manner in which the divine essence is communicated to him—namely, by *spiration*, or out-breathing: spiritus quia spiratus. This is supported by the etymological significance of πνεῦμα, which is breath; and by the symbolical action of Christ in John xx. 22, which suggests the eternal spiration, or out-breathing of the third person. The third trinitarian person is no more spiritual, in the sense of immaterial, than the first and second persons, and if the term "spirit" is to be taken in its ordinary signification, the trinitarian relation, or personal peculiarity, as Augustine remarks, "is not itself apparent in this name"; because it would mention nothing distinctive of the third person, and not belonging to the first and second. But taken technically to denote the spiration or out-breathing by the Father and Son, the trinitarian peculiarity is apparent in the name, and the epithet "Holy" is similarly explained. The third person is the *Holy* Spirit, not because he is any more holy than the first and second, but because he is the source and author of holiness in all created spirits. This is eminently and officially his work. In this way also the epithet "Holy"—which with ordinary use would specify nothing peculiar to the third

person—mentions a characteristic that differentiates him from the Father and the Son.

Dr. Hodge speaks to the same effect:

> The Third Person of the Trinity is called "The Spirit" by way of eminence probably, for two reasons, first, because He is the power or efficiency of God, *i.e.* the Person through whom the efficiency of God is directly exercised; and secondly to express his relation to the other persons of the Trinity. As Father and Son are terms expressive of relation, it is natural to infer that the word Spirit is to be understood in the same way. The Son is called the Word as a revealer or image of God, and the Third Person is called Spirit as his breath or power. He is also predominantly called the Holy Spirit, to indicate both his nature and operations. He is absolutely holy in his own nature, and the cause of holiness in all creatures.[6]

In our study of the name we must not lose sight of the fact that the term Spirit, Holy Spirit was employed in the Old Scripture before the truth of the Trinity had been revealed. Men knew God in the variety of his manifestations and operations long before the distinction of Persons in the Godhead was made known. Monarchianism in its various forms, like many other heresies, is simply a case of arrested development; for it held fast the doctrine of a modal Trinity, as it was apparently presented in the Old Testament, and refused to recognize the truth of the essential Trinity as it was brought to light in the New. Spirit, like breath, signified primarily the power or efficiency of God; and the term designated primarily rather an economic than a Trinitarian relation. The Third

[6] *Syst. Theol.*, Vol. I., beginning of chapter viii.

Person was given the name Spirit as the manifested energy of God rather than upon the ground of this eternal procession.[7]

The New Testament discovers behind the varied manifestations of God the personal distinctions upon which they rest, and the term which in the first place expresses an economic relation is found adequate to express the essential nature of the Spirit. Back of his going forth from God as a power is his proceeding from God as a Person. This truth of the Procession of the Spirit will come before us for fuller consideration when we take up the teaching of Jesus as recorded in the Fourth Gospel. Now it appears that as soon as the Personality of the Spirit is disclosed, the name assumes a new and higher significance, and discovers the essential and eternal relation which he sustains to the Father and the Son. The term Holy is applied to him in virtue of his office; for he is the source and spring of holiness in all the creatures of God.

In the synoptic report of the teaching of Jesus there are found seven distinct references to the Holy Spirit; or if similar sayings spoken on different occasions are reckoned separately, there are ten. Three are peculiar to Matthew—xii. 18,[8] xii. 28, and xxviii. 19; and two are peculiar to Luke—iv. 18 [9] and xi. 13. Two are found in each of the Gospels, though in one instance Luke gives a different setting to the words: the blasphemy against the Holy Spirit—Matt. xii. 31, 32; Mark iii. 29; and Luke xii. 10; while in the other instance, the promise that the Spirit shall teach the disciples what to say in the hour of danger, each of the evangelists places the words in a different connexion— Matt. x. 20; Mark xiii. 11; Luke xii. 12. The reference to David speaking in the Spirit is found in Matt. xxii.

see
pg 196

---

[7] See my *Teaching of the Gospel of John,* p. 162.
[8] (Quotation from Isaiah.)
[9] *Ibid.*

43 and Mark xii. 36. In the course of our study passages of similar import will be brought together, and the points of difference noted.

I. Prophecy Fulfilled in Him

The first passage that invites our attention, as we follow the order of the Harmony, is the quotation of Isaiah lxi. 1, 2, in Luke 4:18:

> And he came to Nazareth, where he had been brought up; and he entered, as his custom was, into the synagogue on the Sabbath day, and stood up to read, and there was delivered unto him the book of the prophet Isaiah. And he opened the book, and found the place where it was written, The Spirit of the Lord is upon me. Because he anointed me to preach good tidings to the poor: He hath sent me to proclaim release to the captives, and recovering of sight to the blind, To set at liberty them that are bruised, To proclaim the acceptable year of the Lord.

The quotation differs in details from both the Hebrew and the LXX, but expresses with sufficient accuracy the sense of the original.

So far as the record indicates, this is the first public appearance of Jesus in Nazareth, his first appeal to the people of the town where he had been brought up. He appropriates and applies to himself the prophecy regarding the Servant of Jehovah, the mysterious figure that dominates the latter part of the book. As kings and priests were anointed with oil, the symbol of the Spirit, he is anointed with the Spirit himself, anointed for service, as the leaders of the people of God under the old covenant were endowed by the Spirit with gifts and grace sufficient for their tasks. The Spirit by whom he was conceived, who descended upon him in visible form at his baptism, abode upon him as the Christ of God throughout his ministry. It is a mission of mercy upon which he is sent, and *the day of vengeance of our God,* of which the prophet speaks, is not named, though the following verses convey to the Jews a veiled warning not to receive the grace of God in vain. When John the Baptist sent messengers from his prison to ask, "Art thou he that cometh, or look we for another?" Jesus answered by pointing to his works of grace and power; and the argument reaches its height in the words of the prophet which he proclaimed to the men of Nazareth: "The poor have good tidings preached to them." [10] The philosopher speaks to the cultured, the prophet of God speaks to the poor.

The passage presents no peculiar difficulties from the point of view of our theme, and it is needless to spend time in elucidating the obvious. It is sufficient to refer to the admirable commentary of Plummer.

II. Blasphemy Against the Holy Spirit

see pg 194

Matt. xii. 22-32; Mark iii. 20-30; Luke ii, 10: Each of the Synoptic Gospels records the difficult saying of Jesus regarding the unpardonable sin; but Luke does not refer it to the same occasion as Matthew and Mark. This difference does not compel us to ask which representation is correct, for there is no reason why both should not be correct. There is every reason to believe from the Gospel record and from the rules of reason that Jesus often repeated himself. His words were not addressed to modern critics, who have the whole record before them, but to his immediate hearers, an audience continually changing. It is preposterous to assume that the greatest of teachers persistently disregarded the primary law of education. The great

[10] Matt. xi. 5.

truths of the Kingdom, we may be sure, were taught again and again throughout his ministry. No reason can be assigned why he may not have spoken of blasphemy against the Holy Spirit according to the representation of Matthew, and again on a different occasion and a later time according to the representation of Luke.

Matthew and Mark agree in substance, though they differ in some matters of detail. Neither Gospel purports to furnish a complete verbal report, and there is no difficulty in supposing that here and elsewhere the narratives must be taken together, in order to obtain a full and detailed record of the facts. We are not shut up to the alternative, Matthew or Mark; but receive both Matthew and Mark. Each supplies details which are lacking in the other. Matthew says that Jesus spoke to the Pharisees; Mark says that he addressed the scribes that came down from Jerusalem. Mark tells us that the scribes said, "He hath Beelzebub, and, By the prince of demons he casteth out the demons." What provoked this charge Mark does not tell us; but Matthew relates the occasion: "Then was brought unto him one possessed with a demon, blind, and dumb; and he healed him, in so much that the blind and dumb both spake and saw. And all the people were amazed, and said, Is not this the son of David? But when the Pharisees heard it, they said, This fellow doth not cast out demons, but by Beelzebub the prince of demons." The answer of Jesus according to Mark is an appeal to reason. "How can Satan cast out Satan?" Is he divided against himself? If so, how can his kingdom stand? And if another has entered the domain of Satan and spoiled his goods, he must be stronger than Satan, he must have mastered him. To this Matthew adds an argument ad hominem: "If I by Beelzebub cast out demons, by whom do your sons cast them out?" If they and I alike cast out demons, why do you ascribe my work to Satan and theirs to God? *Your sons* are your pupils, your followers, or simply those of your own race. Exorcism was a common practice among the Jews.[11] We cannot stop to ask whether Jesus implies that their sons did actually cast out demons, or speaks only by way of concession. It would be interesting to inquire whether Jesus or any New Testament writer ever constructs an argument upon a baseless assumption merely in order to stop the mouth of an opponent; but it would lead us too far from our theme.

"But if I by the Spirit of God cast out demons, then is the Kingdom of God come upon you." Since the casting out of evil spirits transcends the power of man, it must be referred to a supernatural power, either to Satan or to God. It has been shown that it cannot be of Satan; then it must be of God. The conclusion is inevitable: the miracle is wrought by Jesus through the Spirit of God. Mark omits this saying, and Luke has, by the *finger of God* instead of *by the Spirit*.[12] This is probably the sense attached to the term Spirit of God by those who heard Jesus speak. The finger, like the hand, may be used as a symbol of power,[13] and the personality of the Spirit was not yet clearly apprehended. The Spirit of God and the power of God are still equivalent terms to those who had been trained in the law. If these mighty works have been wrought of God, then the Kingdom of God is come upon them. The Kingdom is here in the person of the King. Where the Messiah appears, clothed with the power of the Spirit, there is the Kingdom of God.

The argument is followed by a solemn warning:

[11] Schürer, *HJP*. See Index, Magic.
[12] Luke xi. 20.
[13] Exod. viii. 19; xxxi. 18; Deut. ix. 10; Ps. viii. 3.

31. "Therefore I say unto you, Every sin and blasphemy shall be forgiven unto men: but the blasphemy against the Spirit shall not be forgiven.
32. And whosoever shall speak a word against the Son of man, it shall be forgiven him; but whosoever shall speak against the Holy Spirit, it shall not be forgiven him, neither in this world, nor in that which is to come."

Matthew xii. 31, 32.

28. "Verily I say unto you, All their sins shall be forgiven unto the sons of men, and their blasphemies wherewithsoever they shall blaspheme:
29. But whosoever shall blaspheme against the Holy Spirit hath never forgiveness, but is guilty of an eternal sin:
30. because they said, he hath an unclean spirit."

Mark iii. 28-30.

While these reports differ in certain details, they agree that there is pardon in the mercy of God for every sin but one. "Every sin and blasphemy shall be forgiven." "All their sins shall be forgiven unto the sons of men, and their blasphemies wherewithsoever they shall blaspheme." Blasphemy is specified as a peculiarly heinous form of sin. All sins, even blasphemies. And Matthew singles out one kind of blasphemy as specially abhorrent—blasphemy against the Son of man. The conjecture that Son of man is a misconception of Mark's phrase, *sons of men,* is wholly unnecessary. Here again we must remember that neither evangelist pretends to furnish a detailed and complete report, and there is no reason why Jesus may not have said, "all their sins shall be forgiven unto the sons of men," as Mark records, and also, "Whosoever shall speak a word against the Son of man it shall be forgiven him," as Matthew has it. We are not shut up to the inquiry, Which is true? There need be no hesitation in accepting both as true. Much futile labour would be saved if we should simply apply to the Gospels the principles that guide us elsewhere; and recognize that none of them tells the whole story, but that they must be put together that the full truth may appear.

Mark reads, *blaspheme against;* Matthew has, *speak*

a word against. The comparison of vs. 31, *blasphemy against the Spirit* and vs. 32, *speak against the Holy Spirit* shows that these are equivalent terms. Thus the offences that may be forgiven are named in an ascending scale—sins, the general term; blasphemy; blasphemy against the Son of man.

Blasphemy in Scripture usage signifies abusive, scandalous, injurious language, directed against man or God. Evidently Jesus has here in mind evil speaking against God. Under the Mosaic law he who blasphemed the name of Jehovah was put to death: "The congregation shall certainly stone him." [14] There are sins that may be committed without thought of God, or conscious violation of his law: but blasphemy is a direct and purposed insult to the majesty of the Most High; a deliberate defiance of the Almighty. Yet even blasphemy may be forgiven.

Two kinds of blasphemy are set in contrast—blasphemy against the Son of man and blasphemy against the Holy Spirit. Of the first it is declared that it shall be forgiven. This is not because the blasphemy against the Son of man is treated as a light offense On the contrary, by singling it out from the category of sins and blasphemies and setting it apart it is recognized as an offense of a particularly heinous character. Sin, blasphemy, blasphemy against the Son of man—this is the ascending scale. Already he had asserted and exercised authority to forgive sins;[15] had healed multitudes of the sick;[16] had affirmed that he was lord even of the Sabbath;[17] that all things had been delivered unto him of the Father, and that he alone knew God, and revealed him to whomsoever he would.[18] Luke adds further emphasis to the thought of the greatness of the Son of man. He records the

[14] Lev. xxiv. 16.
[15] Mark ii. 5, 10.
[16] Mark i. 34; iii. 11.
[17] Mark ii. 28.
[18] Matt. xi. 27.

saying about the sin of blasphemy against the Holy Spirit in a different connection, as contained in the words of Jesus to his disciples in chapter xii. The sequence of thought here is very striking, even startling. "Every one who shall confess me before men, him shall the Son of man also confess before the angels of God; but he that denieth me in the presence of men shall be denied in the presence of the angels of God." [19] Here he declares that the destiny of men is determined by their relation to him. Evidently in the mind of Jesus blasphemy against the Son of man is not a minor offence, but a sin of a peculiarly heinous character; yet even this may be forgiven. But there is another step in the ascending scale—sin, blasphemy, blasphemy against the Son of man, blasphemy against the Holy Spirit. By thus leading the thought step by step to this final form of sin, Jesus pictures its appalling nature in the most solemn and impressive way. Here the line is crossed that marks the limit of forgiveness.

The thought that for this sin there is no pardon is differently expressed by the evangelists. Luke has simply, "shall not be forgiven." Matthew reads, "Whosoever shall speak against the Holy Spirit, it shall not be forgiven him, neither in this world, nor in that which is to come"; neither in this present age or dispensation, nor in that which shall be ushered in by the coming of the Son of man in glory to judge the world. Upon the judgment follows the life eternal, so that Jesus' words mean neither now nor forever, and declare in the strongest terms that forgiveness is eternally impossible. The passage of itself neither implies nor denies that there may be sins which are forgiven in the world to come. The question was simply not present to the mind of Jesus at this time, and he throws no light upon it; but his teaching regarding the doctrine of future probation is sufficiently clear elsewhere. Mark

[19] Luke xii. 8, 9.

reads, "whosoever shall blaspheme against the Holy Spirit hath never forgiveness, but is guilty of an eternal sin." Does this mean, a sin that continues forever, or a sin of which the consequences are everlasting? No doubt both are true. But the term used is not ἁμαρτία but ἁμάρτημα,[20] which denotes rather an act than a state of sin, and the second interpretation of the words therefore expresses most clearly what was in the thought of Jesus. This is a sin which is never forgiven and of which the punishment therefore is without end.

Now we turn to inquire what is the nature of the sin against the Holy Spirit, and why it alone is excluded from the divine mercy which is ready to pardon all other sins, however aggravated they may be.

It is not the inner witness of the Spirit to which he refers, the voice of the Spirit speaking in the heart; but the manifestation of the Spirit in the work of the Son of man. His words are spoken in reply to the charge of the scribes and Pharisees, He hath an unclean spirit. The reason why blasphemy against the Son of man may be forgiven while blasphemy against the Holy Spirit is never forgiven, does not lie in the relative dignity of the Son of man and the Spirit. For Jesus, as we have just seen, claimed to have and to exercise the attributes and prerogatives of the Almighty. Blasphemy against him is blasphemy against God. Both Son and Spirit are divine. Only one reason for the greater guilt of this form of blasphemy can be found— the difference in the clearness of the manifestation of God. Blasphemy against the Son of man is distinguished from other forms of blasphemy because in him God is more fully and clearly revealed than he had ever been made known before. Blasphemy under the Gospel is therefore an aggravated sin. "A man that hath set at naught Moses' law dieth without compassion on the word of two or three witnesses: of how

<hr>

[20] Trench, *Synonyms N. T.*, LXVI.

much sorer punishment, think ye, shall he be judged worthy, who hath trodden under foot the Son of God, and hath counted the blood of the covenant wherewith he was sanctified an unholy thing, and hath done despite unto the Spirit of grace?" [21] Paul tells the men of Athens: "The times of ignorance therefore God overlooked; but now he commandeth men that they should all everywhere repent: inasmuch as he hath appointed a day in which he will judge the world in righteousness by the man whom he hath ordained; Whereof he hath given assurance unto all men, in that he hath raised him from the dead." [22]

But while it is true that God is most clearly revealed in his Son, it is also true that the divinity of the Son is obscured by the human nature which he assumed, so that the fulness of the Godhead which dwells in him is at once revealed and veiled by the flesh. In submitting to become man he laid aside his divine glory, emptied himself, exchanged the form of God for the form of man, even of a bondservant. [23] It is possible, therefore, that men may rail against him, resist him, blaspheme him, crucify him, through ignorance, an ignorance which is not without guilt indeed, but which is yet not deliberate and wilful defiance of God. Peter said to the men of Israel, after speaking of the rejection and crucifixion of Christ, "and now brethren, I know that in ignorance ye did it, as did also your rulers." [24] And Paul speaks to the same effect: "We speak God's wisdom in a mystery, even the wisdom that hath been hidden, which God foreordained before the world unto our glory: which none of the rulers of this world hath known: for had they known it, they would not have crucified the Lord of Glory." [25] And Paul says of himself that though he was a blasphemer, and a per-

[21] Heb. x. 28, 29; cf. Heb. ii. 2, 3.
[22] Acts xvii. 30, 31.
[23] Phil. ii. 7.
[24] Acts iii. 17.
[25] I Cor. ii. 7, 8.

secutor, and injurious, to which he adds elsewhere that he strove to make the followers of Christ blaspheme,[26] yet he obtained mercy because he did it ignorantly in unbelief.[27]

Jesus prayed for those who nailed him to the cross, "Father, forgive them: for they know not what they do." [28] Whether or not these words formed part of the original text of Luke, and the manuscript evidence is against it, there is a general agreement that they preserve a precious fragment of tradition which we may accept without hesitation as trustworthy.

But there are works of Jesus which are so obviously and unmistakably wrought by the power of the Spirit of God that only those can fail to see and understand who have wilfully blinded their eyes and hardened their hearts against the truth. The Pharisees recognized that he exercised supernatural power; in the case of their own followers they affirmed that the casting out of evil spirits was accomplished by the power of God; yet when Jesus cast them out they said, "He hath Beelzebub, and by the prince of the demons casteth he out the demons." A work which when wrought by others they ascribed to God, when wrought by Jesus they ascribed to Satan. Moved by envy and pride and hatred they rejected and denied the clearest manifestation of the power of the Spirit, because he wrought through Jesus. Their hatred of Jesus drove them to blaspheme the Holy Spirit who dwelt in him and through him revealed most clearly his grace and power. They set their prejudices and interests over against the manifestation of the Spirit, and exalted themselves above God.

The sin of which Jesus speaks is not a single isolated act; it is an act which betrays a deliberate, determined, malignant spirit of opposition to the Spirit of God when he operates in unwelcome ways or toward unwel-

[26] Acts xxvi. 11.   [27] I Tim. i. 13.   [28] Luke xxiii. 34.

come ends. This is apparently the first time that the charge of having an evil spirit was brought against Jesus; and so terrible is the guilt of confounding the work of the Holy Spirit with the work of Satan that he immediately utters this solemn note of warning, that men may not incur this mortal sin. Yet according to the Gospel record the charge was renewed upon several occasions. In Matt. ix. 34 when he had cast out a demon from one who was dumb, the multitude marvelled, saying, "It was never so seen in Israel"; but the Pharisees said, "By the prince of demons casteth he out demons." The remaining instances are all recorded by the Fourth Gospel alone. In vii. 20 when Jesus had declared that his teaching was of God, and asked "Why seek ye to kill me?" it was the multitude who replied, "Thou hast a demon: who seeketh to kill thee?" In viii. 46-48 Jesus threw out the challenge to his enemies, "Which of you convicteth me of sin? If I say truth, why do ye not believe me?" and affirmed that God spoke through him: "He that is of God heareth the words of God; for this cause ye hear them not, because ye are not of God." Then the Jews inquired, "Say we not well that thou art a Samaritan and hast a demon?" He answered, "Verily, verily I say unto you, If a man keep my word, he shall never see death."[29] And the Jews replied, "Now we know that thou hast a demon." When he represented himself as the good shepherd, who giveth his life for the sheep, "there arose a division again among the Jews because of these words, and many of them said, He hath a demon, and is mad. Why hear ye him?" [30]

It is evident from this review that the words of the scribes and Pharisees which drew from Jesus this solemn warning were not the expression of a passing thought or a sudden burst of anger, but of a deliberate and settled purpose already forming to ascribe to Satan

[29] John viii. 52.   [30] John x. 20.

the teaching and works of Jesus which were manifestly due to the power of the Holy Spirit.

Bunyan has told us how he was tempted to commit this sin: "In these days, when I have heard others talk of what was the sin against the Holy Ghost, then would the tempter so provoke me to desire to sin that sin, that I was as if I could not, must not, neither should be quiet until I had committed it. Now no sin would serve but that. If it were to be committed by the speaking of such a word, then I have been as if my mouth would have spoken that word, whether I would or no; and in so strong a measure was that temptation upon me, that often I have been ready to clap my hands under my chin to hold my mouth from opening; and to that end also I have had thoughts at other times to leap with my head downward into some muck-hole or other, to keep my mouth from speaking." [31] But no single word or act, however atrocious it may be, is sufficient to constitute the sin against the Spirit, unless it is the expression of a deliberate and malignant hatred of good and choice of evil.

The saying of Jesus rests upon the principle frequently set forth in Scripture teaching that responsibility is measured by knowledge. "That servant, who knew his lord's will, and made not ready, nor did according to his will, shall be beaten with many stripes; but he that knew not, and did things worthy of stripes, shall be beaten with few stripes." [32] To the Pharisees Jesus said, "If ye were blind, ye would have no sin; but now ye say, we see; your sin remaineth." [33] The brighter the light, the greater is the guilt of those who will not see. The clearest revelation of the Father and the clearest manifestation of the Spirit are both given through the Son. He who rejects the Spirit working through him rejects the most manifest operation of the Spirit that can be conceived. And beyond

[31] *Grace Abounding*, ch. V.   [32] Luke xii. 47, 48.   [33] John ix. 41.

the Spirit there is nothing. He is the ultimate power in the kingdom of God. To say that Jesus has an unclean spirit is to confound evil with good, and set Satan upon the throne of the kingdom of God.

As Jesus pronounced this the only sin that lies beyond reach of forgiveness, if there are other passages of the New Testament which relate to the subject they must be interpreted in the light of his teaching. There are two passages of this nature which call for consideration.

(a) Heb. vi. 4-6: "For as touching those who were enlightened and tasted of the heavenly gift, and were made partakers of the Holy Spirit, and tasted the good word of God, and the powers of the age to come, and then fell away, it is impossible to renew them again unto repentance, seeing they crucify to themselves the Son of God afresh, and put him to an open shame." In connexion with these verses should be taken iii. 12: "Take heed, brethren, lest haply there shall be in any one of you an evil heart of unbelief, in falling away from the living God"; and x. 26, 27: "For if we sin wilfully after that we have received the knowledge of the truth, there remaineth no more a sacrifice for sins, but a certain fearful expectation of judgment, and a fierceness of fire which shall devour the adversaries." This is evidently the sin of apostasy from Christ.

The passage bristles with difficulties. Is the *impossible* relative or absolute; does it indicate merely that the human teacher is not able to lead men a second time to repentance; or does it signify that there is no hope of repentance and restoration even in God? Does the writer picture in these graphic phrases the condition of those who have been truly regenerated, or simply of those who have been awakened and have made a profession to which there is no corresponding reality? The passage has inevitably become a battleground between the opposing doctrines of the final perseverance of the regenerate and falling from grace.

None of these questions calls for discussion here. It is sufficient for our purpose to inquire what is the relation of this passage to the words of Jesus with which we are engaged. If we accept the truth of Jesus' teaching that there is only one unpardonable sin, two alternatives present themselves; either the sin of apostasy is identical with the sin against the Spirit, or it is not beyond the range of repentance and pardon. The first is evidently to be preferred. The passage in Hebrews differs from the teaching of Jesus not because it deals with another kind of sin, but because it deals with the same sin in another class of persons. Jesus speaks of unbelievers, who continually and malignantly reject the plainest manifestation of the truth; the writer of the Epistle goes further, and speaks of those who had penetrated so deeply into the truth that they had tasted of the heavenly gift, and the word of God, and were made partakers of the Holy Spirit, and then fell away. The sin against the Spirit may be committed by those who are open and avowed enemies of Jesus, and by those who have been his followers, at least in outward profession. And here again the principle is made plain, that men are judged according to the measure of light that they have enjoyed, a principle signally illustrated in the woes pronounced upon Chorazin and Bethsaida and Capernaum in comparison with Tyre and Sidon and Sodom.[34] What hope remains for those who have been partakers of the Holy Spirit, have recognized and acknowledged him, and then have deliberately renounced his guidance and authority, and repudiated the Son in whom he dwells and through whom he works?[35]

(b) The second passage which call for remark is I

[34] Matt. xi. 20-24. [35] See Delitzsch on *Hebrews, in loc.*

John v. 16, 17: "If any man see his brother sinning a sin not unto death, he shall ask, and God will give him life for them that sin not unto death. There is a sin unto death: not concerning this do I say that he should make request. All unrighteousness is sin; and there is a sin not unto death." The Epistle may be called the doctrinal interpretation of the Gospel, or the commentary of the beloved disciple upon the words of the Master. It is natural therefore to associate this passage with the teaching of Jesus regarding the unpardonable sin; and a careful examination shows how closely they are related. "All their sins shall be forgiven unto the sons of men, and their blasphemies wherewithsoever they shall blaspheme"; "there is a sin not unto death." "Whosoever shall blaspheme against the Holy Spirit hast never forgiveness"; "there is a sin unto death." A sin unto death is not merely a sin that naturally issues in death, for that is true of all sin. The distinction is sharply drawn and indicates unmistakably that the sin unto death is a sin that inevitably issues in death, that is, a sin which has no forgiveness. According to John, as in the teaching of the New Testament in general, the destiny of men is determined by their relation to Christ. "He that hath the Son hath the life: he that hath not the Son of God hath not the life." [36] But in the Epistle as in the words of Jesus it is the Spirit of God who dwells in the incarnate Son and works through him. "Hereby know we the Spirit of God: every spirit that confesses that Jesus Christ is come in the flesh is of God; and every spirit that confesseth not Jesus is not of God."[37] In the Gospel and the Epistle alike the sin condemned is the sin of wilful and malignant hostility to the manifestation and operation of the Holy Spirit in the Son of man. For by the Spirit through the Son God grants

[36] I John v. 12.   [37] I John iv. 2.

to men the fullest and clearest revelation of his character and will, makes to them the final offer of his grace. If this be rejected, nothing remains.

Here again it must be noted that the sin is not an isolated act, but rather a state or condition which betrays itself in word or deed. For sin of this nature prayer is not commanded though it is not forbidden. John is speaking of the prayers of believers for one another—"If any man see *his brother* sinning"; and intimates that by this sin a man forfeits his right to the intercession of the Church. How it may be known whether a man has been guilty of this sin is a question that John does not stop to ask.

We conclude, then, that the unpardonable sin of blasphemy against the Holy Spirit is the attitude of deliberate, wilful, malignant hostility to the clearest manifestation of the presence of God which is given by his Spirit dwelling in and working through his Son. It is the most heinous of those sins which the Mosaic law called presumptuous or highhanded.[38] "And if one person sin unwittingly, then he shall offer a she-goat a year old for a sin offering. . . . But the soul that doeth aught with a high hand whether he be homeborn or a sojourner, the same blasphemeth Jehovah; and that soul shall be cut off from among his people. Because he hath despised the word of Jehovah, and hath broken his commandment, that soul shall utterly be cut off; his iniquity shall be upon him." [39] It is the sin of open and persistent defiance of God when his will is clearly revealed which, alike in the Old Testament and the New, is the sin unto death, under the law of Moses the death of the body, under the clearer light of the gospel that loss of eternal life which is termed the second death.

[38] See Delitzsch on Ps. xix. 13; Haupt on I John v. 17, note.
[39] Num. xv. 27-31; *cf.* Deut. xvii. 12.

III. The Promise of the Spirit

When Jesus sent forth the twelve to preach the gospel and to work miracles he gave them a charge, which in Matthew's report is given at length. He warns them of the persecutions which they shall suffer: "But beware of men! for they will deliver you up to councils, and in their synagogues they will scourge you; yea, and before governors and kings shall ye be brought for my sake, for a testimony to them and to the Gentiles." But with the word of warning is given also the word of comfort: "But when they deliver you up, be not anxious how or what ye shall speak; for it shall be given you in that hour what ye shall speak. For it is not ye that speak, but the Spirit of your Father that speaketh in you." [40] Mark and Luke give a meagre report of this charge, and omit the reference to the Holy Spirit. But they both record similar promises given upon different occasions. When Jesus foretold the destruction of the temple, "Peter and James and John and Andrew asked him privately, Tell us, when shall these things be?" [41] Then he pictured to them the signs of the end. These do not concern us here, but again the disciples are forewarned of the sufferings that they shall be called to undergo, and again the assurance is given them of divine assistance. Mark reads, "And when they lead you to judgment, and deliver you up, be not anxious beforehand what ye shall speak; but whatsoever shall be given you in that hour, that speak ye; for it is not ye that speak but the Holy Spirit." [42] In the parallel passage Matthew makes no allusion to the aid of the Spirit. Luke reads, "Settle it therefore in your hearts not to meditate beforehand how to answer; for I will give you a mouth and wisdom, which all your adversaries shall not be able to withstand or gainsay." [43] When these accounts

[40] Matt. x. 17-20.
[41] Mark iii. 3, 4; Luke xxi. 7.
[42] Mark xiii. 11.
[43] Luke xxi. 14, 15.

of Mark and Luke are brought together, they imply the claim of Jesus that he would confer upon his disciples the gift of the Holy Spirit. "It is not ye that speak but the Holy Spirit; I will give you a mouth and wisdom." It is the Holy Spirit, it is Jesus, who speaks through them. This is the nearest approach that the Synoptic Gospels present to the promise of John xvi. 7: "If I go not away, the Comforter will not come unto you; but if I go, I will send him unto you." Though John the Baptist declared, "He shall baptize you in the Holy Spirit," nowhere in the earlier Gospels, and rarely in John, does Jesus explicitly affirm that he will send the Holy Spirit. Ordinarily the Holy Spirit is sent by the Father. But in this instance there is an implicit claim which is clearly brought out by a comparison of the accounts, and this is strengthened by a comparison of this passage in Luke with the similar passage in xii. 11, 12: "And when they bring you before the synagogues, and the rulers and the authorities, be not anxious how or what ye shall say; for the Holy Spirit shall teach you in that very hour what ye ought to say." Each of the evangelists records the promise of the Holy Spirit to aid the disciples in the hour of need, and each places it in a different setting. Here again it is evident that our Lord frequently repeated the lessons that he taught, for men were slow to understand and believe.

The meaning of the promise is clear. God will not forsake his children, nor Jesus his disciples, when danger threatens. Not only shall they be guarded and kept, but they shall be given by the Spirit words of wisdom and of power which none can withstand. The promise has been abundantly verified in the experience of God's people throughout the whole history of the church from the day of Pentecost to this hour. The Person of the Spirit comes more clearly to light. He shall teach, he shall speak. Those personal acts and attributes which are so conspicuously disclosed in the Fourth Gospel already begin to appear.

The promise is designed to meet a special need of the disciples, and therefore falls far short of the rich promises of the Fourth Gospel. Here the inspiration of the Spirit is limited to a particular occasion; there he shall lead them into all the truth, and shall abide with them forever. In one case the Spirit shall help them in the hour of personal peril, in the other case he shall equip them to be the leaders and teachers of the church of God. The second promise is therefore far broader and richer than the first. And in each instance the promise is suited to the particular occasion. Wherever there is need, there is a promise to meet it, according to the assurance given us by Paul: "My God shall supply every need of yours according to his riches in glory in Christ Jesus." [44]   Men are never far from the water-brooks of the Kingdom of God. There are large promises that sweep the whole range of human need; there are particular promises addressed to special necessities and occasions.

IV. The Gift of the Spirit

Luke xi. 13: When the disciples asked Jesus to teach them how to pray, he gave them the form which we call the Lord's prayer. The secret of effective prayer is faith in God, for prayer without faith is a babble of empty words. He went on to show them that faith is rational. There is every reason to believe that God will hear and answer our petitions. Here, as often elsewhere, he makes use of the feelings and habits of men to throw light upon the character of him in whose image they are made. How do men deal with their children? Do they seek to satisfy every just and reasonable desire? "If ye then, being evil, know how to give good gifts unto your children, how much more

[44] Phil. iv. 19.

shall your heavenly Father give the Holy Spirit to them that ask him?" If men, wicked and selfish as they are, love their children and delight to minister to their needs, how much more shall God, who is altogether good, bless those who seek his favour.

This passage is peculiar to Luke. But Matthew records the Lord's Prayer in a different connexion, in the Sermon on the Mount,[45] and later in the same discourse presents the same encouragement to prayer. "If ye then, being evil, know how to give good gifts unto your children, how much more shall your Father, who is in heaven give good things to them that ask him?" [46] Here again there is no need to inquire whether Matthew or Luke has given the more accurate report of Jesus' words. The word is general in one Gospel, specific in the other. As the Holy Spirit is the richest gift that God can bestow, the promise of the Spirit involves all good things. The greater includes the less. This is the most general and comprehensive promise of the Spirit contained in the Synoptic Gospels, and approximates the assurances of the Fourth Gospel. The terms of the promise are very broad—*give the Holy Spirit*. The thought is lifted at once above the realm of the material needs to the highest spiritual sphere—the Father who is in heaven, the Holy Spirit. The Holy Spirit is not given for a specific purpose, but in the fulness of his strengthening and sanctifying power that he may minister to every want of the soul. Only when we study the teaching of Jesus regarding the office of the Holy Spirit in the Fourth Gospel shall we be able to comprehend the breadth and grace of the promise—shall give the Spirit. The condition of receiving the Spirit is that we ask. Blessings of a material kind may be lavished upon men without discrimination: "He maketh his sun to rise on the evil and the good, and sendeth rain

[45] Matt. vi. 9-13.   [46] Matt. vii. 11.

on the just and the unjust." [47] "He is kind toward the unthankful and evil." [48] But for spiritual gifts, and the gift of the Spirit, there must be the preparation of mind and heart. He only receives who desires. Food and raiment, sunshine and rain, men receive of God, though they do not acknowledge or even know him. But the home of the Spirit is the heart, and the heart must seek him and bid him welcome. There is much in life that we receive without asking, find without seeking; but the crowning gifts of God are reserved for the earnest spirit, the eager desire, the hungering and thirsting after the righteousness which is imparted only by the Spirit of God.

V. David's Son and David's Lord

While the Pharisees were gathered together, Jesus asked them a question, saying What think ye of the Christ? Whose son is he? They say unto him, The son of David. He saith unto them, How then doth David in the Spirit call him Lord, saying, The Lord said unto my Lord, Sit thou on my right hand, till I put thine enemies underneath thy feet? If David then calleth him Lord, how is he his son? And no one was able to answer him a word, neither durst any man from that day forth ask him any more questions.
Matt. xxii. 41-46.

And Jesus answered and said, as he taught in the temple, How say the scribes that the Christ is the son of David? David himself said in the Holy Spirit, The Lord said unto my Lord, Sit thou on my right hand, till I make thine enemies the footstool of thy feet. David himself calleth him Lord; and whence is he his son? And the common people heard him gladly.
Mark xii. 35-37.

And he said unto them, How say they that the Christ is David's son? For David himself saith in the book of Psalms, The Lord said unto my Lord, Sit thou on my right hand, till I make thine enemies the footstool of thy feet. David therefore calleth him Lord, and how is he his son?
Luke xx. 41-44.

The quotation is from the hundred and tenth Psalm, verse 1.

These passages record the same event and agree in

[47] Matt. v. 45.   [48] Luke vi. 35.

substance, while they differ in various matters of detail. In Matthew Jesus speaks to the Pharisees, in Luke to the scribes, while in Mark the hearers are not named. The form of the question is not precisely the same, but each evangelist puts it in a somewhat different way. Yet the occasion is obviously the same. In each case Jesus had just put the Sadducees to silence, and he adds a warning against the scribes, with whom Matthew associates the Pharisees.

The comparison of these passages throws light upon the nature and scope of inspiration. The Scriptural doctrine of inspiration must recognize the facts of Scripture and cannot be based upon a priori theories. The Bible must be suffered to bear its own witness, and no doctrine can be maintained which is not in accordance with the method actually employed. Obviously inspiration does not require that events shall be recorded with verbal exactness. There is in Scripture no attempt at painful particularity or precise and literal accuracy. It is sufficient that the substance of the truth shall be correctly conveyed. The writers tell their story as honest witnesses always do, each in his own way, differing in various matters of detail, while yet they are in substantial harmony with one another. The truth of history or doctrine is not tied to a single form of words, but may be expressed in various modes of speech. There are different ways of telling a story, each of which is true, though they do not precisely agree in every particular. The sacred writers are not mere amanuenses, the pen of the Holy Spirit, as Augustine calls them.[49] Yet it must be noted that Augustine recognized also the human element in the Scripture. "For to speak of the matter as it is, who is able? I venture to say, my brethren, perhaps not John himself spoke of the matter as it is, but even he only as he was able; for it was man that

[49] *Conf.* VII, 21.

spoke of God, inspired indeed by God, but still man. Because he was inspired he said something; if he had not been inspired, he would have said nothing; but because a man inspired, he spoke not the whole, but what a man could he spoke." [50]   In these few pregnant sentences Augustine sets forth in his matchless way the relation of the divine and the human factors in the composition of the Scripture.   There is always at work the tendency to magnify one of these elements at the expense of the other.   The supernatural element is denied, and we have a book without inspiration and authority, except that which may spring from the wisdom of the writer.   Or the human element is virtually excluded, and we have a rigid and mechanical view of inspiration which is wholly out of harmony with the phenomena which the Scripture presents.   We must recognize the free movement of the mind of the writer, in his choice of material, his mode of expression, which are his own; and we must recognize also the controlling, restraining, inspiring operation of the Holy Spirit, by which the writer is preserved from error and enabled to convey the truth in such manner as shall serve the purpose of God. The union of the divine and human in this respect is a mystery indeed, but not a mystery peculiar to the nature of inspiration.   It meets us everywhere in the Christian life, and notably in the work of sanctification.   "Work out your own salvation—for it is God that worketh in you!" [51]

In our study of these passages there are two points that call for consideration.

(a) David's authorship of the Psalm.   This is directly and explicitly affirmed.   Mark reads, "David himself said in the Holy Spirit"; and Luke has, "David himself saith in the book of Psalms"; while Matthew puts the assertion in the form of a question: "How

[50] *Tract on John* i. 1.   [51] Phil. ii. 12, 13.

doth David in the Spirit . . . ? If David then calleth him . . . ?"

But it is said that Jesus' knowledge did not extend to matters of a critical nature, questions of date and authorship. Upon one occasion he confessed himself ignorant.[52] These words are sometimes carried far beyond the boundaries of his thought. That in his human nature he was subject to the limitations of other men in respect to knowledge is obvious enough, and is clearly indicated in the Gospel story.[53] But ignorance is not error. To say that he did not know is far removed from saying that he undertook to teach what he did not know. In the very act of confessing his ignorance of the time of his return he drew the line between his knowledge and his ignorance. He knows or he does not know. There is not with him, as with other men, a region of speculation and conjecture lying midway between knowledge and ignorance; he never said, I think, I believe, I suppose. When he spoke, therefore, he claimed to speak with authority. His words are the words of God, for it is God who speaks through him. What he did not know he did not venture to affirm. When he did affirm, the word is true which he spoke to Nicodemus: "We speak that which we know."[54] We may readily dismiss the suggestion of ignorance in this matter as an altogether inadequate explanation of his words.

It is maintained again that he spoke by way of accommodation. He simply accepted the current ascription of the Psalm to David without expressing an opinion regarding it. It is altogether probable, indeed it may be regarded as fairly certain, that Jesus held the common belief of the Jews of his time concerning the divine authority and the human authorship of the various books of Scripture. Every reference that he makes to the Old Testament bears out

[52] Mark xiii. 32.   [53] Luke ii. 52.   [54] John iii. 11.

this view of his attitude toward the sacred writings. But upon certain points he has left no explicit teaching, and his authority cannot be invoked in arrest of historical and critical investigation. The devout believer will welcome the most searching examination of every portion of the Scripture, assured that the results of scientific inquiry cannot be at variance with the word of him who is the truth.

In Matt. xv. 7 and the parallel passage in Mark vii. 6, Jesus said to the Pharisees and scribes, "Well did Isaiah prophesy of you." In Matt. xiii. 13 he said, "Unto them is fulfilled the prophecy of Isaiah." In these instances the question of authorship was not important. There is no reason to doubt that he shared the current belief, but he did not explicitly affirm that Isaiah was the author of the prophecy; he simply cited the book by the name of the reputed author. In his discourse regarding the end he refers to "the abomination of desolation which was spoken of by Daniel the prophet." [55] Here again the question of authorship does not arise. It is the prophecy and not the prophet that is in the mind of Jesus; so that Mark in the parallel passage omits the name of Daniel, and Luke makes no direct reference to the prophecy. Here again we may assume that Jesus shared the common belief of the time, but he gives no explicit teaching. In all these cases the prophecy and not the prophet held the first place in the thought of Jesus and the prophecy was true by whomsoever spoken. Whatever we may infer concerning the opinion of Jesus he did not pronounce explicitly upon the question of authorship.

But here the case is altogether different, and the question of authorship is of prime importance. The whole force of the reasoning turns upon it. If David was not the author of the Psalm, the argument falls to the ground. Nor can it be maintained that we have

[55] Matt. xxiv. 15.

here merely an argument *ad hominem;* that Jesus is simply meeting the scribes and Pharisees upon their own ground, confuting them from their own point of view. That mode of argument he used sometimes to stop the mouths of his foes. But more than that is involved here. For he does not merely accept the authorship, he affirms it in the most direct and explicit manner. "David himself said in the Holy Spirit." "David himself saith in the book of Psalms." "David himself calleth him Lord." We have here not the "hypothetical use of a current tradition," [56] but a categorical assertion as clear and strong as may be conveyed in human speech. The question of authorship is not merely a matter of critical research, but is bound up with the interpretation of Scripture. The meaning of the passage in the Psalm is determined by the person of the writer. If Jesus may not be followed in his interpretation of the Scripture, if he is in error regarding a prophecy which refers to himself, how far may we trust him in other matters?

We appear, then, to be shut up to these alternatives; either Jesus was mistaken in an explicit assertion that related at once to his own Person and to the interpretation of the Scripture; or David was the author of the Psalm. If we reject his teaching here, it is difficult to see upon what ground we may put faith in his exposition of any portion of the Scripture; for nowhere else has he spoken more clearly and particularly than here. [57]

(b) The inspiration of David. "How then doth David in the Spirit call him Lord?" "David himself said in the Holy Spirit." Luke omits the reference to the Spirit. "David himself in the book of Psalms." To speak in the Spirit is to speak by the authority and

[56] Swete on Mark xii. 36.

[57] For David's authorship see Delitzsch and Perowne on Ps. 110 and Broadus on Matthew, *in loc.* Against it, Briggs on the Psalm; *Comms.* of Gould; Swete and Plummer on the Gospels.

inspiration of the Spirit. When we read in Mark i. 23 of a man in an unclean spirit we understand that the evil spirit was his master. Nowhere else in the Gospels is this phrase employed to denote the inspiration of the Old Testament writers, nor indeed is it found elsewhere in the New Testament; but the truth is frequently expressed in various forms that Scripture is given by inspiration of God. Sometimes it is attributed directly to the Holy Spirit. The text of Acts iv. 25 is uncertain, but the weight of evidence favours the reading adopted by the Revised Version—"Who by the Holy Spirit by the mouth of our father David thy servant, didst say," followed by a citation from the Second Psalm. The word of God is the sword of the Spirit.[58] In Heb. iii. 7 a quotation from Psalm xcv is prefaced with the words, "Wherefore, even as the Holy Spirit saith." And in the same manner Jeremiah xxxi. 33 ff. is introduced: "And the Holy Spirit also beareth witness to us." [59] In the Fourth Gospel Jesus repeatedly refers to the Scripture as the word of God, and declares it cannot be broken.[60] Peter sums up the teaching of the New Testament regarding the Old in a sentence—"No prophecy ever came by the will of man; but men spake from God, being moved by the Holy Spirit";[61] words which fully and fairly represent the whole trend of New Testament doctrine.

To say that David speaks in the Spirit is equivalent to saying that the Spirit speaks through David. Jesus regarded the Old Testament with reverence as the word of God, and appealed to it as the final authority in matters of faith and morals. So far as the record indicates, no question of the integrity and the inspiration of the Scripture ever entered the mind of Jesus or his apostles. What is here said of David they would say

[58] Ephes. vi. 17.
[59] Heb. x. 15.
[60] John x. 35.
[61] II Peter i. 21.

with equal confidence of all the sacred writers: they spoke in the Spirit; and their word is therefore the word of God through them. It may be argued that Jesus was mistaken, but that this was his doctrine is too obvious to be denied. In Matt. v. 17, 18 he makes the broad and explicit assertion, "Think not that I came to destroy the law or the prophets: I came not to destroy, but to fulfil. For verily I say unto you, Till heaven and earth pass away, one jot or one tittle shall in no wise pass away from the law, till all things be accomplished." Upon these verses Allen remarks, "Commentators have exhausted their ingenuity in an attempt to explain away this passage, but its meaning is too clear to be misunderstood. Christ is here represented as speaking in the spirit of Alexandrine and Rabbinical Judaism." [62] And the suggestion is made that "These verses did not originally belong to the Sermon, but have been placed here by the editor, who has thus given to πληρῶσαι (-to bring into clear light the true scope and meaning) a sense (viz. to reaffirm and carry out in detail) which is foreign to the general tenor of the Sermon." To eliminate is easier than to interpret. But the difficulty here lies rather in the mind of the commentator than in the words of Jesus, which are in entire accord with the general tenor of his teaching. It must be noted that he draws a clear distinction between the moral and the ceremonial law. "Perceive ye not," he said to his disciples, "that whatsoever from without goeth into the man, it cannot defile him . . . ?" "This he said," the evangelist adds, "making all meats clean." [63] He taught that the temple worship, the centre of the ceremonial system, should be abrogated. [64] [65] How then can he say that "one jot or one tittle shall in

[62] *Comm. in loc.*
[63] Mark vii. 18, 19.
[64] John iv. 21.
[65] See my *Teaching of the Gospel of John,* p. 31.

no wise pass away from the law, till all things be accomplished"? Because the ceremonial law had been fulfilled, accomplished—had served its purpose. All that it signified has been brought to light, all that it sought to do has been performed. All things that it represented and predicted have been accomplished in Christ, and having served its purpose it is done away.[66]

The moral law he represents as of perpetual validity. It is not under the gospel the condition of salvation but remains in force as the rule of duty. He fulfills the moral code primarily by drawing out its full meaning, showing the principles that underlie the letter of the law, and declaring its full scope and purpose. He fulfilled it also by his personal obedience, as he said to John the Baptist, "Thus it becometh us to fulfil all righteousness";[67] but that is not the main thought here. He fulfils the law primarily as a teacher expounding its full significance. When he sets his teaching over against the teaching of the law, he does not contravene the word of Moses, but explains, supplements, enlarges it, in opposition to the narrow literalism of the scribes. The law forbids murder and adultery; Jesus carries the law into the inner region of thought and motive where the sin is conceived.

In certain cases the law permitted practices such as polygamy and divorce—"for your hardness of heart" —which were yet inconsistent with the perfect righteousness which God requires. Jesus claimed the right to set aside the later commandment in favour of the law which was originally enjoined. "From the beginning it hath not been so";[68] and restored the original intent and purpose of the law of marriage. Certain practices were tolerated for a time which fell short of

[66] An interesting and valuable discussion of the subject is found in Turrettin, *Theol. Loc.*, XV, Qu. 26.
[67] Matt. iii. 15.
[68] Matt. xix. 9.

the perfection which he enjoins men to seek. They answered their purpose in confining and restraining within definite limits the customs which had sprung out of the weakness and sinfulness of men, until the time should come when they might safely be annulled. Where the law restrained, Jesus went further in the same direction and forbade outright. Swearing is permitted in certain cases by law; Jesus himself replied when he was put upon his oath by the high priest.[69] But if the law of truth prevailed, there would be no room for the oath. Men are compelled to swear because they do not trust one another. The bare word should be sufficient, and the oath is the fruit of sin. God himself must confirm the promises with an oath that men may believe him.[70] The oath is required for confirmation,[71] but when the Spirit of truth reigns in the hearts of men they will swear not at all. "Let your speech be, Yea, yea; Nay, nay; for whatsoever is more than these is of the evil one." [72] Whatever valuable purposes the oath may answer in the present imperfect state of society, the necessity of it is traced to him who was a liar from the beginning. If the law were observed in its true intent, there would be no place for the oath.

The law of retaliation, "an eye for an eye, and a tooth for a tooth," was designed to limit and restrict the spirit of revenge. Jesus forbids that spirit altogether, and carries the law to its legitimate end.[73] When he commands his disciples to love their enemies, he is not contravening the law, but the Rabbinic tradition, which added to the words of Leviticus—"Thou shalt love thy neighbour as thyself"—the injunction, "and hate thine enemies."

[69] Matt. xxvi. 63.
[70] Heb. vi. 13.
[71] Heb. vi. 16.
[72] Matt. v. 37.
[73] On these passages see the *Comm.* of Plummer and Broadus.

His whole attitude toward the law is indicated in the words, "Ye therefore shall be perfect, as your heavenly Father is perfect."

Thus he claimed and exercised the right to determine what portions of the law had served their purpose, and are done away with; and to interpret the precepts of the law according to their true significance and give them their full effect. This authority he exercised over the law as over the Sabbath, of which he claimed to be the Lord.[74] The moral code remains in full force under the gospel as the rule of duty and of life. We are not saved by keeping the law, but we are not saved without it.

The exposition of the passage does not properly fall within the scope of our inquiry. It is sufficient to observe that the Psalm was generally recognized by the Jews as prophetic of the Messiah;[75] and is frequently applied to him in the New Testament, where indeed it is more frequently cited than any other passage of the Scripture. In his sermon of the day of Pentecost Peter expressly ascribes the Psalm to David.[76] In Heb. v. 6 a quotation from the Psalm is given as the word of God, but David is not named. There are other passages which apparently are based upon the Psalm, though it is not expressly cited.[77] If Abraham could see his day, and Moses could write of him, and all the prophets bear witness to him, why may not David also have been granted a vision of the Christ?

That the Psalm is Messianic, therefore, is attested by the Jews, by Jesus, by the Apostles. In later times indeed this was denied by the Rabbis, but only because of their opposition to the claims of Jesus. The question of Jesus can be answered only by recognizing that

[74] Mark ii. 28.
[75] Edersheim, *Life of Christ*, II, 270.
[76] Acts ii. 33-35.
[77] I Cor. xv. 25; Ephes. i. 20; Heb. i. 3, 13; x. 12; I Peter iii. 22.

the Messiah is both human, as David's son, and divine, as David's Lord. This the Pharisees could not deny without invalidating their own Scripture; nor would they acknowledge it because they feared the claim of Jesus to be the Christ.

CHAPTER VII

THE HOLY SPIRIT IN THE TEACHING OF JESUS—II.

VI. THE BAPTISMAL FORMULA

But the eleven disciples went into Galilee, unto the mountain where Jesus had appointed them. And when they saw him, they worshipped him; but some doubted. And Jesus came to them and spake unto them, saying, All authority hath been given unto me in heaven and on earth. Go ye therefore, and make disciples of all the nations, baptizing them into the name of the Father and of the Son and of the Holy Spirit; teaching them to observe all things whatsoever I commanded you: and lo, I am with you always, even unto the end of the world.[1]

The other Gospels present no precise parallel to this passage, yet each of them records a commission of similar import given by Jesus to his disciples. The closing verses of Mark xvi. 9-20 do not belong to the original text of the Gospel, but it is generally agreed that they may represent a very early tradition. There it is recorded that Jesus charged his disciples to "Go into all the world and preach the gospel to the whole creation. He that believeth and is baptized shall be saved; but he that disbelieveth shall be condemned. And these signs shall accompany them that believe:

[1] Matt. xxviii. 18-20.

227

in my name shall they cast out demons; they shall speak with new tongues; they shall take up serpents, and if they drink any deadly thing, it shall in no wise hurt them; they shall lay hands on the sick, and they shall recover." [2]

Luke presents yet another form. "And he said unto them, These are my words which I spake unto you, while I was yet with you, that all things must needs be fulfilled, which are written in the law of Moses, and the prophets, and the psalms, concerning me. Then opened he their mind, that they might understand the scriptures; and he said unto them, Thus it is written, that the Christ should suffer, and rise again from the dead the third day, and that repentance and remission of sins should be preached in his name unto all the nations, beginning from Jerusalem. Ye are witnesses of these things." [3]

John's record is brief. "Jesus therefore said unto them again, Peace be unto you; as the Father sent me, even so send I you. And when he had said this, he breathed on them, and saith unto them, Receive ye the Holy Spirit; whosesoever sins ye forgive, they are forgiven unto them; whosesoever sins ye retain, they are retained." [4]   Jesus repeated his command in the Acts: "It is not for you to know times or seasons, which the Father hath set within his own authority. But ye shall receive power, when the Holy Spirit is come upon you; and ye shall be my witnesses both in Jerusalem, and in all Judaea and Samaria, and unto the uttermost parts of the earth." [5]

Thus Matthew, Luke, and John, and the unknown author of the addition to Mark unite in testifying that after his resurrection Jesus appeared to his disciples, and laid upon them the duty of preaching the gospel throughout the world, while the most complete account

[2] Mark xvi. 15-18.
[3] Luke xxiv. 44-49.
[4] John xx. 21-23.
[5] Acts i. 7, 8.

of the commission thus conferred is given by Matthew. "Make disciples of all the nations" is the broad and comprehensive command. The gospel is to be preached not simply as a testimony, though that of course is included,[6] but as the power of God unto salvation, the salt, the light, the leaven, by which the world shall be renewed. This *making disciples* is to be by baptism and teaching. By baptism men are inducted into the kingdom; by teaching they are instructed in the nature and duties and rights and privileges of the kingdom.

It is the relation of the Holy Spirit to this work of making disciples of all the nations which specially engages our attention.

We are confronted at once by the question of the text; for the attempt is made to eliminate Matthew xxviii. 19 upon various grounds.

The verse is assailed from the side of textual criticism. It might appear indeed that there is no room for doubt, for the words are found in every manuscript and early version that has come down to us. If further evidence is required, we may turn to the citations of the passage in early Christian literature. In the *Didache*, probably of the first half of the second century, it is written: "Now concerning baptism, thus baptize ye; having first uttered all these things, baptize into the name of the Father, and of the Son, and of the Holy Spirit, in running water." [7] [8] Justin Martyr, about the middle of the second century, says of those who receive the gospel and confess their sins, "they are brought by us where there is water, and are regenerated in the same manner in which we were ourselves regenerated. For in the name of God, the Father and Lord of the

---

[6] Matt. xxiv. 14.

[7] Chap. vii.

[8] Swete, *Holy Spirit in Anc. Ch.*, Add. note, p. 411; Art. "Didache" *HBD*, Extra vol., p. 438, where it is gratuitously observed that the reference to baptism indicates a later hand (p. 477).

Universe, and of our Saviour Jesus Christ, and of the
Holy Spirit, they then receive the washing with
water." [9] These are the earliest references to the
Trinitarian formula of baptism beyond the New
Testament. There is no reason to doubt that the
writers had the words of Matthew in mind; and those
words are explicitly cited by Irenaeus [10] and Tertullian; [11] while Origen affirms that

> the person of the Holy Spirit was of such authority
> and dignity, that baptism was not complete except
> by the authority of the most excellent Trinity of
> them all, i.e., by the naming of Father, Son, and
> Holy Spirit, and by joining to the unbegotten God,
> the Father, and to his only begotten Son, the
> name also of the Holy Spirit. [12]

It is needless to pursue the subject further. Lists of
early writers who refer to the passage are given in
Hastings' *Dictionary Apostolic Church*, Art. "Baptism," pp. 130, 131, and Sophocles' *Lexicon* may be
consulted—βαπτίζω and βάπτισμα. The witness of
the creeds is cited by Swete, and he affirms that
"early baptismal creeds and rules of faith follow,
practically without exception, the Trinitarian scheme,
which appears in St. Matthew's account of the institution of Christian baptism." [13]

Against this weighty array of evidence, however, is
set the fact that Eusebius in quoting this passage often
reads simply, "Go and teach all nations in my name";
and this is conceived to be the original form of Jesus'
words, while the reference to baptism is supposed to
have been added by a later hand for liturgical reasons.
The argument is drawn out at length by Conybeare
in the *Hibbert Journal* i, 102-8, and is sufficiently

[9] *I Apol.* 61.
[10] *Agt. Her.* III. 17, 1.
[11] *On Baptism*, 13.
[12] *De Princ.* I, 3, 2.
[13] *Holy Spirit in Anc. Ch.*, p. 157.

answered by Chase in the *Journal of Historical Studies* vi, 24, p. 483. Allen inclines to the view that the shorter form of Eusebius "is the original text of the Gospel," but leaves the question in doubt.[14]

The weight thus ascribed to Eusebius' form of quotation cannot be justified, unless it is shown that he has occasion to quote the words precisely as they are found in Matthew, and that he was accustomed to quote with verbal exactness. Neither point can be established. Regarding his method of quoting Scripture, Bishop Lightfoot remarks[15] that "he is often careless in his manner of quoting," and gives various illustrations.[16] And again in his *Essays on Supernatural Religion* he says, "The manner in which Eusebius will tear a part of a passage from its context is well illustrated by his quotation from Irenaeus," which is appended.[17] Even though Eusebius "had in the library of his deceased bosom friend Pamphilus, whose name he had added to his own, the finest known copies, the most accurately written copies, of the Bible,"[18] his habit of quotation must be borne in mind.

The fact is so obvious that there would be no need to call attention to it if it were not so often disregarded, that early writers do not quote Scripture with the verbal precision which the modern critic exacts, though he does not always practice it. How precarious is this mode of argument may be copiously illustrated from writers of every age, even those of a high order of scholarship. In his *Authorship of the Fourth Gospel*, discussing "the differences in form between Justin's quotation,[19] and the phraseology of the Fourth Gospel," Ezra Abbot shows in detail that

[14] *Comm. in loc.*
[15] *Dict. Chr. Biog.* II, p. 326.
[16] *Cf.* McGiffert's *Eusebius,* III, 23, note 5.
[17] p. 168, note 1.
[18] Gregory, *Canon & Text N. T.* p. 36.
[19] of John iii. 3-5.

they all admit of an easy and natural explanation on the supposition that he really borrowed from it, and that they are paralleled by similar variations in the quotations of the same passage by Christian writers who used our four Gospels as their exclusive authority.[20]

Numerous examples are given of the loose way in which the passage is cited in early writers; and choosing a modern illustration he notes nine instances of the citation of John iii. 5 by Jeremy Taylor, "who is not generally supposed to have used many Apocryphal Gospels," and shows that "all of these differ from the common English version, and only two of them are alike."[21]

It may also be observed that the writers of the New Testament in quoting from the Old Testament, which they regarded as the very Word of God, used great freedom in modifying the phraseology of the text; sometimes gathering up the significance of various passages in a single sentence, as Jesus did in John vii. 38; sometimes even giving to the words a new form and meaning, as in Ephes. iv. 8, where "Thou hast received gifts among men"[22] becomes, he "gave gifts unto men." To demand precise verbal accuracy in all instances of quotation is to impose a burden which neither we nor our fathers have been able to bear. Johnson remarks:

> Verbal exactness in quoting is a habit only recently introduced in literature. It was impossible, in effect, before the invention of printing made books abundant, and the construction of indexes and concordances rendered it easy to find

[20] pp. 31, 32.
[21] I have gathered a number of instances of inexact quotation and self-contradiction by modern writers in my paper "The Authorship of the Fourth Gospel," *Princeton Theol. Rev.*, 1912, 455-8.
[22] Ps. lxviii. 18.

any passage at will. . . . Yet even today it is far from universal.[23]

It is reasonable to conclude that Eusebius, like every other writer of ancient or modern times, cited Scripture as it suited the particular purpose that he had in mind. Sometimes he quoted Matthew xxviii. 19 in the precise form in which it appears in the Gospel. The passages in which this form occurs are said by Coneybeare, indeed, to have been written at a late date after he had learned from other sources the Trinitarian formula; but this view is sufficiently answered by Chase in the article already cited.

The evidence in favour of the verse is simply overwhelming. If it had not been seriously questioned, we should say that it is beyond reach of question. There should be no hesitation whatever in accepting it as belonging to the original text of the Gospel.

But if the verse be accepted as genuine, the question arises, Are these the words of Jesus, or are they to be ascribed to the author or editor of the Gospel? Moffatt asserts that

> on the whole, the probabilities seem to converge on the likelihood that the Trinitarian form was introduced by the author of the Gospel himself, as a liturgical expansion of the primitive formula of baptism into the name of Jesus.[24]

Prof. Wood takes the same position in his *Spirit of God in Biblical Literature,* asserting that the investigations of Conybeare "throw grave critical doubts upon the Trinitarian formula as a part of the original text," [25] and maintaining that

> the slight reference to baptism in the activity of Christ (baptism seems to disappear totally from

[24] *Intro. Lit. N. T.,* p. 254. That the words should be referred to Christ is maintained by Plummer, *in loc.,* and Zahn, *Intro. N. T.,* II, p. 591.

[25] p. 133, note.

Christ's work after the beginning of the Judean
ministry), the fact that Christ so filled the content of the religion of the early Church, coupled
with the use of Christ's name only in all references to baptism, make it probable that the Trinitarian formula does not come from Christ.[26]

The reasons assigned for referring these words to the
evangelist and not to Jesus must be examined with
care.

What are the facts upon which we must base our
judgment? What is the custom of New Testament
writers in referring to baptism?

Baptism is frequently alluded to with no indication
of form or method.[27]

When allusion is made to the mode of baptism, two
forms appear. (a) the Trinitarian formula occurs
only in the passage before us. (b) ordinarily baptism
is administered in the name of Jesus. And here again
there are variations of form. There is baptism in
the name of Jesus (ἐν τῷ ὀνόματι).[28] In the first of
these passages the Received text has ἐπὶ τῷ ὀνόματι
and this reading is retained by Alford, Meyer and
Nestle. Westcott and Hort read ἐν for ἐπὶ. If we
follow their guidance, there is no example of baptism
ἐπὶ τῷ ὄν. in the New Testament.[29] Again there is
baptism into the name of Jesus—εἰς τὸ ὄν.[30]

Such phrases as *calling on his name*,[31] the *name by
which ye are called*,[32] probably refer to baptism in or
into the name of Jesus. In Gal. iii. 27 the phrase
occurs, "baptized into Christ."

This variety of form is found also in the *Didache*.

[26] p. 134.
[27] Acts iii. 12, 13, 37, 38; ix. 18; xvi. 15, 33; xviii. 8; I Peter iii. 21.
[28] Acts ii. 38; x. 48; I Cor. vi. 11.
[29] Justin Martyr has ἐπὶ with the genitive (*I Apol.*, 61).
[30] Acts viii. 16; xix. 5.
[31] Acts ix. 21; xii. 16.
[32] Jas. ii. 7.

In Chapter VII, as we have seen, the command is given "Baptize into the name of the Father, and of the Son, and of the Holy Spirit"; while in Chapter IX it is written, "But let no one eat or drink of your eucharist, except those baptized into the Lord's name; for in regard to this the Lord hath said: 'Give not that which is holy to the dogs.'" It is altogether natural that in baptism emphasis should be placed upon the name of Jesus as the distinctive feature of the Christian confession, separating the believer from Jew and Gentile alike as no other name could do.

From these facts what conclusion may be drawn? They do not lead us to infer that in Matthew xxviii. 19 we have the words of the evangelist and not of Jesus; but rather that while these are the words of Jesus they do not prescribe a fixed formula which must be rigidly observed. He gave his disciples not a form of words to be repeated, but an interpretation of the nature and significance of the sacrament. In this respect the words are analogous to the phrases, *baptize unto repentance*,[33] *the baptism of repentance unto remission of sins*,[34] indicating the purpose and import of the rite.

This conclusion is confirmed by the habitual attitude of Jesus and of the New Testament in general toward rites and forms of every kind, of which various instances may be noted. The Lord's Prayer is a conspicuous example. Though it is introduced with the injunction, "after this manner therefore pray ye,"[35] "when ye pray, say,"[36] yet it is not recorded in the same form by Matthew and Luke, as is evident at a glance when their reports are set side by side. Matthew reads, "Our Father who art in heaven, Hallowed be thy name. Thy kingdom come, Thy will be done, as in heaven, so on earth. Give us this day our daily bread. And forgive us our debts, as we also have

[33] Matt. iii. 11.
[34] Mark i. 4.

[35] Matt. vi. 9.
[36] Luke xi. 2.

forgiven our debtors. And bring us not into temptation, but deliver us from the evil one." Luke has, "Father, Hallowed be thy name. Thy kingdom come. Give us day by day our daily bread. And forgive us our sins; for we ourselves also forgive every one that is indebted to us. And bring us not into temptation."[37] Moreover there is no citation of the prayer and no indication of its use anywhere in the New Testament. Prof. Lindsay indeed says that "The use of the Lord's Prayer is not mentioned but may be inferred" and quotes from Weizsacker's *Apostolic Age*: "Paul nowhere mentions the Lord's Prayer. But we may assume that we have a trace of it in Rom. v. 11, 15; and Gal. iv. 6. In speaking of the right to call God Father, he gives the Aramaic form for Father, in each instance adding a translation, and this is only to be explained by supposing that he had in mind a formula which was known wherever the Gospel had penetrated, and which, by preserving the original language, invested the name with peculiar solemnity, in order to maintain its significance unimpaired in the believer's consciousness."[38] But the argument thus presented is highly precarious. It cannot be maintained that the term *Father*, so constantly on the lips of Jesus, could have become familiar only through the Lord's Prayer. We may safely affirm that there is no trace of the Prayer in the writings of the New Testament.

The law of the Sabbath fills a large place in the legislation of the old dispensation, and formed one of the main points of contention between Jesus and the Jews. Yet the day was changed from the seventh to the first of the week without the least indication of a command concerning it. We infer that the change was commanded simply because the change was made.

[37] For various readings in Luke's version of the Prayer see Plummer, *in loc.*

[38] *Church and Ministry in the Early Centuries*, p. 44, note 3.

If we turn to the sacrament of the Lord's Supper we find that here too no form is prescribed. The reports of the institution of the Supper given by the Synoptic Gospels differ in several particulars; and Paul gives an account, which he professes he has received directly from the Lord, that does not precisely agree with either of them.[39]

In describing the mode of worship which was observed in the apostolic church, Lindsay remarks that

> St. Paul does not mention the benediction as forming part of the Christian worship, but the way in which it occurs regularly at the beginning of his Epistles, preserving always the same form, warrants us in supposing its liturgical use in the manner above indicated.[40]

But the fact stares us in the face that Paul does not preserve always the same form, but employs a variety of forms. In Rom. i. 7; I Cor. i. 3; II Cor. i. 2; II Thess. i. 2; Philemon 3; Gal. i. 3; Ephes. i. 2; Phil. i. 2, we read "Grace to you and peace from God our (the) Father and from the Lord Jesus Christ"; in Col. i. 2, "Grace to you and peace from God our Father"; to which the Received Text adds, "and the Lord Jesus Christ"; in I Tess. i. 1, after the address "unto the church of the Thessalonians in God the Father and the Lord Jesus Christ," "Grace to you and

[39] I Cor. xi. 23-26. Prof. Machen holds that Paul does not lay claim here to a direct revelation from the Lord, but refers to information which he had gathered from eye-witnesses. (*Origin of Paul's Religion,* pp. 148-9.) But the argument of Hodge upon the other side of the question seems fairly conclusive (*Com., in loc.*). The view that Paul claims a special revelation is held also by Ellicott, Godet, and Meyer. Robertson and Plummer (*Inter. Crit. Com., in loc.*) agree with Machen. In view of the importance of the matter, and of Paul's peculiar position in the apostolic company, as one untimely born (I Cor. xv. 8), it is not surprising that a special revelation should have been granted him, by which he was enabled to speak with the same authority as an eye-witness.

[40] *Church and Ministry in the Early Centuries,* p. 44.

peace"; in I Tim. i. 2 and II Tim. i. 2 "Grace, mercy, peace, from God the Father, and Christ Jesus our Lord"; in Titus i. 4 "Grace and peace from God the Father and Christ Jesus our Saviour."

A similar variety appears in the other Epistles of the New Testament. Hebrews and I John have no benediction, and James has simply Greeting. I Peter i. 2 reads, "Grace to you and peace be multiplied"; and II Peter i. 2, "Grace to you and peace be multiplied in the knowledge of God and of Jesus our Lord." II John 3 has, "Grace, mercy, peace shall be with us from God the Father, and from Jesus Christ, the Son of the Father, in truth and love." In place of benediction III John has a prayer—"Beloved, I pray that in all things thou mayest prosper, and be in health, even as thy soul prospereth." Jude 1 reads, "mercy unto you, and peace and love be multiplied."

It may also be noted as illustrating the attitude of Jesus toward rites and forms that he did not himself administer baptism, as John tells us, correcting a false report which had come to the ears of the Pharisees, but committed it as a ministerial office to his disciples,[41] and the apostles followed his example. Peter commanded Cornelius and those who were with him to be baptized in the name of Jesus Christ (Acts x. 48). Paul thanked God that he had baptized very few in Corinth, "lest any man should say that ye were baptized into my name"; and indicated the nature and purpose of his ministry by affirming that "Christ sent me not to baptize, but to preach the Gospel." [42] [43]

The obvious fact is that the New Testament prescribes no fixed formula of any kind for worship, for prayer, for baptism, for the Lord's Supper. There is no set form of words enjoined for any service or ceremony of the church, no ritual of any kind whatsoever.

[41] John iv. 1, 2.   [42] I Cor. i. 14-17.   [43] See *HDAC*, I, 133.

The endeavour to impose upon the church sacramental theories and methods which have no divine authority has been the most prolific source of division and strife. The New Testament is not a code but a Gospel. Rites and forms have no value in themselves, and are of use only as they serve to convey spiritual truth to the mind and heart of the worshipper.

It is evident in the light of this review that there is no reason to suppose that Jesus is here prescribing a formula to be observed. It is not the ceremony of baptism of which he speaks, but rather the nature and significance of the rite; and he says to his disciples not, You shall use this form of words, but, You shall administer the rite with this purpose and intent, of bringing men into fellowship with the Father, Son, and Holy Spirit. A study of the precise significance of these words will soon demand our attention.

Again it is affirmed that the passage is not in harmony with the general tenor of Jesus' teaching. McGiffert says,

Of the Trinitarian formula, into the name of the Father, the Son, and the Holy Spirit, which later became universal in the Church, we have no trace in the New Testament, except in the single passage, Matthew xxviii. 19, It is difficult in the light of all we know of Jesus' principles and practice, and in the light also of the fact that the early disciples, and Paul as well, baptized into the name of Christ alone, to suppose that Jesus himself uttered the words: "Baptizing them into the name of the Father, and of the Son, and of the Holy Ghost," which are quoted in Matthew xxviii. 19. But it may be that he directed his apostles not simply to make disciples of all the nations but also to baptize them, as they had, perhaps, been in the habit of baptizing those that joined their company. If, then, he simply gave the general direction to baptize (*cf.* the appendix of Mark xvi. 16), it would be very natural for a scribe to add the formula "Into the name of the Father and of the Son and of the Holy Ghost," which was in common use in his day. On the other hand, the fact must be recognized that Paul's indifference about performing the rite of baptism (see I Cor. i. 14 *seq.*) is hardly what we should expect if the eleven apostles received from Christ a direct command to baptize; and it is not impossible that the entire passage (Matt. xxviii. 19b) is a later addition, as maintained by some scholars.[44]

The assumption which underlies the argument that these words of Jesus contain a prescribed formula has already been sufficiently answered. The question at once arises, if, as Prof. McGiffert asserts, this Trinitarian formula "involves a conception of the nature of the rite which was entirely foreign to the thought of these primitive Christians, and indeed no less foreign to the thought of Paul," what could induce a scribe to insert it at a date so early that no trace of any other reading appears? Prof. McGiffert recognizes that "we find it expressly enjoined in *The Teaching of the Apostles,* and that it was in common use in the middle of the second century is clear from the old Roman symbol which was based upon it, and also from Justin Martyr's *Apology.*" How can we account for the early and widespread use of this form of words? With the Gospel record before us, why should we resort to conjectures regarding the origin of the formula? There is no need of ingenious hypotheses to account for the words. The simplest explanation of the use of them throughout the church is that they came from the lips of Jesus.

[44] *Apostolic Age,* p. 61.

The fact is that the formula is not foreign to the thought of the time, and contains nothing that is out of harmony with the teaching of Jesus. The constituent elements of the formula are two, the act of baptism, and the Trinitarian formula with which it is administered. Which of these is out of harmony with the teaching of Jesus? With the rite of baptism he was familiar; he recognized the baptism of John as of divine authority, and himself submitted to it that he might fulfill all righteousness. Though he did not himself baptize, his disciples administered the rite under his direction.[45] He said to Nicodemus, "except one be born of water and the Spirit, he cannot enter into the Kingdom of God"; where baptism is evidently meant. And from the day of Pentecost throughout the whole history of the church the sacrament of baptism has held its place side by side with the Lord's Supper.

No less familiar to the thought of Jesus was the conception of the Trinity. He spoke constantly of the Father, often of the Holy Spirit, and called himself the Son. The last words of Jesus which Luke records unite the Father and the Spirit with himself: "And behold, I send forth the promise of my Father upon you." [46] The *promise of the Father* is the Holy Spirit.[47] The early addition to Mark refers to baptism,[48] and John [49] as well as Luke to the Holy Spirit.

If then both baptism and the Trinity were familiar to the thought of Jesus, what reason may be given why he should not have brought them together in this form of words which Matthew records? And if both parts of the command, the act and the form, are evidently embraced in our Lord's teaching, how can the

[45] John iv. 1, 2.
[46] Luke xxiv. 49.
[47] Acts i. 4, 5; ii. 33.
[48] Mark xvi. 16.
[49] John xx. 22.

command itself be out of harmony with his doctrine? Each of the Synoptic Gospels represents the Father and the Spirit as present at the baptism of Jesus; how then could the use of the threefold name in baptism appear strange to those who wrote and to those who read the Gospels? And how could he to whom the word was spoken from heaven, "Thou art my Son," upon whom the Spirit came, when he was baptized of John—how could he fail to associate baptism with the presence of Father, Son, and Spirit? Matthew's report simply gathers up in one comprehensive phrase elements of Jesus' teaching with which all the Gospels have made us acquainted. There is no reason whatever in the light of the Gospel record why Jesus should not have commanded his disciples to baptize, and why he should not have commanded them to baptize in the name of the Father, the Son, and the Holy Spirit. And there is every reason to believe that the practice of the early church was founded upon the word of Jesus.

Our judgment is confirmed when we turn to the other books of the New Testament. The longer form of the apostolic benediction is as thoroughly Trinitarian as the baptismal formula.[50] Paul's letters abound in reference to the several Persons of the Trinity. In I Cor. vi. 11 he associates baptism with the Trinity: "but ye were washed, but ye were sanctified, but ye were justified in the name of the Lord Jesus Christ, and in the Spirit of our God."

In view of these obvious, even obtrusive, facts, it is difficult to understand how the conception of baptism into the name of the Trinity can be represented as "entirely foreign to the thought of these primitive Christians, and indeed no less foreign to the thought of Paul." On the contrary, it is in entire harmony

[50] II Cor. xiii. 14.

are now concerned, especially the baptismal formula; "Go ye therefore, and make disciples of all the nations, baptizing them into the name of the Father, and of the Son, and of the Holy Spirit."

The first question of an exegetical nature that meets us relates to the rendering of the preposition εἰς. Shall we read *in* or *into* the name? Or is the rendering a matter of indifference because no material distinction between the terms can be drawn? Robertson goes far in affirming that "it is quite immaterial whether one uses εἰς ὄνομα as in Matt. x. 41-42; xii. 41, or ἐν ὀνόματι, as in Matt. xxi 9; Mark ix. 49. Hence we find either baptized ἐν the name of Jesus Christ [59] or baptizing εἰς the name of the Father, and of the Son, and of the Holy Spirit.[60] It is splitting a hair to insist on into the name because of the use of εἰς." [61]   Moulton speaks more cautiously: "There are many New Testament passages where a real distinction between εἰς and ἐν is impossible to draw without excessive subtlety . . . the argument that because εἰς often denotes rest *in* or *at,* and sometimes represents that motion *towards* (as distinguished from motion *to*) which may perhaps have been the primitive differentia of the dative, therefore it is immaterial whether εἰς or ἐν or the simple dative be used with any particular word, would be entirely unwarrantable. It depends upon the character of the word itself." [62]

The fact that the language found it necessary to evolve εἰς from ἐν indicates that they are not merely synonyms; and the evident fact that they are sometimes used interchangeably does not prove that they are never distinguished.[63] εἰς τὸ ὄνομα does not mean

[59] Acts ii. 38.
[60] Matt. xxviii. 19.
[61] *Biblical Review,* Jan., 1923, p. 68.
[62] *Gram. N. T. GR.,* Vol. I, pp. 63, 66.
[63] For a discussion of the question see Robertson *Gram. N. T. Gr.,* pp. 59 ff, 649. *HDAC* Vol. I, p. 134. Meyer on *Rom.* vi. 3. Ellicott on *Gal.* iii. 27. Burton on *Gal.* iii. 27.

simply, with reference to or by authority of. Such phrases as Rom. vi. 3, "Or are ye ignorant that all we who were baptized into Christ Jesus, were baptized into his death?"; and Gal. iii. 27, "For as many of you as were baptized into Christ did put on Christ," evidently denote union, incorporation with. How intimate the union designated by the preposition may be in any particular case is determined by the context, and particularly by the object of the preposition. To be baptized into (εἰς) Moses [64] means into the relation of discipleship and obedience. To be baptized into Christ means to be brought into that oneness of life with him which he set forth in the figure of the vine and the branches. To be baptized into one body [65] is to be incorporated into the body of Christ, which is his church. In the light of New Testament teaching to be baptized into the name of the Trinity is to be introduced to that mystical or spiritual union with Father, Son, and Spirit which Jesus dwelt upon in his last discourse to his disciples before his death, and which finds frequent expression in the teaching of Paul. To baptize men into the divine name is not merely to pronounce over them that name, but to bring them into living fellowship and union with him to whom that threefold name belongs.

If now we seek to draw a distinction between baptizing *in* and *into* the name, the difference appears to lie in this: Baptism *in* the name regards the relation of fellowship and union as already established, and now recognized and confirmed by the administration of the ordinance; baptism *into* the name signifies the introduction into that fellowship. In one case the believer is baptized because he is in Christ; in the other case, that he may be in Christ.

Both these conceptions are in accord with the general teaching of Scripture. The believer is baptized be-

[64] I Cor. x. 2.   [65] I Cor. xii. 13.

cause he is ingrafted into Christ; he is ingrafted into
Christ by baptism. To baptize *in* is to recognize a
relation; to baptize *into* is to constitute a relation.
Faith in Jesus and fellowship with him are the conditions on which baptism is administered, and therefore
the believer is baptized in his name, on the ground of
his relation to him. On the other hand baptism is the
rite by which the believer is publicly and formally admitted to that fellowship. Associated as it is with open
confession of sin, the public acknowledgment of Jesus
as Saviour and Lord, and the reception into the visible
church and incorporation with the people of God,
baptism marks the beginning of a new stage in the
spiritual life, of a closer fellowship with Jesus through
obedience to his command and the public recognition
of his authority in the manner which he has prescribed.
To be baptized into Christ Jesus is to be baptized into
his death, to be brought into such a union with him
that we die with him unto sin.[66] To be baptized into
Christ is to put on Christ.[67] To the Colossians Paul
writes, "In whom (Christ) ye were also circumcised
with a circumcision not made with hands in the putting
off of the body of the flesh, in the circumcision of
Christ; having been buried with him in baptism,
wherein (ἐν ᾧ) ye were also raised with him through
faith in the working of God, who raised him from the
dead." [68] The *wherein* of our English versions and the
ἐν ᾧ of the Greek are ambiguous, and may mean
in whom, that is, in Christ, as interpreted by Meyer
in loc.; or to baptism, as held by Ellicott, Lightfoot,
and Abbott. The reference to baptism is decidedly to
be preferred. "Baptism is the grave of the old man,
and the birth of the new. As he sinks beneath the
baptismal waters, the believer buries there all his corrupt affections and past sins; as he emerges thence, he
rises regenerate, quickened to new hopes and to new

[66] Rom. vi. 3, 4.   [67] Gal. iii. 27.   [68] Col. ii. 11, 12.

life. This it is, because it is not only the crowning act of his own faith, but also the seal of God's adoption and the earnest of God's Spirit. Thus baptism is an image of his participation both in the death and in the resurrection of Christ." [69] Paul affirms that Christ cleansed the church by the washing of water with the word; [70] and that we are saved "through the washing of regeneration and renewing of the Holy Spirit." [71] In both cases baptism is evidently meant. Ananias said to Saul at Tarsus, "Arise and be baptized, and wash away thy sins, calling on his name." [72] And Peter writes, after referring to the ark in which Noah and his household were saved through water, "which (i.e. water) also after a true likeness, doth now save you, even baptism, not the putting away of the filth of the flesh, but the interrogation of a good conscience toward God, through the resurrection of Jesus Christ." [73]

It is evident from these passages that the New Testament attaches great importance to the sacrament of baptism. But it contains no doctrine of baptismal regeneration. It is clearly taught that "The sacraments become effectual means of salvation, not from any virtue in them, or in him that doth administer them; but only by the blessing of Christ, and the working of his Spirit in them that by faith receive them." The sacraments are means of grace in the same sense as the Word, which does not save men simply by the hearing of the ear, but only as it is applied by the Spirit to lead them to faith and obedience.

The sacraments are given to be a badge of discipleship, a bond of union, a means of grace. Baptism may be regarded either as the seal of a relationship already established (ἐν) or as the rite by which initiation into

[69] Lightfoot, in loc.
[70] Ephes. v. 26.
[73] I Peter iii. 20.
[71] Titus iii. 5.
[72] Acts xxii. 16.

that relationship is procured (εἰς). But it must always be borne in mind that according to the doctrine of Scripture the sacraments are means of grace, not conditions of salvation.[74]

In his *Commentary* on Galatians iii. 27 Burton holds it an "outstanding fact" that "the use of βαπτίζω εἰς τὸ ὄνομα was in all probability derived from the usage of the mystery religions, and to one familiar with that usage would suggest the ideas associated with such phraseology." But in view of the opinion which Paul entertained and vigorously expressed regarding the moral and spiritual condition of the pagan world, as in Romans i., it is in the highest degree improbable, may even be pronounced impossible, that in connexion with one of the most solemn rites of Christian worship he would introduce a formula associated with the beliefs and practices of heathen worship.[75] Surely it is immeasurably more probable that these are the words of Jesus, and that they were used by Paul and received by the church not as derived from the system of pagan worship against which they protested and contended without ceasing, but as taught by him whom they revered as Saviour and Lord. Why should we seek for another origin of the phrase, when this lies close at hand?

The significance of the phrase *into the name of* now invites our attention. To baptize into Christ and into the name of Christ are equivalent terms. Tertullian says correctly that Jesus commands his disciples "to baptize into the Father, and the Son, and the Holy Ghost."[76] The name is the mark by which the person is known and recognized, by which he is distinguished and represented. The use of the term *name of God*

[74] The significance of baptism is treated by Prof. Chas. Hodge with his usual clearness in his *Comm.*, on Ephes. v. 26. See also Machen, *Origin of Paul's Religion,* p. 286.
[75] See Machen, *ibid.,* pp. 280 ff. Gray, *HBD,* III, p. 480.
[76] *Agt. Praxeas* XXVI. *Prescr. agt. Her.* XX.

for *God* is frequent in the Old Testament, and expresses the sum-total of those attributes by which he is known as God. In Luke vi. 22: "they shall . . . . cast out your name as evil"; Acts i. 25; "there was a multitude of persons (literally names, ὀνομάτων) gathered together"; Rev. iii. 4: "Thou hast a few names in Sardis that did not defile their garments"; Rev. xi. 13: "There were killed in the earthquake seven thousand persons" (literally names of men, ὀνόματα ἀνθρώπων), *names* is obviously equivalent to *persons*. To baptize into the name of is to baptize into the person of—into a relation of fellowship and union such as is expressed in the term *one with Christ.* "Even as thou, Father, art in me and I in thee, that they also may be in us." [77]

No doctrinal significance may be attached to the use of the singular (ὄνομα) instead of the plural. The singular is often used in classic Greek where the plural might appear to be called for; and this is found also in the New Testament, Luke vi. 22: "Cast out your name"; Rev. xvii. 8: "And they that dwell on the earth shall wonder, they whose name (ὄνομα) had not been written in the book of life from the fountion of the world." The unity of the three Persons is apparent from the whole scope of the passage, but it is not established by the use of the singular *name,* instead of the plural.[78] On the other hand, the term is in entire harmony with Scripture teaching, and we cannot fail to recognize its eminent fitness here.

In view of the place filled by the Holy Spirit in the life and teaching of Jesus and in the faith and life of the church, it must appear strange that the New Testament contains neither direction to pray to him, nor

[77] John xvii. 21.
[78] See McLean, Art. "Baptism," *DAC* 1:134. Deissman, *Bible Studies,* pp. 146 and 196. He says "The hypothesis of a Hebraism is unnecessary; the Papyri demonstrate the same usage." Robertson *Gram. GK. N. T.,* p. 649.

any instance of such prayer. Some scholars have thought that prayer to the Spirit is found in II Thess. iii. 5: "And the Lord direct your hearts into the love of God, and into the patience of Christ,"[79] understanding by *Lord, Holy Spirit*. But the term is properly referred to Christ in accordance with New Testament usage. [80] Hort has found an example in Acts ix. 31, which he renders, "So the Ecclesia throughout all Judaea and Galilee and Samaria had peace; being built; and walking by the fear of the Lord and by the invocation (παρακλήσει) of the Holy Spirit (probably the invoking his guidance as Paraclete to the Ecclesia) was multiplied." [81] But παράκλησις does not appear to be used in this sense in the New Testament, and it is properly rendered *comfort,* as in our English versions.

The nearest approach to the invocation of the Holy Spirit is seen in the Apostolic benediction: "The grace of the Lord Jesus Christ, and the love of God, and the communion of the Holy Spirit, be with you all." [82] The benediction is both a wish and a prayer, and there is nothing incongruous in supposing that Paul is here invoking the Holy Spirit. But it is more in harmony with customary New Testament modes of thought and speech to conceive of him as praying to God for the gift of the Holy Spirit, who is usually represented as given or sent; and the same may be said of the salutation in Rev. i. 4, where by "the seven spirits that are before his throne" we should understand the Holy Spirit in the variety and perfection of his operations.[83] Charles holds that the phrase denotes angels, and must therefore be an interpolation "probably early in the second century." How an interpola-

[79] Hastings, *Great Christian Doctrines; Prayer,* p. 390.
[80] See Ellicott, *in loc.*
[81] *The Christian Ecclesia,* p. 55.
[82] II Cor. xiii. 14.
[83] See Swete, *in loc.* Trench, *Eps. to Seven Churches.*

tion so contradictory to the whole teaching of the book should have crept unchallenged into the text, at a date so early, is not explained. We may safely say, then, that there is no command to pray to the Spirit and no example of prayer to the Spirit to be found in the pages of the New Testament. According to the Scripture representation believers pray for the Holy Spirit;[84] they pray and serve in the Spirit;[85] and the Spirit prays within them,[86] but nowhere are they enjoined to pray to him.

For this omission, at first sight so singular and surprising, two reasons may be assigned. (a) The full significance of the truth of the Personality of the Spirit with all its doctrinal and experimental implications was not immediately apprehended by the church. A truth which though in harmony with earlier Scripture teaching yet marked so great an advance upon it could not be grasped at once in the fulness of its meaning. Time was required to assimilate it, and give it its proper place in the system of revealed truth.

This omission gave occasion to some in the early church to ask questions that Gregory Nazianzen found it necessary to answer in a discourse which Swete pronounces the "greatest of all sermons on the doctrine of the Spirit." [87] These are the questions asked as late as the closing years of the fourth century, as he states them in his sermon:

> Who in ancient or modern times ever worshipped the Spirit? Who ever prayed to Him? Where is it written that we ought to worship Him, or to pray to Him, and whence have you derived this tenet of yours? [88]

[84] Luke xi. 13.
[85] Ephes. ii. 18; Phil. iii. 13.
[86] Rom. viii. 26.
[87] *Holy Spirit in Anc. Ch.*, p. 240.
[88] "Fifth Theol. Oration," *Nicene Fas.*, VII, p. 321.

His opponents accused him of bringing in a strange God.

> Of the wise men amongst ourselves, (he says) some have conceived of Him as an activity, some as a creature, some as God; and some have been uncertain which to call Him.
>
> It is the Spirit in whom we worship, and in whom we pray . . . . therefore to adore or to pray to the Spirit seems to me to be simply Himself offering prayer or adoration to Himself. And what godly or learned man would disapprove of this, because in fact the adoration of One is the adoration of the Three, because of the equality of honour and dignity between the Three?

He goes on to mark the progress of the Scripture revelation of God.

> The Old Testament proclaimed the Father openly and the Son more obscurely. The New manifested the Son, and suggested the Deity of the Spirit. Now the Spirit Himself dwells among us, and supplies us with a clearer demonstration of Himself. For it was not safe, while the God-head of the Father was not yet acknowledged, plainly to proclaim the Son; nor when that of the Son was not yet received to burden us further (if I may use so bold an expression) with the Holy Ghost; lest perhaps people might, like men loaded with food beyond their strength, and presenting eyes as yet too weak to bear it to the sun's light, risk the loss even of that which was within the reach of their powers; but that by gradual additions, and as David says, Goings up and advances and progress from glory to glory, the Light of the Trinity might shine upon the more illuminated.

And he adds the suggestion that the Deity of the Spirit was one of the things which Jesus promised his disciples should be taught them by the Spirit.

These somewhat extended citations may serve to illustrate the difficulties which confronted the early church as it sought to find a place for the doctrine of the Spirit in the scheme of Christian truth.[89] As the Son precedes the Spirit, in the order of the Trinity, and as it is the office of the Spirit to interpret and apply the teaching and work of the Son, the doctrine of the Son necessarily precedes the doctrine of the Spirit; and only when the Person and work of Christ were fully apprehended were the Person and work of the Spirit made the theme of particular investigation. Schaff says therefore, after speaking of the doctrine of the Person of Christ, "The doctrine of the Holy Spirit was far less developed, and until the middle of the fourth century was never a subject of special controversy." [90]

It was natural that before the doctrine of the Spirit was developed in the theology of the Church many crude ideas of his Person should be entertained. Origen identified him with the little child whom Jesus set in the midst of the disciples to illustrate the truth that only the childlike may enter into the kingdom of heaven.[91] We learn from Jerome [92] and Epiphanius that there were those who identified him with Melchisedec.[93] Justin Martyr taught that by the Spirit and

[89] For fuller treatment of this subject see Swete, Art. "Holy Ghost" in *DCB* and *Holy Spirit in Ancient Church.* Smeaton, *Doctr. of the Holy Spirit,* Third Division. Schaff, *Church Hist.,* II, 560 and III, 663. Fisher, *Hist. Chr. Doctr.* Index "Holy Spirit." For references to Holy Spirit in Apostolic Fathers, see Winstanley, *Spirit in N. T.,* p. 156.

[90] *Ch. Hist.,* II, 560.

[91] Matt. xviii. 2.

[92] *Letter 73.*

[93] See Art. "Melchisedec" in *Smith BD,* which is much more complete and satisfactory than the art. in *HBD.* Swete, *Holy Spirit in Anc. Ch.,* p. 149, note 3.

the power of God that came upon Mary we must understand the Word, the Logos.[94] In this Justin "has put into words the thought which was probably in the minds of most Christians in the second century." [95] Purves affirms that Justin's "own thought strongly *tended away from the doctrine of the Trinity*," and shows how this lends great weight to his witness that the church worshipped three divine Persons.[96]

(b) It is also true that the church was accustomed to think of the Holy Spirit, according to the prevailing representation of the New Testament, as given or sent by the Father and the Son; and it was natural, therefore, that prayer should be directed to them rather than to him, that believers should pray for the Spirit rather than to the Spirit, even when his Personality was clearly recognized and his particular office was in mind.

But though the doctrine of the Holy Spirit was not fully developed for centuries, his Personality and Deity were recognized by the church from the beginning, and he was worshipped and adored side by side with the Father and the Son. Creeds are the fruit at once of experience and of controversy; they are the endeavour of the church to express and to guard its faith. Before the church could formulate the doctrine of the Holy Spirit, there must be rich experience of his regenerating and sanctifying power; and the truth may be precisely and adequately defined only by answering the doubts and objections which it is called to meet. The earliest creed that has come down to us, the so-called Apostles' Creed, in its original form probably of the second century, recognizes the Spirit in the fewest possible words—"I believe . . . . in the Holy Spirit." But though the doctrine was slowly unfolded, the

[94] *I Apol.* 33.
[95] Swete, *Holy Spirit in Anc. Ch.*, p. 387.
[96] *Test. of J. M. to Early Christianity,* pp. 275 ff.

Spirit held a large place from the beginning in the devotional life of the church. There is an unbroken chain of testimony from the days of the apostles that the church worshipped the Spirit with the Father and the Son. To illustrate this by examples belongs to Church History, or the History of Doctrine, and does not fall within the scope of the present work. The student who desires to pursue the subject will find abundant material in the article on the Holy Ghost in the *Dictionary of Christian Biography*, by Swete; Smeaton's *Doctrine of the Holy Spirit*, Third Division; Swete's *Holy Spirit in the Ancient Church;* and the Introduction to Kuyper's *Work of the Holy Spirit*, by B. B. Warfield, which is decidedly the most valuable part of the book.

B—IN THE FOURTH GOSPEL

CHAPTER VIII

THE HOLY SPIRIT IN THE TEACHING OF JESUS—III.

The first passage that claims our attention is the conversation with Nicodemus recorded in chapter three. We may trace in outline the course of Jesus' thought, and then take up in detail the references to the Holy Spirit.

Nicodemus addresses Jesus as a teacher come from God. Jesus answers that more than a teacher is needed by him who would see the kingdom of God; he must be born again. There is only one way by which men may enter the kingdom, whether they be Jews or Gentiles, the way of the new birth. The Jews are not, as they were prone to fancy, birthright members of the kingdom by virtue of their descent from Abraham. They too must be born again. When Nicodemus could not understand, Jesus proceeded to unfold to him the origin and nature of the new birth. "Except one be born of water and the Spirit, he cannot enter into the kingdom of God."

But the regenerating work of the Spirit rests upon the atoning work of the Son; and this Jesus presents to Nicodemus in a figure drawn from a familiar story of the Old Scripture. "And as Moses lifted up the serpent in the wilderness, even so must the Son of man be lifted up; that whosoever believeth may in him have eternal life." The new birth is of the Holy Spirit, but the eternal life which is thus begun is in him, the Son of man. He has purchased for men the right to become children of God;[1] they are actually made children of God by the renewing power of the Spirit.

The work of the Spirit rests upon the work of the Son, the work of the Son rests in turn upon the sovereign grace of the Father. Jesus ascends to the ultimate source of salvation in the love of God. "For God so loved the world, that he gave his only begotten Son, that whosoever believeth on him should not perish, but have eternal life." This is the gospel in a sentence. The Son is represented as the gift of love, the object of faith, the source of eternal life. God loves and gives, man believes and lives. Eternal life is the gift of God, offered to men in his Son, imparted to men by his Spirit. "God gave unto us eternal life, and this life is in his Son."[2] The Holy Spirit is the "Spirit of life in Christ Jesus," imparting in regeneration the new life, the eternal life, which God proffers to men in his Son. The new life is begotten by the Holy Spirit upon the ground of the redemption accomplished by the Son, who is the gift of the Father's love that men may live in him.

Verses 16-21 are correctly regarded as the words of Jesus by Meyer and Godet. Westcott ascribes them to the evangelist, but his reasoning is far from convincing. The chief arguments adduced are: (1) "The secondary character" of the section, which "adds no new thoughts." But in fact the passage is not secondary, but of primary importance, for, as we have seen, the thought here reaches its climax; the new birth is traced from the work of the Spirit to the gift of the Son, and thence to the love of the Father, as its source and spring. These are new thoughts of the first importance. Where in the preceding words of Jesus is the

[1] John i. 14.   [2] I John v. 11.

Father named, his love for the world, his gift of his Son? These are new thoughts without which the teaching would be incomplete and would leave the final truth untouched. (2) The use of certain phrases which are not elsewhere employed by Jesus, but by the evangelist—only begotten Son, believe in the name of, to do the truth. But the preceding section furnishes a sufficient answer. There we find the phrase, "born of water and the Spirit," which occurs nowhere else in the teaching of Jesus. If the particular words which Westcott cites are nowhere else ascribed to Jesus, yet the thoughts which they convey are obviously contained in his teaching. We must remember how small a portion of his words has been preserved, and must permit so great a teacher to use upon appropriate occasions terms which he does not ordinarily employ.

With this survey of the course of Jesus' thought we are prepared to take up in order the points which are of special interest in our study of the Holy Spirit.

The Authorized Version renders verse 3, "Except a man be born again." For *again* the English and American Revisers read *anew*, with *from above* in the margin. Scholars are divided in opinion between these renderings, and the question which is to be preferred requires our consideration. The word ἄνωθεν has several meanings in the New Testament. (a) Ordinarily in accordance with its derivation it signifies *from above*.[3] (b) From the beginning.[4] (c) Over again, anew. This sense of the word is found in the New Testament unless the verse in hand be an exception, only in Gal. iv. 9, where it is joined with πάλιν.[5] These with the present passage are the only instances of the use of the word in the New Testament. The

[3] Matt. xxvii. 57; Mark xv. 38; John iii. 31; x. 11; xix. 23; Jas. i. 17; iii. 15, 17.
[4] Luke i. 3; Acts xxvi. 5.
[5] See Ellicott and Burton, *in loc.*

usage of New Testament writers, and of John in particular, is obviously and strongly in favour of the rendering *from above,* which is also in accord with the characteristic teaching of the Fourth Gospel and the First Epistle of John, that the new birth is of God.[6] But New Testament usage is not uniform, and yields some support, though slight, to *anew.*

There are other considerations to be borne in mind, however, as we attempt to fix the meaning of the term. If Jesus spoke in Aramaic, the precise word that he employed has not been preserved, so that our judgment must be based upon the Greek. Nicodemus evidently understood Jesus to mean *anew.* But are we bound by Nicodemus' understanding or misunderstanding of the term? It might be ambiguous to him as to us; he was bewildered and may easily have misapprehended Jesus' teaching, as even his disciples often did; and he was slow of understanding in this spiritual realm of which Jesus spoke. The word of Nicodemus therefore carries with it no decisive weight.

Much is made of the fact that "in the traditional form of the saying[7] a word is used ($\dot{\alpha}\nu\alpha\gamma\varepsilon\nu\nu\tilde{\alpha}\sigma\vartheta\alpha\iota$) as equivalent to the ambiguous phrase of St. John ($\gamma\varepsilon\nu\nu\eta\vartheta\tilde{\eta}\nu\alpha\iota$ $\dot{\alpha}\nu\omega\vartheta\varepsilon\nu$) which unquestionably can only mean 'to be reborn'."[8] [9] But against this may be set the fact that Greek writers from Origen usually adopt the sense *from above.* The word was of doubtful meaning to them as to us. Chrysostom recognizes the ambiguity: "The word 'again' in this place, some understand to mean 'from heaven,' others 'from the beginning'."[10] In his eighth *Homily* on the Epistle to

[6] John i. 13; I John ii. 29; iii. 9.

[7] e. g. Just. M. *I. Apol.*

[8] Westcott, *Addl. note.* Abbot, *Auth. Fourth G.,* pp. 20 ff. Drummond, *Char. and Auth. of Fourth Gospel,* ch. ii.

[9] *cf.* I Peter i. 3, 23.

[10] *Hom. on John, in loc.*

the Colossians he uses the word in the sense of *anew, afresh*.

The case is argued with learning and ability by Ezra Abbot, Westcott, and Godet in favour of the rendering *anew,* and by Meyer and Dwight [11] in favour of *from above*. After scholarship and critical skill have done their utmost, the ambiguity remains. Both renderings have support in Greek usage; both are appropriate to the course of the thought, and we cannot pronounce with confidence in favour of either; though the weight of evidence appears to incline toward the reading *from above*. Happily the question is of no great importance, for the words that follow make it abundantly clear that the new birth is a birth from heaven. "Except one be born of water and the Spirit, he cannot see the kingdom of God."

There are those who regard *water* (ὕδατος) as an interpolation; [12] but as it is found in all manuscripts and versions and appears in frequent citations by early Christian writers, the attempt to elide it must be pronounced an instance of the pernicious habit of determining a text by the critic's judgment of what should have been said, instead of examining the evidence with open mind to discover what actually was said.

The question what is meant by *water* has given rise to much debate, for both exegetical and theological considerations are involved. That water signifies baptism was the view generally held by the church until the time of the Reformation, when Calvin, recoiling from the doctrine of baptismal regeneration as maintained by the church of Rome, taught that water is merely the symbol of the Spirit's work, representing his cleansing and renewing power, and has no relation to

[11] Add. note in Godet.

[12] Swete, *Holy Sp. in N. T.,* p. 132. Wendt, *Gospel Acc. to St. John,* p. 120.

baptism. "Spiritum et aquam pro eodem posuit." Theologians of the Reformed faith have commonly followed Calvin in this opinion.

The older view, however, is maintained by many of the ablest modern expositors, as Meyer, Westcott, and Godet, and is indeed so obviously correct that it would seem to be impossible to miss it, if it were not so often missed.

Others again have thought that by water is meant the word. It is true that the new birth is said to be accomplished by the word of God. "Of his own will he brought us forth by the word of truth";[13] "Having been begotten again, not of corruptible seed, but of incorruptible, through the word of God which liveth and abideth";[14] and that the word is compared to the rain and the snow that come down from heaven to water the earth and make it fruitful;[15] but the narrative gives no indication that this was in the mind of Jesus here.

It is hardly possible that Nicodemus should have attached to the word any other meaning than baptism. The land was ringing with the name of John the Baptist; his fame was in all men's mouths; and of his ministry baptism was the central feature, outstanding and conspicuous. This natural and obvious sense of the word should be retained unless it is at variance with the course of the argument or with the general tenor of Scripture teaching. But it is in fact in entire harmony with the context and with New Testament doctrine, as may readily be shown. From every point of view water suggests the rite of baptism.

If we regard water as merely a symbol, signifying spiritual renewing and cleansing, is not the sacramental water set apart by divine command for the very purpose of representing the inward work of the Spirit; and is it not therefore the highest form of the symbol

[13] Jas. i. 18.   [14] I Peter i. 23.   [15] Isa. lv. 10.

and the one which Jesus would naturally employ? If common water may signify the Spirit, how much more the water of the sacrament? Why then should Jesus pass by the most obvious symbol of the Spirit's work; the rite administered by John, his forerunner and herald, sent by God to baptize men unto repentance; the rite to which he had himself submitted that he might fulfil all righteousness; the rite which he himself had already begun, or was soon to begin, to administer by the hands of his disciples? [16]

Smeaton understands that our Lord has in mind "the *sprinklings, ablutions, lustrations* common in the Mosaic law."

> The water referred to by our Lord in this connexion was but the ceremonial expression for the cleansing of our person by His own obedience or atoning sacrifice, proving the complete removal of guilt and of everything that could exclude us on the ground of law from the Kingdom of God.[17]

But again we ask, If the washings of the Mosaic law may be signified by the water, why may not baptism, the divinely appointed rite of the New Testament, be regarded as the highest expression, the fulfilment, of the Old Testament symbolism? Did not these Old Testament cleansings reach the height and fulness of their symbolic significance in baptism? Why then should Jesus choose the earlier and lower form of the symbol, and pass by the later and higher form in which the truth was expressed? When Jesus would use water as a sign of spiritual cleansing, why should he not use the water of the sacrament, ordained of God for the very purpose of signifying the cleansing and renewing work of the Spirit?

But baptism is more than a symbol; it is a sacrament. As a sacrament it is appointed to be a badge of

[16] John iii. 34, 36; iv. 1, 2.   [17] *Doct. of Holy Spirit,* p. 183.

discipleship, a bond of union, a means of grace. Here the analogy which has been drawn between the phrases, the *Holy Spirit and fire*, and *water and the Spirit*, breaks down. It is said that if in one case fire is used in a merely symbolic sense, water may be used in the same sense as the other. But the difference is plain; fire is merely a symbol and has no sacramental significance; there is no sacrament of fire. But there is a sacrament of water. Water is not merely a symbol but a sacrament.

The place here accorded to baptism is in harmony with the general teaching of the New Testament. It must be borne in mind, of course, that the term regeneration is used in a narrower and wider sense. It may signify the immediate and instantaneous act of the Spirit, or it may denote the whole complex process that we are accustomed to call conversion, including on the part of man, repentance and faith; on the part of God, the forgiveness of sin and the imparting of the new life in Christ. If *born of the water and Spirit* be understood in the larger sense of the term, there is no difficulty in conceiving that the Spirit imparts renewing grace in baptism as he imparts sanctifying grace in the Lord's Supper. We find therefore that baptism is associated with repentance,[18] and faith;[19] and with the washing away of sin and spiritual cleansing and renewing.[20] In Rom. vi. 3 Paul asks, "Or are ye ignorant that all we who are baptized into Christ Jesus were baptized into his death?" Through baptism we are united with him in his death, and the benefits of his atoning sacrifice are ours.

What is here said of baptism is repeatedly affirmed elsewhere in the New Testament. In Ephes. v. 25, 26 we read: "Husbands, love your wives, even as Christ also loved the church, and gave himself up for it; that he might sanctify it, having cleansed it by the washing

[18] Matt. iii. 11.   [19] Col. i. 12.   [20] Acts ii. 38; xxii. 16.

of water with the word." The general term, *word*, (ϱήματι) takes its particular meaning here from its association with baptism, and signifies the word of the rite, that is, the formula of baptism and the promises connected with it. Augustine has expressed the truth in his familiar saying, *Accedit verbum ad elementum, et fit sacramentum*—the word is added to the element, and the sacrament is made. The water and the word compose the sacrament; for by the word the water is set apart for a sacramental purpose.[21] In Titus iii. 4, 5 baptism and the Spirit are joined together as in the passage before us.

> But when the kindness of God our Saviour, and his love toward man appeared, not by works done in righteousness, which we did ourselves, but according to his mercy he saved us, through the washing of regeneration and renewing of the Holy Spirit.

The reference of this passage to baptism has also been denied,[22] but upon wholly insufficient grounds.[23] The washing or laver (λουτϱῷ) of water in Ephes. v. 26 is the washing or laver of regeneration, and the reference to baptism is as obvious in one case as in the other. Peter expresses the same thought in the strongest possible way: "Because Christ also suffered for sins once, the righteous for the unrighteous, that he might bring us to God; being put to death in the flesh, but made alive in the Spirit; in which also he went and preached unto the spirits in prison, that aforetime were disobedient, when the long-suffering of God waited in the days of Noah, while the ark was a preparing, wherein few, that is, eight souls, were saved through water: which also after a true likeness

[21] On this verse see Ellicott and Hodge, *in loc.*
[22] Hodge, *Syst. Theol.*, III, 595. On the place of baptism in Paul's teaching, see Weiss, *Bib. Theol. N. T.*, p. 84.
[23] See Ellicott, *in loc.*

doth now save you, even baptism, not the putting away
of the filth of the flesh, but the interrogation of a good
conscience toward God, through the resurrection of
Jesus Christ." [24] The closing words are obscure, but
the general sense of the passage is plain: baptism does
not avail as a mere outward ceremony, but only as it
is accompanied by that spiritual disposition which
is acceptable to God through Christ. [25]

In his First Epistle John says of Jesus, "This is he
that came by water and blood, even Jesus Christ; not
with the water only but with the water and with the
blood." [26] He evidently has in mind the flow of water
and blood from the side of Jesus pierced by the spear of
the Roman soldier as he hung upon the cross. This
John saw, and it was to him not a natural sequence of
the wound but a miracle, and he interprets it in this
passage of his Epistle. That the issue of blood and
water had a spiritual significance is plainly indicated
in the Gospel: "And he that hath seen hath borne
witness; and his witness is true; and he knoweth that
he saith true, that ye also may believe." [27] These strong
words would be unmeaning if he was speaking of a
merely natural phenomenon. Evidently he speaks of
a miraculous event which conveys a spiritual truth, and
what that truth is he shows in this comment upon the
matter in his Epistle. Christ came by blood and
water; the aorist ($\ἐλθὼν$) points to a historical fact. He
came, that is, he manifested himself as the Christ, and
this manifestation was through blood and water. These
general terms find more precise definition in the words
that follow—"not with water only, but with the water
and with the blood"; that is, the well-known water of
baptism and blood of atonement. The transition from
the general, water and blood, to the particular, the
water and the blood, is marked by the change of prepo-

[24] I Peter iii. 18, 21.   [26] I John v. 6.
[25] On this passage see Leighton, *in loc.*   [27] John xix. 35.

sition from διὰ *by,* to ἐν, *with* or *in.* Through water and blood he reveals himself as the Christ; and the water and the blood of his baptism and his sacrifice are the sphere in which he exercises the office of the Christ. The baptism with water marked the beginning of his Messianic ministry, the blood marked the close of his work of expiation. His Messianic work on earth is bounded by the baptism and the cross. "He not only undertook, when he came to baptism, the task of fulfilling all righteousness,[28] but he also completed it by pouring out *his blood;*[29] and when this was done, *blood and water* came forth from the side of Jesus Christ, being dead on the cross."[30] Calvin speaks to the same effect:

> Water is a figure of ablution, and blood of satisfaction. These things are both found in Christ, who as John says "came by water and blood"; that is, to purify and redeem. Of this the Spirit of God is a witness: or rather there are three that bear witness, the Spirit, the Water, and the Blood. In the water and the blood we have a testimony of purgation and redemption; and the Spirit as the principal witness confirms and secures our reception and belief of this testimony. This sublime mystery was strikingly exhibited upon the cross, when blood and water flowed from Christ's sacred side; which on this account Augustine has justly called 'the fountain of our sacraments.'[31] [32]

It is evident from this review that the reference of water to baptism is abundantly justified by Scripture usage.

[28] Matt. iii. 15.
[29] John xix. 30.
[30] Bengel, *in loc.*
[31] *Instt.* IV. 14, 22.
[32] I have treated at length of I John v:6-8 in connection with John xix. 34-37 in my *Teaching of the Gospel of John.*

And it may be shown with equal clearness that the reference to baptism is in harmony with that system of theology which is known as the Reformed faith. The Westminster Confession of Faith teaches that

> The efficacy of baptism is not tied to that moment of time wherein it is administered; yet, notwithstanding, by the right use of this ordinance the grace promised is not only offered, but really exhibited and conferred by the Holy Ghost, to such (whether of age or infants) as that grace belongeth unto, according to the counsel of God's own will in his appointed time.[33]

The Shorter Catechism inquires, "What are the outward and ordinary means whereby Christ communicateth to us the benefits of redemption?" and gives the answer in these terms:

> The outward and ordinary means whereby Christ communicateth to us the benefits of redemption are his ordinances, especially the Word, Sacraments, and prayer; all of which are made effectual to the elect for salvation.[34]

A sacrament is defined as "a holy ordinance instituted by Christ, wherein, by sensible signs, Christ and the benefits of the new covenant are represented, sealed, and applied to believers." [35] "Baptism is a sacrament, wherein the washing with water, in the name of the Father, and of the Son, and of the Holy Ghost, doth signify and seal our engrafting into Christ, and partaking of the benefits of the covenant of grace, and our engagement to be the Lord's." [36]

It is interesting to note that the verse we have in hand is cited in both the Larger and Shorter Cate-

[33] XXVIII. 6.   [34] Qn. 88.   [35] Qn. 92.   [36] Qn. 94.

chisms as one of the proof texts establishing the Scripture doctrine of baptism.

It is evident then that neither the general tenor of Scripture teaching nor the principles of the Reformed faith forbid us to recognize the rite of baptism in the water which is here associated with the Spirit; on the contrary, both Scripture and the Reformed faith are in entire accord with this interpretation.

There is here no doctrine of baptismal regeneration, as the term is commonly understood. Renewing grace is not inseparably attached to the ordinance. Not all who are baptized are regenerated, not all who are regenerated are baptized. In commenting on this passage Smeaton says, "The term water has been variously interpreted. (1) Some refer it to baptism—an opinion current in Patristic theology from the earliest times, and asserted in the Greek and Latin church and in some of the Protestant formularies. But it is untenable, as will be evident to every mind that weighs the matter in the light of common observation. The water to which the Lord refers *certainly regenerates,* and entitles those who receive it to enter the Kingdom of God, from which no true member can ever be cast out again—which cannot be affirmed of baptism in every case." [37] If this be true, it weighs equally against his own view of the water. Did the washings prescribed by the law of Moses "certainly regenerate"? But it is not true. Jesus does not say that men must be born of water that they may enter the kingdom of God, but of water *and the Spirit.* The very form of the phrase shows how closely these words are linked together —not ἐξ ὕδατος καὶ ἐκ πνεύματος, as if water and Spirit might be severed; but ἐξ ὕδατος καὶ πνεύματος . They are united, the Spirit, who is the power by which regeneration is accomplished, and baptism, the means of grace which he employs. The water has no efficacy

[37] *Doctr. Holy Spirit,* p. 183.

whatever apart from the Spirit. Water and the Spirit do certainly regenerate, and the Spirit may use the water to this end. Renewing grace may be imparted through the sacrament of baptism as sanctifying grace is imparted through the sacrament of the Supper. The Spirit uses the sacraments not merely as signs and symbols of his gracious work, but as the means by which in part that work is accomplished. We must not, on the one hand, ascribe to the sacraments an efficacy of their own, nor, on the other hand, may we deny their efficacy when they are employed by the Holy Spirit. That baptism is simply one of the means which the Spirit uses, and that regeneration is not inseparably attached to it, is indicated by the fact that the water does not again appear, but the Spirit alone is named: "That which is born of the Spirit is Spirit." Baptism is treated in the same way in the early addition to Mark, xvi. 16—"He that believeth and is baptized shall be saved; but he that disbelieveth shall be condemned." In Rom. x. 16 the confession of the mouth is joined with the faith of the heart. "There is in every sacrament a spiritual relation, or sacramental union, between the sign and the thing signified; whence it comes to pass, that the names and effects of the one are attributed to the other." [38] The same truth is taught in John vi. Jesus declares emphatically and repeatedly that men must eat his flesh and drink his blood if they would have eternal life. Language could not be more clear and explicit. But he goes on to explain the deeper meaning of his words. It is the spirit that giveth life; the flesh profiteth nothing." [39] He is not speaking directly of the Lord's Supper, but sets forth the principle which underlies it and gives it spiritual value. The eating his flesh and drinking his blood is represented sensibly and visibly in the Supper. Whether

[38] *Westminster Confession of Faith*, ch. xxvii. 2.
[39] John vi. 63.

we take πνεῦμα here to refer to the Holy Spirit or not
—a question that we shall presently consider—the
contrast is sharply drawn between the material and
the spiritual, and it is taught that the material has no
value or power of itself. It is true of the elements of
baptism and the Lord's Supper alike that they avail
only as they are employed by the Spirit to apply to
those who worthily receive them the benefits of Christ's
atoning work.[40]

The question has been raised whether Jesus speaks
of the baptism of John or of Christian baptism. Probably he spoke in general terms to include both forms
of baptism; for it is the sign and seal alike of John's
ministry and of the new covenant in Christ Jesus. And
the words gain added weight when we remember that
Nicodemus was of the sect of the Pharisees, who "rejected for themselves the counsel of God, being not
baptized of him (John)." [41] To the Pharisees the
injunction not to slight or neglect the ordinance of God
was particularly appropriate; for the baptism of John
was from heaven.[42]

We need have no hesitation in the light of these
considerations in referring the water to baptism. Dr.
Hodge denies the reference in his *Systematic Theology,*
but in his commentary on Rom. vi. 3 and Ephes. v. 26
he teaches everything with regard to the nature and
effect of baptism which this interpretation requires.
That this obvious and appropriate and Scriptural significance of the word has ever been abandoned must
be pronounced one of those instances, unhappily not
rare in the history of the church, in which the exposition of Scripture has been warped by the supposed
necessities of a theological system.

Twice again in this passage the Spirit is named.

[40] See Denney, *Jesus and the Gospels,* pp. 87-90.
[41] Luke vii. 30.
[42] Mark xi. 30.

"That which is born of the flesh is flesh; that which is born of the Spirit is Spirit." [43] The flesh is man in his natural state of sin and condemnation. "Flesh and blood cannot inherit the kingdom of God; neither doth corruption inherit incorruption." [44] The kingdom is a spiritual kingdom, and only they may enter it who are born of the Spirit: "not of blood, nor of the will of the flesh, nor of the will of man, but of God." [45] In the natural and the spiritual world alike the child bears the image of the parent.

Ambrose accepted and defended a reading of the verse which has no manuscript authority, and is evidently a gloss: "that which is born of the flesh is flesh, because it is born of the flesh; and that which is born of the Spirit is Spirit, because the Spirit is God." [46] The last clause he accused the Arians of expunging from the text: "Which passage you, Arians, so expressly testify to be said concerning the Spirit, that you remove it from your copies, and would that it were from yours, and not also from those of the Church." [47] We may suppose that the words were inserted by a scribe in order to furnish additional witness to the Deity of the Spirit, as the famous passage I John v. 7 was introduced to give support to the doctrine of the Trinity. [48]

The analogy between the natural and spiritual realms which Jesus so often traces is drawn here: "The wind bloweth where it will, and thou hearest the voice thereof, but knowest not whence it cometh and whither it goeth; so is every one that is born of the Spirit." [49] It is possible to tender πνεῦμα by Spirit in both clauses

[43] John iii. 6.
[44] I Cor. xv. 50.
[45] John i. 13.
[46] *On the Holy Spirit*, III, 59 and 63.
[47] *Ibid.*, III, 59.
[48] Gregory, *Canon & Text of N. T.*, pp. 374, 508. Westcott on *Eps. of John*, Addl. note *in loc.*
[49] John iii. 8.

of the verse, and read as the margin of the Revised Version suggests, "The spirit breatheth." But in that case the free self-determination of the regenerate soul is compared to the free self-determination of the Spirit — a conception wholly foreign to the course of Jesus' thought. As flesh and spirit are contrasted, so wind and Spirit are compared. "Every one that is born of the Spirit" is elliptical, and must be understood to signify, "so is it with every one that is born of the Spirit." For it is not the freedom of the soul that is born again of which Jesus speaks, but the freedom of the Spirit in the work of regeneration. His action is likened to the blowing of the wind in these particulars: it is self-determined: "Where it will"; it is known by its effects: "thou hearest the sound thereof"; it is mysterious in its origin and operation: "thou knowest not whence it cometh and whither it goeth."

Thus our Lord makes plain the truth that in order to enter the kingdom of God there is need of a new birth, a spiritual birth, a divine birth, a sovereign birth. All this is involved in the phrase, "born of the Spirit," and belongs to the logical unfolding of the doctrine of regeneration.

In his discourse on the bread of life recorded in the sixth chapter of John, though Jesus does not directly refer to the sacrament of the Lord's Supper, yet he sets forth the principle which underlies it and gives to it spiritual value and power. Because baptism was an established ordinance, he speaks of it distinctly and directly to Nicodemus: but the sacrament of the Supper had not yet been instituted, and therefore it is not expressly named. But the truth which it symbolizes is expressed, a general truth which finds a particular application in the sacrament; as the cleansing which is symbolized by water comes to its full significance in baptism. "I am the bread of life"; "The bread which I will give is my flesh, for the life of the world"; "Ex-

cept ye eat the flesh of the Son of man and drink his
blood, ye have not life in yourselves"; "He that eateth
my flesh and drinketh my blood abideth in me and I
in him."

His disciples found this a hard saying, and Jesus
expounded to them the spiritual significance of his
words: "It is the spirit that giveth life; the flesh
profiteth nothing." The bold figure of eating his flesh
and drinking his blood was employed to arrest attention and awaken interest; but it is not to be taken
literally. Through the material the spiritual appears.
If this verse stood alone, and no further comment was
made, we should naturally infer that Jesus is speaking
of the Holy Spirit, the giver of spiritual life. And this
would be in entire accord with his teaching regarding
the Spirit in John iii. Thus he would ascribe to the
Spirit, though indirectly, the same efficacy in the administration of the Supper that he had already ascribed
to him in the administration of baptism. The sacraments derive all their power from him.

But the words that follow forbid this interpretation.
"The words that I have spoken unto you are spirit, and
are life." It is the life-giving power of his words
of which he speaks, a truth that often finds a place in
his doctrine. The story of the two builders [50] teaches
that every man is building, that every building shall be
tested, that the result of the testing depends upon the
foundation; that the only sure foundation is obedience
to his word. By his word his disciples are made clean,[51]
as they are sanctified by the word of God,[52] the word
which he has given them.[53] Therefore he said, "If a
man keep my word, he shall never see death." [54] But
the word and the sacraments and all other means that
may be employed to renew and cleanse the hearts of

[50] Matt. vii. 24-27; Luke vi. 47-49.
[51] John xv. 3.
[52] John xvii. 17.
[53] John xvii. 14.
[54] John viii. 57.

men owe their efficacy to the Holy Spirit. Only as he applies them to the soul do they accomplish the end for which they are given. They are simply the instruments which he employs to fulfil his sovereign work of grace in the lives of men. The word of God avails only as the Spirit of God brings it home to the heart and gives it power over the life.

II. "Now on the last day, the great day of the feast, Jesus stood and cried, saying, If any man thirst, let him come unto me and drink. He that believeth on me, as the Scripture hath said, from within him shall flow rivers of living water. But this spake he of the Spirit, which they that believe on him were to receive; for the Spirit was not yet given; because Jesus was not yet glorified." [55]

The text presents two subjects for our consideration, the words of Jesus and the interpretation of them by the evangelist.

(a) *The words of Jesus.* The occasion that suggested the figure is commonly supposed to have been the ceremony of bringing water in a golden bowl from the pool of Siloam and pouring it into vessels near the altar, a ceremony which according to Jewish tradition was derived from Isaiah xii. 3—"Therefore with joy shall ye draw water out of the wells of salvation." This rite was observed every day of the feast of Tabernacles, except perhaps the eighth, of which we lack sufficient knowledge to speak with confidence.

The Spirit in his refreshing and lifegiving power is frequently represented in the Old Testament and the New by water, the indispensable condition of all created life. In the story of the creation it is written, "And no plant of the field was yet in the earth, and no herb of the field had yet sprung up; for Jehovah God had not caused it to rain upon the earth." [56] Some of the fathers taught that the river of the water of life

[55] John vii. 37-39.   [56] Gen. ii. 5.

in Revelation xxii. 1 [57] represents the Holy Spirit.[58] To the woman of Samaria Jesus said, "If thou knewest the gift of God, and who it is that saith to thee, Give me to drink; thou wouldest have asked of him, and he would have given thee living water." [59]   There as here the water is the gift of Jesus. And it is living water, water not drawn from Jacob's well or the pool of Siloam, but springing from an everflowing fountain, water that ministers refreshment and life not to the body, but to the soul. There the water is represented as quenching the thirst of the spirit; here it flows forth as a lifegiving stream. The gift shall not be confined to him who receives it but in turn shall be imparted to others through him. It is the law of the kingdom that as every man has received a gift, so shall he minister it, as a good steward of the manifold grace of God.[60]

What is the Scripture to which Jesus refers? Where in the Old Testament shall we find the words, "from within him shall flow rivers of living water"? There is nothing in the Old Scripture which answers precisely to the words of Jesus. How then may the quotation be explained? It is a forced expedient to refer the words, "as the Scripture hath said," to the preceding clause, "He that believeth in me"; though it has been resorted to also in John xix. 28, where "that the scripture might be accomplished" is by some scholars [61] connected with the words preceding, "knowing that all things are now finished," and not with "I thirst." Smeaton affirms that the promise here given intimates "precisely the same thing as Christ said to the woman of Samaria.[62] The meaning is not that the Spirit

[57] Swete, *Procession of the Spirit,* pp. 8, 216; *Comm.* of Swete and Charles, *in loc.*
[58] Copious selections from ancient and modern writers bearing upon this passage are given in Hare's *Mission of the Comforter,* note H.
[59] John iv. 10.
[60] I Peter iv. 10.
[61] See Meyer, *in loc.*
[62] John iv. 14.

flows from one disciple to another—for none can so give the Spirit—but that the Spirit as a flowing river quenches the thirst and satisfies the desires, so that the soul no longer thirsts for any other object." [63] But the difference of phraseology clearly indicates a difference of meaning: "Shall become in him a well of water springing up unto eternal life"; "from within him shall flow rivers of living water." The water does not simply spring up in the believer, it flows from him. If believers may be called the light of the world and the salt of the earth, there is no reason why they may not be represented as ministering to others of that divine grace with which their own hearts are filled. That Christ works through men, and through them imparts his grace to others is plainly declared in the figure of the vine and the branches. The life is of the vine, the branches bear the fruit: The vine bears fruit through the branches. This thought underlies the whole conception of the church as the body of Christ, in which he dwells and through which he works, as he dwelt in the body of his flesh, and through it accomplished his work on our behalf. It is the outflowing of the grace and power of the Spirit in the ministry of believers of which Jesus here speaks. At a later stage of our study we shall see that the witness of the Spirit is ordinarily borne through the disciples.

Obviously this is one of those quotations, frequent in all literature, and found elsewhere in the New Testament, which gather up the substance of various passages in a sentence. They are termed "Quotations of Substance" by Prof. Franklin Johnson in his Quotations of the New Testament from the Old, Chapter VI; and he gives illustrations from the New Testament, in which he discovers only three or four examples, and specifies Matt. ii. 23; John vii. 38; and Ephes. v. 14; while Rom. iii. 10 is regarded rather as a citation from

[63] *Doct. of the Holy Spirit,* p. 48.

Psalm xiv. 3. Illustrations are drawn also from Greek and Latin authors.[64] This mode of quotation, indeed, is so common that it need cause neither difficulty nor surprise. And there is not the slightest occasion here or elsewhere in the Gospels to suppose that the words are drawn from some lost apocryphal writing; nor is the accuracy of the record affected by the fact that the precise form of words cannot be found in the Old Testament. The endeavour is sometimes made to force upon the speakers and writers of the New Testament a rigid and formal accuracy of quotation to which they will not submit, and which is constantly transgressed by authors of the first rank in every age. It is interesting to note that one of the foremost Bible scholars in citing this passage gives it in this fashion: "If any man thirst let him come unto me, and drink living water." [65] The citation is correct in substance though verbally inexact.

The words of Jesus are not the citation of a specific Old Testament prophecy, but rather a summary of those passages which portray the beneficent out-flowing of the life which is in fellowship with God; such as Prov. xviii. 4: "The words of a man's mouth are as deep waters; the wellspring of wisdom is as a flowing brook"; Isa. lviii. 11: "Thou shalt be like a watered garden, and like a spring of water, whose waters fail not." He who receives the living water through faith in Christ shall in turn become to others a fountain of blessing. It is highly significant that Jesus thus gathers up in a sentence the Old Testament teaching concerning the Holy Spirit, and relates it to his own Person and work.

(b) *The interpretation of the words of Jesus by the evangelist.*

Among the evangelists the beloved disciple alone ventures to interpret the thought of the Master. The

[64] See also Art. "Quotations" in *HDC & Gs*.
[65] Calvin, *Instt.*, Bk. IV, ch. xix., vi.

earlier writers simply report what they had seen and heard and gathered from tradition; John interprets. They tell us what Jesus said; John goes further, and tells us what he meant. To this general rule there is a single striking exception in Mark vii. 19—"Perceive ye not, that whatsover from without goeth into the man, it cannot defile him; because it goeth not into his heart but into his belly, and goeth out into the draught?" The Authorized Version renders the words that follow by "purging all meats." If the participle is neuter, as in the received text, καθαρίζον. it evidently refers to the phrase, "that which goeth into the draught." But the participle according to the decisive weight of evidence is masculine, καθαρίζων. [66] To what then should it be referred? Meyer says to the draught, which he regards as the logical subject, though it is in the accusative case in the text. It is much better, however, to refer it to Jesus, the subject of λέγει in the verse preceding, and read with the Revised Version, "*This he said*, making all meats clean." In view of "the freedom of the Greek from artificial rules and its response to the play of the mind" [67] the separation of the participle from the verb presents no serious difficulty. The objection is raised that we have no other example of such interpretation of Jesus' words in Mark; and that is true. Sometimes we are called on to reject a passage because something like it is found elsewhere; and again because nothing like it is found elsewhere. The New Testament writers observe no rules of this kind, and each case must be determined upon the evidence presented. In this instance we naturally inquire, Have we not here a reminiscence of Peter, recalling and interpreting the words of Jesus in the light of his own experience on the housetop in Joppa? [68]

This interpretation, which was recognized by

[66] See Swete, *in loc.*   [67] Robertson, *Gram. Gk. N. T.*, 417.
[68] Acts x. 11-15.

Origen,[69] and lifts the teaching of Jesus to the high spiritual level which was characteristic of all his teaching, may be accepted without hesitation.[70]

How does John interpret the words of Jesus? "This spake he of the Spirit, which they that believed on him were to receive." Why "which"? Surely neither Jesus nor John conceived of the Spirit as neuter, an impersonal force or energy; yet that is the sense that "which" inevitably conveys to modern ears.

In the light of this interpretation it is natural to refer the *living water* of John iv. 10 also to the Spirit. But there are several possible explanations of the phrase in that passage: by the living water Jesus may mean himself, God's grace and truth, faith, salvation; and the truth conveyed may be conceived under so many different aspects that we cannot determine precisely what lay in the mind of Jesus. He promised the Samaritan woman water that would quench her thirst, the thirst of the soul, and it is obvious that this may be represented in various ways. The soul thirsts for God;[71] for the word of God;[72] for the Spirit;[73] for righteousness.[74] God is the fountain of life,[75] but there are many ways through which he imparts himself to men, and any one of these may answer to the living water by which the thirst of the soul is quenched. We cannot affirm, therefore, that Jesus here is speaking of the Spirit, though the resemblance of the two passages may seem to point in that direction; and it is probable that he makes use of the phrase to signify in the most general sense the satisfaction of the soul in God.

[69] Matt. xi. 12.
[70] In favour of this rendering see Swete and Gould; against it, Meyer and Riddle.
[71] Ps. xlii. 1, 2; lxiii. 1; cxliii. 6; Isa. lv. 3.
[72] Amos viii. 11-13.
[73] Isa. xliv. 3.
[74] Matt. v. 6.
[75] Isa. lv. 1; Ps. xxxvi. 9; Jer. ii. 13; xvii. 13.

Here the living water is expressly declared to be the Spirit. But what is meant by the words that follow: "For the Spirit was not yet given; because Jesus was not yet glorified"? *Given* is not in the text, but is evidently required in translation. The Spirit was present and active in the world from the beginning; in the Old Testament is represented as the efficient energy of God, in the New Testament, disclosed as a divine Person. Without him is nothing accomplished, for he is the agent of the Godhead in the realm of nature and of grace. By him every soul is regenerated that has ever entered the kingdom of God throughout the whole course of human history. He rested upon judge and prophet and king under the old dispensation. John the Baptist was filled with the Holy Spirit. The power of the Spirit was conspicuously displayed in the conception of Jesus, through which the Word became flesh. How then can it be said that the Spirit was not yet given?

It is evident that the words must be understood not in an absolute, but in a relative sense, a mode of speech of which there are many examples both in the Old Testament and in the New. It is not meant that the Holy Spirit was not in the world until Jesus was glorified, but that he was not disclosed in the fulness of his grace and glory, did not put forth the greatness of his power. Jesus received the Spirit without measure, but he did not impart the Spirit to his disciples in the height and fulness of his power until he was seated at the right hand of the Majesty on high, and crowned Lord of all.

All revelation is gradual and progressive, for it is limited by the capacity of men to receive. The Son was in the world from the beginning, as the maker of the universe, the light which lighteth every man. "Abraham rejoiced to see his day; and he saw it and was glad." Moses wrote of him. He followed the children of Israel in their long journey through the wilderness.[76] The Old Testament was a continual foreshadowing of him and of his redeeming work. Yet of him too it might be said, He was not yet given. For the incarnation ushered in a new era of revelation immeasurably surpassing all that had gone before. Pentecost holds in the revelation of the Spirit the place that the incarnation holds in the revelation of the Son. Then men began clearly to apprehend his Personality, and to experience in a measure unknown before, his sovereign power. The revelation of the Spirit follows and keeps pace with the revelation of the Son. When the Person of the Son is disclosed by his birth in Bethlehem, the Person of the Spirit begins to appear. And when the atoning work of Jesus is accomplished, and he is exalted at the right hand of God, the Spirit begins to exercise the full power of his ministry in the church and in the world. It is his office to witness to Jesus, and the work of Jesus must be finished before the witness can be borne. Calvary and Olivet are the conditions of Pentecost. Jesus therefore may say to the disciples, though they have been born again of the Spirit, "If I go not away, the Comforter will not come unto you; but if I go, I will send him unto you." [77] [78] As under the old dispensation there was a partial anticipation of Christ, so there was a partial manifestation of the Spirit. He accomplishes more widely and perfectly under the Gospel what he wrought more narrowly and imperfectly under the law. For it is through the truth that he regenerates and sanctifies the soul; the truth comes to its full expression in the finished work of Christ, and the more fully and clearly the truth is revealed and apprehended the richer is the fruit in character and life.

In these respects, then, the revelation of the Spirit

[76] I Cor. x. 14.
[77] John xvi. 7.
[78] Swete, *Holy Spirit in N. T.*, note F, p. 375.

after the ascension of Christ transcends all earlier revelation.

(a) His Personality is clearly brought to light. He is no longer a divine energy or power, but a divine Person. Our Lord's clearest and fullest teaching regarding the Spirit was reserved until the night he was betrayed; but though some perception of the truth began to dawn upon the minds of the disciples, it was not until the Spirit came upon them in mighty power that the full import of the Master's words was apprehended. It is only after Pentecost that the work of the Spirit is clearly distinguished from the work of the Father and the Son; and regeneration and sanctification which the Old Testament ascribes to God, are seen to pertain to the special office of the Spirit.[79] Yet the truth was so thoroughly in harmony with the representation of the Old Testament, sprang so naturally from it, that it apparently provoked no opposition or dissent on the part of the Jews when it was presented to them, and found its place without difficulty or hindrance in the theology and life of the church. When the truth was plainly disclosed, it was seen to be the logical and inevitable sequel of Old Testament teaching. We need not wonder that the disciples were not able to grasp at once the full significance of this great truth; for it is singular to observe how in our own time, and in the writings of men who hold without question the Personality of the Spirit, the practice of using the neuter pronouns in referring to him still persists. Thayer's Lexicon defines the Spirit as God's power and agency and recognizes in him no distinct personality; yet there is a curious interchange of *it* and *he* in the treatment of the theme. We

[79] On the whole subject of the progressive disclosure of the Spirit, see Swete, *Holy Spirit in N. T.*, notes E and F. Kuyper's *Work of the Holy Spirit,* ch. xxvi. The most valuable part of the work is the introduction by B. B. Warfield, where the unfolding of the doctrine of the Spirit is admirably presented.

find the same phraseology in places where we should
not expect it. The Authorized Version in Rom. viii. 26
reads, "The Spirit *itself*," which is properly altered in
the Revised Versions to *himself*. But in John xv. 26
both the English and American Revisions read: "But
when the Comforter is come, whom I will send unto
you from the Father, even the Spirit of truth *which*
proceedeth from the Father." It is true of course that
in one clause the Greek pronoun is masculine, referring to παράκλητος, and in the other neuter, referring to
πνεῦμα; but to designate the Spirit by a pronoun
which in modern usage is not applied to persons, and
that in a passage which explicitly sets forth his Personality, cannot be justified by niceties of grammar. The
thought must determine the rendering. In the same
way the Spirit is spoken of as neuter in the Revised
Versions, both English and American, in I Peter i. 11:
"Searching what time, or what manner of time, the
Spirit of Christ which was in them did point unto,
when it testified beforehand the sufferings of Christ,
and the glory that should follow them." However it
may have been with the Old Testament prophets,
Peter certainly did not conceive of the Spirit as impersonal, for in the beginning of this Epistle he associates him with the Father and the Son. And in the
rendering of Peter's words, Peter's thought should control. In Titus iii. 6 both Revisions read "renewing of
the Holy Spirit (Ghost) which he poured out upon
us richly."

In his *Spirit of God in Biblical Literature* Prof.
Wood habitually speaks of the Spirit as *it*. He holds,
upon altogether insufficient grounds, that the teaching ascribed to Jesus regarding the Spirit in John xiv.
16 was probably "a Christian addition."[80] Yet on
page 256 the Spirit appears as *he*.

Prof. J. A. Alexander in the first line of his *Com-*

[80] p. 242.

mentary on Acts xix. 2 uses *it* with reference to the Spirit, but throughout the exposition *he* is always used. The neuter pronoun is employed in similar fashion in Sanday & Headlam's *Commentary* on Romans, following the Authorized Version: "The Holy Spirit itself";[81] and in Ellicott's *Commentary* on Galatians: "The Holy Spirit itself."[82] Prof. Swete in his *Holy Spirit in the New Testament* interchanges the masculine and neuter in a strange and perplexing fashion throughout the whole course of the work, and even in the same sentence—"We see the Spirit manifesting itself in the events of our Lord's life, and in the experience of believers after his ascension; and we also receive direct teaching upon the work of the Paraclete and upon the relation of Christians to Him." [83] We read again, "When any personal action or relation is ascribed to the Spirit the article at once reappears, *e.g.*, . . . when it is co-ordinated with the Father and the Son." [84] It is curious to observe that in the closing paragraphs of the book, which form a summary of the discussion, in which the Personality of the Spirit is clearly shown, *it* and *itself* are the only pronouns employed. In Hastings' *Dictionary of Christ and the Gospels*, Art. "Holy Spirit," by James Danney, *it* frequently occurs, even in passages where the Personality of the Spirit is explicitly affirmed. And in the *Dictionary of the Apostolic Church* the Spirit appears in the same paragraph as both *He* and *it*.[85] In the closing paragraph of F. W. Robertson's fine sermon on "The Principle of the Spiritual Harvest" we read that the reward of the Christian life, "is the Holy Spirit of God in man, making itself felt." In Leighton's *Commentary* on I Peter iii. 21, note, the Spirit is twice referred to by the neuter pronoun.

These illustrations, which might be indefinitely in-

[81] Rom. viii. 26. [83] p. 7. [85] Vol. I, p. 580.
[82] Gal. v. 16. [84] p. 397.

creased, indicate how closely the conceptions of the Spirit as a divine energy and as a divine Person are related, and how easily the mind turns from one to the other.

(b) Under the old covenant the Spirit was given to chosen individuals, particularly to those who represented and served the theocracy; at Pentecost he was poured out upon the church and the church became his abiding place, his temple. Here again it must be borne in mind that the words are true in a relative sense. He was present in the church of the Old Testament as truly as in the church of the New; and to him must be ascribed the faith of Abraham, the wisdom of Moses, the patience of Job, the inspiration of psalmist and prophet, as well as the guidance of the apostolic company. But now he whose gifts had been conferred for special purposes upon chosen men, is poured out in the fulness of his sanctifying grace upon all the people of God.

(c) Not only is the Person of the Spirit clearly made known, and his power more widely diffused, but he operates more energetically and fruitfully in the individual life, in the church, in the world. As men of the Old Covenant — like Abraham and Moses and David—saw the Christ but dimly through the mist of the intervening centuries, so the full work of the Spirit was not wrought in them, for the work of the Spirit is determined by the revelation of the Son. His office in regeneration and sanctification, with which the New Testament is chiefly concerned, is rarely alluded to in the Old Scripture. His ministry could not be clearly apprehended until his Person was disclosed. Only after Pentecost is the work of the Spirit plainly and explicitly distinguished from the work of the Father and Son.

The transcendent nature of his work appears in the change which his coming at Pentecost accomplished in the lives and character of the apostles. After three years of fellowship with the Master they had been timid as sheep; they became bold as lions. They had been weak; they were clothed with power, and turned the world upside down: they had been foolish and slow of heart to understand and to accept the plainest teaching of Jesus, and stumbled at his word; they began to speak with wisdom that none could withstand. They were lifted to an immeasurably higher plane of life, intellectual and spiritual. When we cross over from the Gospels to the Acts, we are introduced to a new world. We ask, Is this John? Can this be Peter? They were narrow-minded, bigoted Jews; now they have learned to look with the eyes of the Master upon the great world for which God gave his Son to die. They have grown mightily in strength and in spiritual stature, and are ready for the enterprise to which Jesus has called them, the conquest of the world.

CHAPTER IX

THE HOLY SPIRIT IN THE TEACHING OF JESUS—IV.

In his *Christian Ecclesia* Dr. Hort affirms that chapters xiii-xvii of the Fourth Gospel are "on the whole the weightiest and most pregnant body of teaching on the ecclesia to be found anywhere in the Bible." [1] With even greater confidence a similar judgment may be pronounced upon the teaching of these chapters regarding the Person and work of the Holy Spirit. It may be said with truth that they explicitly assert or clearly imply all that is taught in the New Testament upon this theme. The Spirit is mentioned eight times by name. Once he is called the Holy Spirit; [2] three times the Spirit of truth; [3] and four times the Paraclete. [4] But this enumeration falls far short of defining the place which the Spirit holds in this discourse, for the whole passage is pervaded and inspired by the thought of his gracious ministry. Jesus is about to complete his atoning work, and the life which has been rendered in service shall be offered in sacrifice. When the atonement has been provided in the body of his flesh, it must be made known to men throughout the world from generation to generation and from age to age until the glorious consummation of the kingdom of God. This work he carries on through his spiritual body, the church, which is the pillar and ground of the truth, the fulness of him who filleth all

---

[1] p. 223.
[2] John xiv. 26.
[3] John xiv. 17; xv. 26; xvi. 12.
[4] John xiv. 16, 26; xv. 26; xvi. 7.

288

in all. As the church is the soul of the world, the Holy Spirit is the soul of the church. It is by the Spirit that Jesus dwells in the hearts of his people and works through them as in the beginning through the body of his flesh. Through the Eternal Spirit he offered himself to God;[5] through the Spirit dwelling in his mystical body, the church, he proclaims to men the gospel of redeeming grace.

The teaching of Jesus upon this theme, as upon every other, is not philosophical, but practical; not abstract, but concrete; not general, but specific; not systematic, but occasional, drawn out by the questions and the needs of those to whom he spoke. When men asked him about matters of doctrine or duty, he often replied with a story, as the parables attest. He was accustomed to speak with immediate reference to the case of those whom he addressed. He never attempted, for example, a formal definition of God, nor did he employ those high-sounding titles with which men often seek to veil their ignorance. Usually he called him by the simple and familiar name of Father. And when he spoke of him in any other way, it was always to give him a name that answered to the need of the hour. To the woman of Samaria who conceived of God as a local divinity, confined to Gerizim or Jerusalem, he said, God is a Spirit, not subject to the limitations of place and time. She asked, Where shall we worship? Jesus answered, Everywhere. Not a holy place is required, but a holy heart. Worship not here or there, but in spirit and in truth; not in form, as the Jews, nor in error, as the Samaritans. Not the temple is the true sanctuary, but the soul. "Wouldest thou pray in a temple? Pray in thyself. But be thou first a temple of God, for he in his temple heareth him that prays."[6]

When Moses prayed, Tell me thy name, God an-

[5] Heb. ix. 14.   [6] Augustine.

swered, "I AM." Imagine with what breathless interest Moses listened. God is about to reveal himself,
to give himself a name. But the answer returned upon
itself, and denied what it seemed about to reveal—
I AM THAT I AM.[7] What form of speech can contain him for whom the heavens are too small? When
again Moses prayed, Show me thy glory, God said to
him, "Thou shalt see my back, but my face shall not
be seen." [8] Throughout the Old Testament the back
of God is turned toward men. God laboured, if we
may so speak, by priest and prophet and law giver, by
rite and ceremony and sacrifice, to give himself a name.
But throughout the old dispensation the sentence was
never finished. No predicate was found for I AM.
Some disclosure of his nature and will was given, but
it was obscure, and still the cry rose upward to the
stars, Tell me thy name. Jesus appropriated the sentence which the Old Testament had begun, and finished
it, found the predicate so long desired. He translated
the enigmatic phrase, I AM THAT I AM, into the
speech of daily life. Sometimes he said, I AM, as
God said it; and in the words, "Before Abraham was,
I am" [9] we catch the echo of Exod. iii. 14. But ordinarily he completed the sentence by attaching a predicate suggested by the needs of those to whom he spoke.
To the hungry he said, I am bread; to the blind, I am
light; to the outcast, I am the door, the shepherd; to
the perplexed, I am the way; to the bereaved, I am
the resurrection and the life. He put himself in the
place of God, and in his own Person uttered the word
which God had left unspoken. He never spoke in
vague and general terms, saying, God is this; but
always with specific reference to the case of those who
heard him, saying, To you God is this.

, It is this quality of freshness, of spontaneity, of
adaptation to immediate needs, which gives to his

[7] Exod. iii.   [8] Exod. xxxiii. 23.   [9] John viii. 58.

words their unfailing charm. There is nothing formal or stereotyped in his teaching, but it springs from a heart filled with love and keenly sensitive to the wants of men, and eager to answer them.

It is in accordance then with his habitual mode of teaching, that the whole representation of the Holy Spirit in these chapters is shaped and coloured by the circumstances of the hour and the state of the disciples. He does not undertake to give a systematic account of the Person and the ministry of the Spirit, such as the theologian properly endeavours to provide. He speaks directly to the eleven, and tells them what the Spirit will be to them, what offices he will perform in their behalf, and how he will work through them for the increase of the kingdom. His teaching, indeed, was rather a conversation than a discourse, and again and again the disciples broke in with question or comment.

So radically alike are men in their nature and their needs, however they may differ superficially in outward circumstances and conditions, that these words spoken to a little company in Jerusalem nineteen hundred years ago with particular reference to their peculiar necessities speak to our hearts today, and will continue to quicken and comfort the hearts of the people of God while the world stands. When Jesus speaks to a single soul, he speaks to all men everywhere for his words are eternal truth; spirit and life to all who put their trust in him.

In view of the character of Jesus' teaching we may hope to gain a more complete and adequate conception of the doctrine of the Holy Spirit as here set forth, if instead of taking up the references to him in the order of the text, the method thus far employed in our study, we group them under four heads, and consider

1—The relation of the Spirit to the Father;
2—The relation of the Spirit to the Son;

3—The relation of the Spirit to the disciples;

4—The relation of the Spirit to the world.

Thus the theme may be treated in an orderly and systematic manner, and every phase of the Personality and work of the Spirit as here presented may find its proper place. To each of these themes a chapter will be devoted. We take up then as the foundation of Jesus' teaching:

1. The relation of the Spirit to the Father.

In harmony with the uniform representation of the Old Testament and the early Gospels the Spirit is said to be sent or given by the Father.[10] It is also affirmed that the Spirit is sent in answer to the prayer of Jesus: "And I will pray the Father, and he shall give you another Comforter";[11] and in the name of Jesus: "But the Comforter, even the Holy Spirit, whom the Father will send in my name." [12] Again the Persons of the Trinity are brought together; the Father sends the Spirit in the name of the Son. The phrase *in my name* is susceptible of various interpretations as a glance at the Commentaries will suffice to show. Reference may also be made to Westcott on the Epistles of John, additional note on III. 7; and Cremer's Lexicon of New Testament Greek, ὄνομα, p. 457.

We may perhaps most readily and clearly apprehend the fulness of meaning which lies in the phrase as here employed if we recognize in it a twofold significance, as it is related on one side to Jesus and on the other to the disciples.

(a) The name of Jesus, the name in which alone salvation may be found, is the sphere in which the Spirit moves and operates. Beyond that name his saving and sanctifying ministry does not extend. As the Son came in the name of the Father,[13] so the Spirit is sent in the name of the Son. The Son came in the

[10] John xiv. 16, 26.
[11] John xiv. 16.
[12] John xiv. 26.
[13] John v. 10; x. 25.

name of the Father as he makes the Father known to men; the Spirit comes in the name of Jesus as he makes Jesus known to men. To send the Spirit in the name of Jesus is to send him as the revealer or interpreter of Jesus, as Jesus was the interpreter of the Father.[14] Thus he performs for the Son the same office that the Son performs for the Father.

(b) *In my name* in its relation to the disciples signifies *on the ground of your relation to me,* because you are mine. This meaning the phrase often conveys and it is eminently appropriate here. In the name of Jesus believers pray,[15] and in his name the Spirit is sent, because they are his. "All things are yours; and ye are Christ's; and Christ is God's." [16] The gift of the Spirit follows the gift of the Son, and is conferred upon those by whom the Son has been received.

The purpose for which the Spirit is sent will claim our attention when we turn to consider his relation to the disciples.

Since the Holy Spirit holds the foremost place in the teaching of Jesus here, it may appear strange that there is no allusion to him in the prayer recorded in John xvii, the only extended prayer of Jesus which has been preserved. Though he has told the disciples of the value, the necessity, of the Spirit's ministry, and promised them to pray that the Spirit might be sent, the Spirit is never named in the prayer that follows directly upon the discourse. If the mind of Jesus was so filled with the thought of the Spirit, and if the Spirit was so intimately and essentially related to the life and ministry of the disciples, how could he refrain from interceding for them that the Spirit might be sent? When we examine the prayer, we find that though there is no direct allusion to the Holy Spirit, it is the work of the Spirit which Jesus has in mind throughout. The prayer contains four distinct peti-

[14] John i. 18.   [15] John xiv. 13, 14.   [16] I Cor. iii. 22, 23.

tions for the disciples and each of them involves the
ministry of the Spirit. (1) Keep them from the evil
one. This is the peculiar office of the Spirit according
to the New Testament, to purify and preserve the
believer from the power of sin. (2) Sanctify them in
the truth. And it is the Spirit who shall guide them
into all the truth. (3) Unite them in love. Love is
the fruit of the Spirit, and believers are enjoined to
keep the unity of the Spirit in the bond of peace.[17]
(4) Glorify them with me. To behold his glory is to
be transformed, transfigured, into the same image,
from glory to glory, and this is the work of the Spirit.[18]
Every petition which Jesus offers for his disciples rests
upon the ministry of the Holy Spirit, and is accomplished only through him.

Thus Jesus teaches that the Father sends the Spirit
in the name of the Son and in answer to the prayer of
the Son, that he may minister to the children of God,
supplying every need of theirs, according to his riches
in glory in Christ Jesus.[19]

Now the question arises whether beyond the sending
of the Spirit Jesus speaks of that eternal relation of
the Spirit to the Father which the church is accustomed
to designate by the term Procession. The only passage in these chapters, or in the New Testament, which
may be cited in support of the doctrine of the eternal
procession of the Spirit from the Father is xv. 26—
τὸ πνεῦμα τῆς ἀληθείας ὃ παρὰ τοῦ πατρὸς ἐκπορεύεται. The
Vulgate reads, qui a Patre procedit, and from procedit the term procession is derived. The church doctrine affirms that as the Son is eternally begotten of
the Father, so from the Father the Spirit eternally
proceeds. Is that the meaning of these words of
Jesus? Does he teach both the mission and the procession of the Spirit, or do both clauses refer to the
mission alone? It is evident that the form of the

[17] Ephes. iv. 3.   [18] II Cor. iii. 18.   [19] Phil. iv. 19.

phrase, ὃ παρὰ τοῦ πατρὸς ἐκπορεύεται is not decisive. The procession is neither required by the ἐκ of the verb, nor forbidden by παρά. It is said indeed that ἐκ points conclusively to the eternal procession of the Spirit, and the clause cannot be interpreted to refer simply to his mission. But a similar phrase is used of Jesus—ἀπὸ θεοῦ ἐξῆλθεν, where the following clause—καὶ πρὸς τὸν θεὸν ὑπάγει shows that the reference is not to his eternal generation but to his mission to the world.[20] In xvi. 27 Jesus says of himself, ἐγὼ παρὰ τοῦ πατρὸς ἐξῆλθον; and the words following are yet stronger—ἐξῆλθον ἐκ τοῦ πατρὸς; while the appended clause, καὶ ἐλήλυθα εἰς τὸν κόσμον again indicates that he refers to the mission upon which he was sent, and not to his eternal relation to the Father. Coming forth from the Father into the world is contrasted with leaving the world and going to the Father. In John viii. 42—ἐγὼ γὰρ ἐκ τοῦ θεοῦ ἐξῆλθον καὶ ἥκω which the R. V. renders, I came forth and am come from God, the thought is different, and the eternal relation of the Son to the Father and his coming into the world are set side by side. It may also be noted that ἐξῆλθον παρά is frequently used in the LXX in the sense, went forth from the presence of.[21] [22]

In the light of this review it may be seen that the phrase does not require the reference to the Procession of the Spirit.

On the other hand, it is affirmed that as the reference to the mission of the Spirit is not forbidden by ἐκ it is required by παρά, which must bear a merely local sense. But in John i. 14 we read that the Word became flesh and dwelt among us, and we beheld his glory, δόξαν ὡς μονογενοῦς παρὰ πατρὸς, where the allusion is evidently to the eternal generation of the Son.

[20] John xiii. 3.
[21] Gen. iv. 16; xxvii. 34; Exod. xxxv. 20; II Kings v. 2; Job i. 12; ii. 7.
[22] Swete, Procession, p. 9.

It is plain that the form of the phrase is not decisive in favour of either interpretation; yet it may be admitted that the choice of prepositions throws at least a slight balance of probability on the side of the reference to the mission rather than to the procession of the Spirit. It is significant that the early fathers and the early creeds when they appeal to this verse in support of the doctrine of the Procession habitually and instinctively substitute ἐκ for παρά with the purpose conscious or unconscious of strengthening the foundation on which the doctrine rests. Illustrations are given by Swete, *Procession*, pp. 6, 10, 76; and by Hort, *Two Dissertations*, pp. 86, 141, 144, 149.

It is maintained, however, as by Godet, that the verbs employed draw a manifest distinction between the mission and the procession of the Spirit. There are those who "refer the words, *who proceeds from the Father*, to the same fact as the preceding words—*whom I will send you from the Father*—to the sending of the Holy Spirit to the disciples. The attempt is made to escape the charge of tautology by saying that the first clause indicates the relation of the Spirit to Christ, and the second his relation to God (Keil), as if in this latter were not already contained the *from God*, which, repeated in the second clause, would form the most idle pleonasm. It must be observed that the second verb differs entirely from the first; ἐκπορεύεσθαι, *to proceed from*, as a river from its source, is altogether different from *to be sent*; the ἐκ, *out from*, which is added here to παρά, *from the presence of*, also marks a difference. But especially does the change of tense indicate the difference of idea; whom *I will send* and *who proceeds from*. He whom Jesus will send (historically at a given moment) is a divine being, who emanates (essentially, eternally) from the Father. An impartial exegesis cannot, as it seems to me, deny this sense."

But the argument is rather specious than substantial, and the answer is obvious. There is no difficulty in supposing that the present tense signifies the continual going forth of the Spirit from the Father as the perpetual executive of the divine purpose, while the future refers to a specific mission upon which he shall be sent after the return of Christ to the Father. There is neither tautology nor repetition of thought; but the promise, I will send, is confirmed by reminding the disciples that the Spirit is always going forth from the Father to fulfil his purposes of grace. The Spirit whose peculiar office it is to execute the will of the Father I will send to you.

The arguments drawn from the verse itself for and against the doctrine of the Procession of the Spirit carry no decisive weight. The utmost that may be affirmed is that the doctrine cannot be firmly established upon this foundation. We must turn then to the general tenor of our Lord's teaching here, and endeavour to discover which interpretation of the verse will accord most fully with the course of thought that the discourse presents. Jesus is speaking throughout, in harmony with his habitual mode of instruction, for a definite purpose. He has an immediate and particular end in view, to comfort and strengthen his disciples, as he is soon to leave them. The law which governs all his teachings finds its application here: he speaks in order to meet a present and urgent need. And this he does by giving the disciples the promise of another Helper, who shall take his place, shall be to them what he has been and do for them what he has done. He represents the Spirit as always engaged in errands of mercy and of grace, continually going forth from the presence of the Father to perform his holy will. There was no apparent occasion to speak of the eternal and mysterious relation which subsists between the Father and the Spirit. We may readily believe that so great a truth lay beyond the reach of. their understanding and was numbered among those mysteries of which he said, "I have yet many things to say unto you but ye cannot hear them now." [23] Again it must be acknowledged that the argument is not conclusive. That Jesus referred to the procession of the Spirit in these words is not impossible, nor would the reference be altogether inappropriate. The mission may be regarded as resting upon the procession, and Jesus may seek to strengthen the faith of the disciples by assuring them that the Spirit, as the Son, is of the Father.

But the reference to the mission of the Spirit is more in keeping with the general drift and purpose of the discourse. Of the sending of the Spirit by the Father, from the Father, Jesus speaks on various occasions, while nowhere, unless this passage be an exception, does he allude to that eternal and metaphysical relation, which we term *procession*. He confirms the faith of the disciples by the assurance that the Spirit whom they shall receive is the Spirit of the Father, the Spirit through whom the Father carries out his will in nature and in grace, of whom they have learned from the Old Scripture, of whom he himself has taught them. In like manner after declaring, "My sheep hear my voice, and I know them, and they follow me: and I give unto them eternal life; and they shall never perish, and no one shall snatch them out of my hand," as though men might doubt his power, his ability to save, he adds immediately, "My Father who hath given them unto me is greater than all and no one is able to snatch them out of the Father's hand." [24] He always sought to establish the faith of men by referring all things to the Father.

That the doctrine of the Procession of the Spirit is taught in this verse is ably though inconclusively

[23] John xvi. 12.   [24] John x. 27-29.

argued by Godet, with whom Swete agrees; while the reference to the mission of the Spirit is maintained by Meyer and Westcott, and apparently most modern scholars. Swete gives a number of examples of the patristic exegesis of the verse, and adds: "In later times the opposite view—that by procession no more is intended than simple mission, and that the passage in S. John has therefore no real bearing on the ecclesiastical dogma of the productio naturalis, seems to have been put forth first by Beza, who has been followed by a host of modern expositors," [25] But in his *Commentary* on Revelation xxii. 1 he says that the reference here is probably to the mission of the Spirit rather than his Procession.

It may be said, therefore, while the question cannot be determined with certainty, that the weight of the argument drawn from the text itself, and yet more the argument drawn from the general purpose and tenor of the discourse, are in favour of the reference to the temporal mission rather than the eternal procession of the Spirit. And if this view be accepted, there is no explicit teaching to be found anywhere in the New Testament upon which the doctrine of the Procession of the Spirit, a doctrine which has filled so large a place in the theology and the history of the church, may be established.

This is not to say, however, that the doctrine has no basis in Scripture. There is good reason to believe that the church has been guided by the Spirit himself according to the promise of Jesus in framing the doctrine of the Procession and in giving it a place in the formularies of Christian faith. The doctrine of the Procession is intimately related to the doctrine of the Trinity, and both doctrines are deduced from the Scripture in the same manner. Neither can point to explicit Scripture statement. Since I John v. 7 has

[25] *Procession*, p. 7, note.

been eliminated from the text,[26] there is no passage
which explicitly sets forth the doctrine of the Trinity;
but it is drawn by just and necessary consequence from
the whole range of Scripture teaching regarding God,
and thus rests upon a broader and firmer foundation
than could be furnished by isolated text. God is one
in the first principle of Scripture teaching. But divine
attributes and acts are ascribed to Three Persons, who
are termed Father, Son, and Spirit. The Father is
God, the Son is God, the Spirit is God. When these
representations are set side by side, they can be harmonized only by recognizing that God is One in Three
Persons. The doctrine of the Trinity simply brings
together in complete and systematic form the various
representations of the nature and work of God which
the Scripture presents. The Bible does not provide a
system of theology, but simply the materials from
which a theology may be fashioned, and is related to
theology as nature is related to science. As soon as
the various statements of Scripture regarding God are
brought together, the doctrine of the Trinity emerges,
and cannot rationally be denied.

The doctrine of the Procession of the Spirit is established by a similar course of reasoning. No explicit
warrant for it may be adduced, but it is drawn from
the general tenor of Scripture teaching. Not only is
it evident that God is One in Three Persons, but it is
also manifest that while the Three are One God, equal
in power and glory, yet side by side with this essential equality there is a personal or official subordination
of the Son to the Father and of the Spirit to the Father
and the Son. Son and Spirit are sent by the Father;
it cannot be conceived that the Father should be sent
by the Son or the Spirit. This manner of subordination is indicated by the very terms Son and Spirit in

[26] On this text see Gregory, *Canon and Text of N. T.*, p. 508.

contrast with Father, and is everywhere evident. Both Son and Spirit are consistently represented as the agents of the Father's will, and it is a natural and inevitable conclusion that this subordination which appears in all the relations of the Godhead to nature and to men rests upon a distinction which is inherent in the very nature of the Trinity. From the economic we reason to the Trinitarian relation, and with Augustine recognize in the Father the *Fons Trinitatis*—the fountain or source of the Trinity—from whom both the Son and the Spirit are derived. The derivation of the Son we designate by the Scriptural term, generation; the derivation of the Spirit we designate by Procession. The doctrine of the Procession is therefore entirely Scriptural, while the word though not Scriptural is a convenient term to signify an incomprehensible relation. He is derived from the Father in a manner which is distinguished from the generation of the Son, and to that mode of derivation we apply the term Procession, the most general term that we can command. Thomas Aquinas teaches, "Since processions in the divine nature follow immanent actions, which in the intellectual and divine nature are only two, to understand and to will; there are only two processions in the divine nature, of the Word and of love." [27] These are the generation of the Son and the procession of the Spirit, for the Son is wisdom and the Spirit is love. John of Damascus, the great theologian of the Greek church, says,

> The Son is derived from the Father after the manner of generation, and the Holy Spirit likewise is derived from the Father, yet not after the manner of generation, but after that of procession. And we have learned that there is a differ-

[27] *Theol.* I, xxvii. 5.

ence between generation and procession, but the nature of that difference we in no wise understand.[28]

A summary of the doctrine of this great teacher of the eighgth century, whose theology is still regarded by the Greek church as the standard of orthodoxy, is given by Swete, *D C B*, Art. "Holy Ghost," p. 131, and *Procession*, pp. 201, 204.

We need have no hesitation then in accepting the doctrine of the eternal procession of the Holy Spirit from the Father as drawn by just and necessary inference from the teaching of Scripture regarding his Person and work, and the relation of the Persons of the Trinity to one another. It is constantly taught that the Spirit is sent by the Father to execute his will in the realm of nature and of grace. The mission implies the procession. Together with the equality of nature there is a subordination of office, implied in the name *Spirit* and in the office which he performs as *sent* by the Father. The economic or official subordination which is everywhere apparent in Scripture is carried back into the eternal Trinitarian relation of the Persons of the Godhead one to the other, and we have as the inevitable result the truth of the Procession of the Spirit from the Father. Whether he proceeds from the Father only, as the Greek church maintains, or from the Father and the Son, as is held by the Roman Catholic and Protestant churches generally, will engage our attention in the next chapter, "The Relation of the Spirit to the Son."

[28] *Orthodox Faith,* 8.

CHAPTER X

THE HOLY SPIRIT IN THE TEACHING OF JESUS—V.

2. The Relation of the Spirit to the Son

The Spirit is sent by the Son as by the Father. Twice in chapters xiv.-xvi. Jesus promises that the Father will send or give the Spirit,[1] and twice he says, I will send the Spirit.[2] Here for the first time, beneath the shadow of the cross, he clearly and explicitly affirms that he too will send the Spirit; though, as we have seen, the comparison of Mark xiii. 11—"It is not ye that speak, but the Holy Spirit," and Luke xxi. 15—"I will give you a mouth and wisdom," shows that the claim was implied in his earlier teaching. No loftier claim can be conceived, for who may send the Spirit of God but God himself? Men are sent by the Spirit, the Spirit is sent by God. He who affirms that he will send the Spirit of God affirms that he is God.

He promises that he will send the Spirit to his disciples after he has ascended to the Father. "It is expedient for you that I go away; for if I go not away, the Comforter will not come unto you; but if I go, I will send him unto you."[3] In his estate of humiliation he receives the Spirit, in his estate of exaltation he sends the Spirit. That is the office of the glorified Redeemer. "The Spirit was not yet given, because Jesus was not yet glorified."[4] As it is the purpose of

[1] John xiv. 16, 26.
[2] John xv. 26; xvi. 7.
[3] John xvi. 7.
[4] John vii. 29.

303

the Spirit's ministry to carry forward and complete the work of the Son, the Spirit is sent only when that work has been accomplished.

The Spirit is sent by the Father and the Son. Yet here too, as always, the primacy is accorded to the Father. Side by side with the essential unity and equality of the Persons of the Godhead, the New Testament recognizes an economic or official subordination which is inherent in the very terms Son and Spirit, terms which express derivation; and the subordination of office which everywhere appears rests upon an essential distinction between the Persons of the Trinity. The Son is eternally begotten of the Father, the Spirit eternally proceeds from the Father. The Father is unbegotten and underived, and is therefore properly termed by Augustine, *Fons Trinitatis*. Paul sets forth the same truth—"The head of every man is Christ; and the head of the woman is the man; and the head of Christ is God." [5] He is treating of the relation of man and woman, and he represents that relation as one of equality in Christ Jesus, in whom there "can be no male and female," [6] and yet of personal subordination of the woman to the man, who is her head. This he compares to the relation of the Father and the Son, who are by nature equal, while yet the Son is subordinate to the Father, as he is derived from him and is sent by him. It is not of Christ in his human nature alone of whom Paul here speaks, but of Christ the Godman. As the incarnate Son he is subject to the Father, but this relation must rest upon an eternal relation inherent in the very nature of the Trinity. In the light of Scripture teaching we cannot conceive of the Son sending the Father; for the terms Father and Son, which belong to the Eternal Persons of the Trinity, indicate at once equality of nature and subordination of office.

[5] I Cor. xi. 3.   [6] Gal. iii. 28.

On I Cor. xi. 3 see especially Ellicott. In commenting on I Cor. iii. 13 Hodge remarks: "The Scriptures speak of a threefold subordination of Christ. 1. A subordination as to the mode of subsistence and operation, of the second to the first person in the Trinity; which is perfectly consistent with their identity of substance and equality in power and glory.

2. The voluntary subordination of the Son in his humbling himself to be found in fashion as a man, and becoming obedient unto death, and therefore subject to the limitations and infirmities of our nature.

3. The economic or official subordination of the anthropos. That is, the subordination of the incarnate Son of God, in the work of redemption and as the head of the church. He that is by nature equal with God becomes, as it were, officially subject to him." It is simpler to combine 2 and 3, and recognize a twofold subordination of the Son, economic or official in his incarnation, and personal in his eternal generation.

I will send the Spirit, said Jesus, from the Father.[7] The Spirit is conceived as residing with the Father and going forth from the Father, and only when Jesus has returned to the Father will he send the Spirit. Until his humiliation is ended and his atoning work completed, to send the Spirit pertains to the Father alone.

That the Spirit is sent by both the Father and the Son is so clearly taught as to leave no room for doubt. But a more difficult question remains:. Does the Spirit proceed from the Son as from the Father? Few questions of a purely theological character have played so large a part in the history of the church as the question of the single or double procession of the Spirit. The *filioque* is as famous as *homo-ousion,* though immeasurably less important both in its doctrinal and practical aspects. It does not properly fall within

[7] John xv. 26.

the scope of our inquiry to trace the long course of theological and ecclesiastical controversies which gathered about the phrase, and rent the church asunder. That is a theme for Systematic Theology and Church History; but it will not be out of place to note some of the salient points in the development of the doctrine of the Procession. For a complete account of the matter in its doctrinal and historical aspects the student may consult Schaff, *Ch. Hist.* IV. 304 ff and 476 ff. Swete, *Procession of the Holy Spirit* and Art. "Holy Ghost" in *Dictionary of Christian Biography*. Smeaton, *Doctrine of the Holy Spirit,* Third Division. The important literature on the subject ancient and modern is cited in these volumes. See also Gibbon, opening pages of Chapter LX.

Not until the fourth century did the doctrine of the Holy Spirit begin to engage in an adequate way the interest and attention of the church. The earlier controversies were concerned with the doctrine of the Person of Christ, for it was at this point that the Christian faith was most vigorously attacked by Jews and Gentiles alike. The church rightly judged that the Person and work of the Son were matters of supreme moment as the very foundation of the gospel of redeeming grace, and addressed itself to the task of setting forth and maintaining the teaching of the Scripture upon this great theme. Until the questions concerning Christ were answered, and the doctrine of the Son in his divine and human natures had been established, all other questions, however important they might be, must be deferred to a more convenient season. Only when the Son was fully known and acknowledged by those who bore his name was the development of the doctrine of the Spirit attempted by the church. In the development of doctrine, as in the history of redemption, the Spirit follows the Son.

Yet a doctrine of such importance as the Person

and work of the Holy Spirit, the Third Person of the Trinity, so intimately and vitally related to the life of the individual believer and of the universal church, could not be wholly neglected or forgotten. The early writers and teachers of the church, however, were engaged with the practical rather than the theological side of the truth, the work of the Spirit in regeneration and sanctification rather than his place and order in the Trinity. Tertullian, about 200, is apparently the first of the fathers of the church to give distinct and definite form to the common faith regarding the relation of the Spirit to the Father and the Son. He teaches that the Spirit proceeds from the Father;[8] that he proceeds from the Father through the Son;[9] and that "the Spirit indeed is third from the Father and the Son. . . . Nothing, however, is alien from that original source whence it derives its own properties."[10] Whether Tertullian would have consented to go beyond the phrase *from the Father through the Son,* and affirm that the Spirit proceeds alike from the Father and the Son, remains an open question, upon which there is ample room for difference of opinion. But *per filium* and *filio* are not equivalent terms, and his doctrine of subordination would appear to lead him logically to confine the doctrine within the limits of the phrase which he actually employs. He is not indeed always clear and consistent in his teaching, but in general he inclines to a somewhat rigid view of the subordination of the Son and the Spirit to the Father, as is indicated by the treatise which has just been cited.

Origen's doctrine is often confused and obscure, especially as it comes to us through the medium of a translation; but he held, apparently, the same view of the Procession of the Spirit from the Father through the Son.

[8] *Agt. Praxeas,* 2.   [9] *Id.* 4.   [10] *Id.* 4.

> On the whole we conclude that Origen held sub-
> stantially the Eternal Procession of the Holy
> Spirit from the Father through the Son; a view
> which we shall find supported by the great Greek
> theologians of the next century, and which differs
> in little more than expression from the present
> doctrine of the Western Church (Swete, *Proces-
> sion*, p. 65).

From the last clause of this quotation the Greek
Church would emphatically dissent. Athanasius appears to have been of the same opinion.[11]
The general attitude of the Greek Church toward
the doctrine of the Procession is indicated by Swete.

> The procession of the Holy Ghost through the
> Son was undoubtedly maintained by a majority
> of the great church teachers who flourished in the
> East during the Fourth Century; by one of them,
> perhaps by two, the Father and the Son were
> regarded as the joint source from which the Spirit
> issues forth. But the church, as represented by
> her Councils and Creeds, was content to assert
> that He "proceedeth from the Father;" or if any
> attempt was made to supplement the words of
> Christ, this was done by appending to them other
> words bearing the same Divine sanction—'And
> which receiveth of the Son.'[12]

It is to the greatest of the fathers, Augustine, that
the church owes the full and clear development of the
doctrine of the Procession from the Father and the
Son.

> If, therefore, that also which is given has him
> for a beginning by whom it is given, since it has

[11] "The conception common to Dionysius, Gregory Thaumaturgus
and Athanasius is ultimately derived from Tertullian, for whom as
a Montanist the subject had especial interest" (Hort, *Two Dissertations*, p. 87 note).
[12] *Procession*, p. 109.

received from no other source that which proceeds from him; it must be admitted that the Father and the Son are a Beginning of the Holy Spirit, not two Beginnings; but as the Father and the Son are one God, and one Creator, and one Lord relatively to the creature, so are they one Beginning relatively to the Holy Spirit. But the Father, the Son, and the Holy Spirit is one Beginning in respect to the creature as also one Creator and one God.[13]

Shedd's note upon this passage is interesting and instructive.

The term "beginning" (principium) when referring to the relation of the Trinity, or of any person of the Trinity, to the creature, denotes *creative* energy, whereby a new substance is originated from nothing. . . . But when the term refers to the relations of the persons of the Trinity to each other, it denotes only a modifying energy, whereby an existing uncreated substance is communicated by generation and spiration.

When it is said that the Father is the "beginning" of the Son, and the Father and Son are the "Beginning" of the Spirit, it is not meant that the substance of the Son is created ex nihilo by the Father, and the substance of the Spirit is created by the Father and Son, but only that the Son by eternal generation receives from the Father the one uncreated and undivided substance of the Godhead, and the Spirit by eternal spiration receives the same numerical substance from the Father and Son. The term "beginning" relates not to the essence, but to the personal peculiarity. Sonship originates in fatherhood, but deity is unoriginated. The Son as the second person "begins"

[13] *On the Trinity*, V., ch. xiv.

from the Father, because the Father communicates the essence to him. His sonship, not his deity or Godhead, "begins" from the Father. And the same holds true of the term "beginning" as applied to the Holy Spirit. The "procession" of the Holy Spirit 'begins' by spiration from the Father and Son, but not his deity or Godhead." [14]

But while Augustine teaches that the Spirit proceeds from the Father and the Son, he teaches also that he proceeds principally from the Father, as the ultimate source.

But from Him, of whom the Son has it that He is God (for He is God of God), he certainly has it that from Him also the Holy Spirit proceedeth; and in this way the Holy Spirit has it of the Father Himself, that he should also proceed from the Son, even as he proceedeth from the Father.[15]

Yet he did not say, whom the Father will send from *me,* as he said, whom *I* will send unto you from the Father — showing, namely, that the Father is the beginning *(principium)* of the whole divinity, or if it is better so expressed, deity. He, therefore who proceeds from the Father and from the Son, is referred back to Him from whom the Son was born (natus).[16]

Again the comment of Dr. Shedd may be quoted.

The term "beginning" is employed "relatively and not according to substance," as Augustine says. The Father is "beginning of the whole Deity," with reference to the personal distinctions of the Father, Son and Spirit — the Son being from the Father, and the Spirit from the Father and Son. The Trinitarian relations or modes of the

[14] *Nicene & Post-Nicene Fathers.*
[15] *Tract on John,* 99, 8.
[16] *On the Trinity,* IV, xx.

essence, "begin" with the first person, not the second or the third. The phrase "whole deity" in the above sentence, is put for Trinity, "not for essence." Augustine would not say that the Father is the "beginning" *(principium)* of the divine essence considered abstractly, but only of the essence as *trinal*. In this sense Trinitarian writers designate the Father *"fons trinitatis"* and sometimes *"fons deitatis."* Turrettin employs this latter phraseology (III. XXX. 1:8); so does Owen *(Communion with Trinity,* Ch. III); and Hooker *(Polity,* V. LIV). But in this case the guarding clause of Turrettin is to be subjoined; *"fons deitatis, si modus subsistendi spectatur."* The phrase *"fons trinitatis"* or *"principium trinitatis"* is less liable to be misconceived and more accurate than *"fons deitatis"* or *"principium deitatis."* [17]

The development of the doctrine is reflected in the Creeds of the church. The Apostles' Creed reads simply, "I believe in the Holy Ghost." To this the Nicene Creed adds an anathema against those who teach falsely regarding the Spirit, but makes no explicit reference to his Procession. The Constantinopolitan Creed, 381, the second as the Nicene was the first Ecumenical creed, which still remains the doctrinal standard of the Eastern or Greek Catholic Church, adds the words *who proceedeth from the Father* (τὸ ἐκ τοῦ πατρὸς ἐκπορευόμενον). [18]

The Athanasian Creed in its laboured attempt to compass the mystery of the Godhead affirms that "the Holy Ghost is of the Father and the Son; not made; neither created; nor begotten; but proceeding." [19] The

[17] On the teaching of Augustine see also Schaff, *Ch. Hist.* III, p. 684.

[18] Hort, *Two Dissertations,* p. 143; Schaff, *Ch. Hist.* II, p. 537.

[19] The Creeds are given in full, in Latin and English, by Schaff, *Ch. H.* III, pp. 690-695.

origin and date of this document are highly uncertain.
Loofs [20] refers it to the period 450-600. Swete thinks
it unsafe to assume that it "existed as a whole before
the time of Charlemagne." [21]   Schaff places it about
the middle of the fifth century. [22]

In view of the authorities thus cited it may be said
that the whole church, Eastern and Western, would
probably have united with few dissenting voices in
the doctrine propounded by Tertullian that the Holy
Spirit proceeds from the Father through the Son. John
of Damascus, the great theologian of the Greek
Church, affirmed that the Spirit proceeds from the
Father, is communicated through the Son. [23]   But the
question pressed for an answer, Does the Spirit proceed
from the Father only, or from the Father and the Son?
And the line of division was sharply drawn.   The
Western or Latin Church carried the doctrine to its
logical issue, and affirmed the double Procession of
the Spirit.   This the Greeks refused to acknowledge.
The doctrine was never ratified by a general council
of the church, but was explicitly enunciated by the
national Synod of Toledo in Spain, in the year 587;
and an anathema was pronounced against those by
whom the doctrine should be denied.

The Greek Church took its stand upon the words of
Jesus in xv. 26—"Who proceedeth from the Father"—
and would not go beyond them.   Thus the Eastern
and Western churches began to drift apart, and the
conflict grew more heated as the doctrine of the double
Procession was more dogmatically affirmed.   About
the middle of the ninth century a long and bitter
struggle ensued between Photius, Patriarch of Con-
stantinople, and Nicolas, Pope of Rome, in which each
in turn was anathematized and excommunicated by
the other; and finally in 1054 the church was rent in

[20] *Schaff-Herzog Encycl.*   [22] *Ch. Hist.* III, 696.
[21] *Procession,* p. 176, note 1.   [23] *On the Orthodox Faith,* ch. viii.

twain. The *filioque* was the doctrinal, as the suprem-
acy of the pope was the ecclesiastical, cause of the
division which still prevails between the Greek or
Eastern and the Latin or Western churches.

For further study of the points of resemblance and
difference between the Greek and Latin doctrine of
the Holy Spirit, see Schaff, *Ch. H.*, IV., 484.

To the theologians of the Greek Church must be
accorded the honour of determining and defining the
doctrine of the Person of the Son in his divine and
human nature against the heresies by which the Scripture teaching was assailed.

> The Messiahship and Divine Sonship of Jesus
> of Nazareth, first confessed by Peter in the name
> of all the Apostles and the eye witnesses of the
> divine glory of his Person and his work, as the
> most sacred and precious fact of their experience,
> and after the resurrection adoringly acknowledged
> by the sceptical Thomas in that exclamation, "My
> Lord and my God!" is the foundation stone of the
> Christian Church; and the denial of the mystery
> of the incarnation is the mark of anti-Christian
> heresy.
>
> The whole theological energy of the anti-Nicene
> period concentrated itself, therefore, upon the
> doctrine of Christ as the God-man and Redeemer
> of the world.[24]

In this great conflict Athanasius is the commanding
figure.

The doctrine of the Holy Spirit, which follows logically the doctrine of the Son, was developed by the
fathers of the Latin Church, beginning with Tertullian
and culminating in the work of Augustine. When the
Son had been accorded his rightful place in the faith
and worship of the church, the Holy Spirit, whose office

[24] Schaff, *Ch. Hist.*, II, 545.

it is to interpret and apply the work of the Son, was given a place by his side.

If we turn from the history of the doctrine as it was developed by the church to the study of the doctrine itself, we must observe that as the procession of the Spirit from the Father is nowhere explicitly affirmed in the New Testament, if our interpretation of John xv. 26 is correct, so neither is the procession from the Son. But we have also seen that while the procession of the Spirit from the Father is nowhere directly and explicitly affirmed, yet it is deduced by just and necessary consequence from the general tenor of New Testament teaching. And we have seen, moreover, that the Spirit sustains the same economic relation to the Son as to the Father, that is, he is related to the Son as to the Father in the exercise of his office in the economy of redemption; is called the Spirit of the Son as of the Father, and is sent by both the Father and the Son. From this outward or economic relation of the Spirit to the Father we argue that the inner or Trinitarian relation must be of the same nature, involving a subordination of office side by side with equality of nature. And the same line of reasoning leads us to the same conclusion regarding the relation of the Spirit to the Son. If he is subordinate to the Son as to the Father in respect of office, it is a just inference that this subordination also rests upon that Trinitarian relation which we term Procession. In the case of Father and Son alike the subordination of the Spirit rests upon a distinction inherent in the nature of the Trinity. The doctrine of the Procession of the Spirit from both Father and the Son as maintained by the Western church, Roman Catholic and Protestant alike, is not only legitimate, but is required by the general teaching of the New Testament, even though no explicit warrant for it may be adduced. How intimately the Persons of the Godhead are united in the revelation and operation of redeeming grace appears in this, that the Son sends the Spirit from the Father, and the Father sends the Spirit in the name of the Son.

Of greater interest and importance than the question of the procession of the Spirit is the inquiry how his ministry is related to the ministry of the Son. He is sent by the Son as by the Father, and it is his office to bear witness to the Son. There is a close and striking analogy between the relation of the Son to the Father and the relation of the Spirit to the Son. The parallel is drawn out at length by Jesus himself, especially in the passage we have in hand. The Son reveals the Father, the Spirit makes known the Son; the Father is manifested in the Son through the Spirit. The Son does not speak from himself, but from the Father—"The words that I say unto you, I speak not from myself; but the Father abiding in me doeth his works";[25] the Spirit "shall not speak from himself; but whatsoever things he shall hear"—from the Father through the Son—"these shall he speak."[26] It is the mission of the Son to glorify the Father—"I glorified thee on the earth";[27] it is the office of the Spirit to glorify the Son; "for he shall take of mine and shall declare it unto you."[28] To glorify God is to make him known, and as the Son declares the Father,[29] so the Spirit declares the Son. As no man can see the Father except as he is revealed in the Son,[30] no man can say that Jesus is Lord but in the Holy Spirit.[31] The Son is the interpreter of the Father, the Spirit is the interpreter of the Son; and as no one comes to the Father but by the Son, no one comes to the Son but by the Spirit. The relation between the Father, the Son, and the Spirit is set forth by early Christian

[25] John xiv. 10; viii. 38; xii. 49.
[26] John xvi. 13.
[27] John xvii. 4; vii, 18; viii. 50.
[28] John xvi. 14.

[29] John i. 18.
[30] John xiv. 6.
[31] I Cor. xii. 3.

writers in various figures. Ignatius writes, "nevertheless, I have heard of some who have passed from this to you, having false doctrine, whom ye did not suffer to sow among you, but stopped your ears, that ye might not receive those things which were sown by them, as being stones of the temple of the Father, prepared for the building of God the Father, and drawn up on high by the instrument of Jesus Christ, which is the Cross, making use of the Holy Spirit as a rope (σχοίνῳ). while your faith was the means by which you ascended and your love the way which led up to God." [32] Lightfoot's paraphrase brings out the force of this singular passage:

> For ye are stones of a temple, prepared for the building of God, hoisted up by the Cross of Christ, the Spirit being the rope and your faith the engine, while love is the way leading to God. [33]

He adds by way of comment,

> The metaphor is extravagant, but otherwise not ill-conceived. The framework, or crane, is the Cross of Christ; the connecting instrument, the rope, is the Holy Spirit; the motive power, which sets and keeps the machinery in motion, is faith; the path (conceived here apparently as an inclined plane) up which the spiritual stones are raised that they may be fitted into the building, is love.

Irenaeus represents the Son and the Spirit as the hands of God.

> Now man is a mixed organization of soul and flesh, who was formed after the likeness of God, and moulded by his hands, that is, by the Son and

[32] *Ep. to the Ephesians*, ch. ix; *Ante-Nicene Fathers*, I, p. 53.
[33] *Apost. Fathers*, Part II, Vol. II, p. 52.

Holy Spirit, to whom also He said, Let us make man.[34]

The most natural and obvious figure to express the relation of the Spirit to the Son represents them as the word and the breath of God, inseparable as breath from speech. The comparison occurrs frequently in the writings of the fathers. "Moreoever the Word must also possess Spirit ($\pi\nu\epsilon\tilde{\upsilon}\mu\alpha$). For in fact even our word is not destitute of spirit; but in our case the spirit is something different from our essence." [35] The note upon this passage in *Nicene and Post-Nicene Fathers,* Vol. IX., observes that "The Greek theologians . . . spoke of the Holy Ghost as proceeding from the Father like the breath of His mouth in the utterance or emission of His Word." And various examples are given.[36]

The office of the Spirit will call for fuller consideration when we enter upon the study of his relation to the disciples. Here it may suffice to indicate how absolutely and completely his ministry is determined by the work of the Son. The relation of the Son to the Father and of the Spirit to the Father and the Son is summed up in the words of Jesus recorded in xvi. 14, 15—"He shall glorify me; for he shall take of mine, and shall declare it unto you. All things whatsoever the Father hath are mine; therefore said I, that he taketh of mine and shall declare it unto you." The Son receives all things from the Father, the Spirit interprets and imparts all things unto those by whom the Son is received. The Spirit therefore cannot be fully known, nor can he put forth the full measure of his power, until the redeeming work of the Son has been accomplished; for it is his peculiar office to inter-

---

[34] *Agt. Her.,* Pref. Bk. IV. See also *Id.,* ch. x. *cf.* Swete, *Procession,* p. 52.

[35] John of Damascus, *Orthodox Faith,* Bk. I, ch. vii.

[36] See also Swete, *Procession,* p. 202.

pret and apply that work to the hearts and lives of men.

Thus the Spirit is related to the Son as the Son is related to the Father. In each case identity of nature is accompanied by subordination of office. But a broad difference stretches across the face of the analogy. The revelation of the Father by the Son is an outward historical manifestation. "The Word became flesh, and dwelt among us, and we beheld his glory." "He who was manifested in the flesh, justified in the Spirit, seen of angels, Preached among the nations, Believed on in the world, Received up in glory."[37] The Son took upon him flesh and blood that men might see him and hear him. He was found in fashion as a man, in all things made like unto his brethren.

But while the revelation of the Father by the Son is a historical manifestation, the revelation of the Son by the Spirit is an inward experience. Never does the Spirit appear, never does the Spirit speak, in his own Person. The sacrifice of Calvary is offered for the sins of the whole world; it is the office of the Spirit to apply the benefits of that atoning sacrifice to the individual soul. The work of the Son was wrought before the eyes of the world; the work of the Spirit is accomplished in the silence and solitude of the heart. The work of the Son is general and conspicuous; the work of the Spirit is personal and obscure. The Holy Spirit has never appeared to the eyes of men. It is said indeed that he descended upon Jesus at his baptism in the form of a dove, but that was a manifestation of his presence and his power, not a glimpse of his Person. The tongues of fire that rested upon the disciples at Pentecost were the evidence that the promise of his coming had been fulfilled; but the Spirit himself was present in their hearts. Throughout the Old Testament and the New, he speaks through law-giver and

[37] I Tim. iii. 16.

prophet and Christ; but his own voice is never heard. Never does he speak to the outward ear, but only with still small voice to the ear of the spirit. Wherever we read, The Holy Spirit saith, the agent or organ through whom he speaks is indicated. He speaks to the heart of the prophet, and through the prophet his message is conveyed. The voice of the Father, the voice of the Son, are heard in Scripture, but the Spirit speaks only within the individual soul; or if he has a message for the ears of men it is conveyed by human instruments. It is the Spirit who speaks in the Word—"Wherefore, even as the Holy Spirit saith," [38] but he speaks with human voice: "the Holy Spirit spake before by the mouth of David";[39] "who by the Holy Spirit, by the mouth of your father David, thy servant, didst say." [40] When in Acts xiii. 2 we read, "And as they ministered to the Lord, and fasted, the Holy Spirit said, Separate me Barnabas and Saul for the work whereunto I have called them," according to the analogy of Scripture we understand that the Spirit communicated his will to the assembled company of believers by one of their number through whom he spoke. Each of the Epistles to the Seven Churches contains the admonition, "He that hath an ear, let him hear what the Spirit saith to the churches." But it is Christ who speaks; the word of the Spirit is conveyed to the church through the Son. It was not unnatural, therefore, that for centuries the Person of the Spirit should be hidden or obscured by the Person of the Son, and not until the dignity, the majesty, the deity of the Son was fully established in the faith of the church did the Person of the Spirit receive the full place and honour which belong to him as the third member of the Godhead.

In accordance with the New Testament representation, therefore, the Son is the visible representative of his people before the Father's throne, and there makes

[38] Heb. iii. 7.   [39] Acts i. 16.   [40] Acts iv. 25.

continual intercession for them; while the Holy Spirit prays within us with inarticulate groanings that cannot clothe themselves in the form of human speech.[41] The fountain of redeeming grace is the love of the Father; and his love is revealed to men in the gift of His Son, in his life of service and death of loving sacrifice; and imparted and applied to men one by one through the Holy Spirit.   The benefits of the atonement of the Lamb of God who taketh away the sin of the world are communicated to individual men through the regenerating and sanctifying operations of the Holy Spirit, by whom the love of God is shed abroad in the hearts of them that believe upon the Son.

[41] Rom. viii. 26.

CHAPTER XI

THE HOLY SPIRIT IN THE TEACHING OF JESUS—VI.

3. THE RELATION OF THE SPIRIT TO THE DISCIPLES

It is in accordance with Jesus' habitual method of instruction that he does not undertake to give a complete and systematic account of the Person and the work of the Holy Spirit. His teaching is dominated here as always by an immediate practical purpose. The relation of the Spirit to the Father and the Son is not revealed in an abstract and formal way, but, as it were, indirectly and incidentally. Only so much is said upon this theme as may prepare the disciples to receive the truth which they particularly need to learn, the ministry of the Spirit to their own condition and needs. As he taught of the Father, not by philosophic terms and definitions, but by portraying his relation to the particular wants and circumstances of individuals, so he speaks of the Holy Spirit. *To you* the Spirit is the Paraclete, *to you* the Spirit ministers. The relation of the Spirit to them, the offices which the Spirit performs for them, is the burden of his teaching. The Procession of the Spirit, the inner Trinitarian relation that he sustains to the Father and the Son, which has filled so large a place in the theology of the church, is not even alluded to, or alluded to but once, in the whole discourse. His thoughts are engaged with the ministry of the Spirit to the little company of his disciples, and through them to the world.

Our study of this theme may be fitly introduced by an examination of the distinctive title which is given to the Spirit. He is called the Paraclete (παράκλητος). The word is derived from the verb παρακαλέω, to call to one's side, to one's aid. The Greek fathers ordinarily give to the word the active sense of helper or comforter; but it is generally agreed by modern scholars that it is passive both in form and meaning, and signifies one who is called in to help. One sense of the term, indeed, implies the other, for he who is called in to help becomes a helper. The particular purpose, the precise need, which the Paraclete is called to serve must be gathered in every case from the context.

For our present purpose it is not necessary to trace the history of the word as it appears in classic Greek, in the Septuagint, in Philo, and in Jewish and early Christian literature. The student has abundant material at his command, and may consult Thayer's and Cremer's *Lexicons;* Hare's *Mission of the Comforter,* note K;[1] Westcott, add. note on John xiv. 16, *H B D.,* art. "Paraclete"; *H D C G S.,* art. "Paraclete"; Brooke, *Intern. Crit. Com. on I. John,* ii. 1; Godet on John xiv. 16, and add. note by Dwight, whose notes in general are eminently judicious and satisfactory; Watkins, *Com. Excursus H.;* on Philo's use of the word see Hatch, *Essays in Biblical Greek,* p. 82. He says,

> This word (παράκλητος) is found in the N. T. only in the Gospel and first Epistle of St. John. The facts upon which any induction as to its meaning there must be sought in the first instance in contemporary writings cognate in character to those of S. John.[2] They are found in Philo in sufficient numbers and in a sufficiently clear connexion to render the induction from them free

---

[1] The notes are by far the most valuable part of the book.
[2] The sentence is obviously incomplete, but the meaning is clear.

from doubt, they show that Philo used the word (a) in a sense closely akin to its Attic sense of one who helps or pleads for another in a court of law, and hence (b) in the wider sense of helper in general. . . . The meaning consoler or comforter is foreign to Philo, and is not required by any passage in S. John.

In view of all the evidence in the case the word appears to be used in the general sense of helper, and in the more restricted sense of an advocate or counsel who pleads a case in a court of law. In this second sense it answers precisely in etymology and meaning to the Latin advocatus.

How then should the term be rendered in our English speech? It occurs only five times in the N. T., and is peculiar to John. Four times it is found in the Gospel,[3] and once in the First Epistle, ii. 1. There are three possible translations. (1) Comforter. This is the rendering of the A. V. in the passages in the Gospel without alternative reading, and of the English and American Revisions, which, however, place in the margin "or, Advocate, or Helper, Gr. Paraclete." This translation we owe to Wicklif, who indeed seems to have coined the word, for the earliest instances of its use are found in him. He was followed by Tyndale, and by all later English versions except the Rhenish, which reads *Paraclete*.

According to its etymology and early use, comfort means strength;[4] but in our modern use it has come to signify simply consolation, and comforter is therefore wholly inadequate to express the office of the Spirit as Jesus represents it here. Consolation is indeed a part, and a blessed part, of the Spirit's work, as to bind up the broken-hearted is the office of the Christ

[3] John xiv. 16, 26; xv. 26; xvi. 7.
[4] See Trench, *Select Glossary*.

upon whom the Spirit rests;[5] but it is only a part, and by no means the most important part, of the service which the Spirit renders to the children of God.

We may glance for a moment at the kindred term παράκλησις. In Acts iv. 36 the name Barnabas is said to signify υἱὸς παρακλήσεως; which is rendered by the A. V., son of consolation. But according to the generally accepted derivation, Barnabas in the Aramaic means literally son of prophecy, one who prophesies or teaches.[6] *Consolation* is therefore an inappropriate rendering, though it is retained in the margin of both Revised Versions, while they properly place *exhortation* in the text. In commenting on this passage Alexander observes that the word "has its primary senses of *exhortation* (or persuasion)[7] rather than its secondary sense of consolation."[8] These citations show the breadth of meaning that lies in the term, and unless there is clear indication that the words are employed in a restricted sense, comfort and comforter are usually inadequate renderings of παράκλησις and παράκλητος. In Acts ix. 31 it is recorded that the church throughout all Galilee and Judaea and Samaria "walking in the fear of the Lord and in the comfort of the Holy Spirit (τῇ παρακλήσει τοῦ ἁγίου πνεύματος), was multiplied." This is the rendering of the A. V. and Revised Versions, but appears to be obviously inadequate unless *comfort* is given a larger significance than it conveys to modern ears. It is the gracious operation of the Spirit in his quickening and sanctifying power that is indicated. Perhaps *encouragement* would bring out most clearly the meaning of the term as here employed.

[5] Isa. lxi. 1.

[6] *Cf.* I Cor. xiv. 3; I Thess. ii. 3.

[7] Acts xiii. 15; xv. 3; Rom. xii. 8; I Cor. xiv. 3; II Cor. iii. 4; I Tim. iv. 13; Heb. xii. 5; xiii. 22.

[8] Acts ix. 31; Luke ii. 25; Rom. xv. 5; II Cor. i. 3; vi. 7; vii. 4; vii. 13; Phil. ii. 1; II Thess. ii. 16; Philem. vii.; Heb. vi. 18.

It is not in accord with the teaching of the N. T. to regard consolation as the chief purpose of the Spirit's ministry; and this is conspicuously clear in the passage to which our thoughts are turned. Only once does Jesus intimate that the Spirit shall come to console the disciples in view of his return to the Father. "I will not leave you orphans: I come unto you." [9] For *orphans* (ὀρφανούς) the A. V. reads *comfortless,* and the Revised Versions, *desolate,* with *orphans* in the margin. The word occurs in the N. T. only here and in James i. 27, where it is rendered by A. V. and Revised Versions *fatherless.* The definite and graphic *orphans* is peculiarly appropriate here, because he has just addressed them as "little children," [10] and is about to leave them. In the light of the preceding verse—"And I will pray the Father, and he shall give you another Comforter, that he may be with you for ever; even the Spirit of truth; whom the world cannot receive; for it beholdeth him not, neither knoweth him: ye know him, for he abideth with you, and shall be in you"—the promise that he will come to them is naturally referred to his return in the Spirit. This at least is apparently the main thought that he has in mind, even if the promise should be enlarged to include his personal and visible manifestations after he rose from the dead. Here only is the thought of consolation suggested in connexion with the ministry of the Spirit. His approaching departure is elsewhere represented as an occasion not of sorrow but of rejoicing. The separation is only for a little time—"a little while, and ye behold me no more; again a little while, and ye shall see me," [11] and though they sorrow when he is taken from them, their sorrow shall soon be turned to joy. [12] "It is expedient for you that I go away"; [13] and "If ye loved me, ye would have rejoiced because

[9] John xiv. 18.   [11] John xvi. 16.   [13] John xvi. 7.
[10] John xiii. 33.   [12] John xvi. 22.

I go unto the Father; for the Father is greater than I."[14]

Nor, again, is it represented as the main office of the Spirit to console them amid the trials and persecutions to which they shall be exposed. Of this the passage contains no suggestion, though Jesus warns them of the hatred of the world, and of the tribulation that they shall encounter at the hands of their enemies. Their comfort lies in the assurance that for them he has overcome the world.[15] This, too, is certainly included in the things which the Spirit shall bring to their remembrance, but no explicit indication is given of this phase of his ministry.

That *Comforter* is not a satisfactory rendering is made still clearer by the phrase *another* Paraclete.[16] The word is ἄλλον, another of the same kind, not ἕτερον, of a different kind. The Spirit shall take the place of Jesus with the disciples, and shall minister to them as Jesus had ministered; and the work of Jesus was not primarily to console, but to teach, to guide, to save.

It may be of interest here, as throwing light upon Eusebius' habit of quotation to which allusion was made in an earlier chapter, to note that he cites the phrase twice in a single passage, and in one instance uses ἄλλον and ἕτερον in the other.

From every point of view it is evident that Comforter is an inadequate and misleading interpretation of the word Paraclete. This was recognized by the majority of the American Revisers, as is indicated near the close of the Preface to the N. T.:

It is not superfluous to mention expressly the fact that in this edition the variant readings and renderings are placed at the foot of the pages, but in as close juxtaposition as possible with the pas-

[14] John xiv. 28.   [15] John xvi. 33.   [16] John xiv. 16.

sages to which they relate. The reader's attention is thereby drawn to the circumstance that
some degree of uncertainty still cleaves, in the
judgment of scholars, either to the text of the
passage before him, or to its translation, or to
both. Accordingly, when he remembers that, by
the rule of procedure which the Committee followed, the translation of 1611 held its place in
every instance until an alteration commanded the
votes of two-thirds of the revisers, it will become
evident to him that a rendering given in the margin may have commended itself to a majority,
while still falling short of the degree of approval
necessary to enable it to supplant the text. It is
known that this was the case in a considerable
number of instances, of which the established term
"Comforter" as the appellation of the Holy Spirit
in the fourteenth Chapter of the Gospel of John
is a notable representative.

In his *Companion to the Greek Text and the English
Verson* Schaff remarks that comforter "is an inadequate rendering of παράκλητος, which means *advocate,
helper, intercessor, counsellor* . . . but after long de-
liberation the Revisers retained the dear old word
which expresses one important function of the Spirit."[17]
We are not dealing here simply with the technical
and critical question of the proper translation of a
Greek word, but the rendering of the term has a direct
and important bearing upon the conception that we
form of the office of the Holy Spirit, the nature and
purpose of his ministry. There are those who are led
by the term Comforter to conceive of the Spirit as
simply a minister of consolation in time of trouble.
They confine him to the sick-room, the house of mourning, and call upon him as they send for the physician

[17] p. 446.

or the pastor in their sickness and sorrow. The term obscures or conceals the large and gracious operation of the Spirit as the life of our life, the spring of wisdom and strength and peace and joy, God within us, renewing the soul in his own image. While the word admirably expresses a single aspect of the Spirit's work, it hides the breadth and amplitude of his ministry, which covers the whole of life, and supplies every need of the soul. We must find a word that will more adequately set forth the magnitude of the Spirit's work in his quickening, sanctifying, transforming power.

(2) The rendering Advocate is preferred apparently by the majority of modern scholars, and has much to commend it. The word has this significance in classic Greek, in Philo, and in Rabbinical writings, which have appropriated the term.[18] This is the evident sense of the word in I John i. 7: "And if any man sin, we have an Advocate with the Father, Jesus Christ the righteous." Both revisions place "or, Comforter. Or, Helper. Gr. Paraclete," in the margin; but the meaning here is so obvious that there seems to be little need of an alternative reading. It is undoubtedly desirable to retain the same rendering in the Gospel and Epistle provided that no violence is offered to the thought of the passage. But it appears upon examination that advocate as well as comforter is too restricted to express in an adequate way the office of the Spirit. If he is not represented in the Gospel primarily as a comforter, neither is he represented primarily as an advocate. Neither word is large enough, for each expresses a single aspect of the ministry which is as broad as the life of man. In the Epistle a particular feature of Jesus' ministry on behalf of his disciples is represented, his intercession for them in their sin. But no such limit is assigned to the office of the

[18] Meyer on xiv. 16; Westcott, add. note on xiv. 16.

Spirit here; and he is not portrayed by Jesus as an advocate in any proper sense of the term. The attempt to show that he is an advocate because he "pleads the believer's cause against the world—John xvi. 8 ff.;"[19] and also Christ's cause with the believer—John xiv. 26; xv. 26; xvi. 14"[20] does not carry conviction. It is true that the Spirit intercedes for us on earth,[21] as Jesus intercedes in heaven, but this is not the aspect of his work which is presented here. Meyer adopts the translation *advocate,* but gives the word a liberal interpretation: "Another advocate (instead of myself), another, who will as counsellor assist you." And he adds that the word is used by Greek writers "both in the proper judicial sense (advocate) and also in general as here." The judicial sense of the term falls far short of expressing the thought of Jesus.

(3) It is better therefore to give the word the largest meaning that it will bear in order to express the breadth of the Spirit's ministry as Jesus represents it. It would have been well if our early translators had followed the example of the Rhenish version and the Vulgate and introduced the term Paraclete. Turrettin in commenting on Luke xxii. 44 says that Jesus "*angelo paracleto opus habuerit.*"[22] The language would have been enriched; the word would soon have grown familiar and have made for itself a place in our English speech with other words borrowed from the Hebrew and the Greek; and the thought of Jesus would have been conveyed with greater precision and completeness. But since that course was not followed, the word should be rendered by the nearest English equivalent, a term which may preserve and reproduce as nearly as possible the amplitude of the original. If we were compelled to choose a more specific term, *teacher*

[19] *Cf.* John III, xvii. 3.
[20] Westcott, add. note on John xiv. 16.
[21] Rom. viii. 26.
[22] *Theol. Locus* 13 Qu. 14, 4.

would commend itself as in harmony with the general tenor of the passage; and some scholars have favoured that rendering. *Guide* may also be suggested. But the broadest term that the language affords is to be preferred, that the whole range of the Spirit's operation as it lay in the mind of Jesus may be embraced. *Helper,* the second alternative reading of the English and American Revisers, appears to be the most adequate rendering that has been proposed, commended at once by the literal significance of the Greek word, and by the tenor of Jesus' teaching.

With this preliminary discussion we are prepared to consider precisely and particularly the nature of the ministry of the Spirit as Jesus unfolds it here. What is the office that he performs for the disciples, the service that he renders them? It is very clearly and definitely set forth: "He shall guide you into all the truth." [23] This includes the whole range of his renewing and sanctifying operation in the hearts of men. Three times in this passage he is called the Spirit of truth,[24] because by him alone the truth revealed in the Son is imparted to men, not merely in outward manifestation but in inward experience of its saving power. By him all the gifts that pertain to the new life in Christ are conferred,[25] from him all the graces of the renewed soul proceed.[26] He is fitly represented in the wide extent, the varied operations, and the perfection of his ministry, by the seven Spirits that stand before the throne.[27]

The work of the Spirit like the presence of the Son is perpetual and unbroken. "And I will pray the Father, and he shall give you another Comforter, that he may be with you for ever, even the Spirit of truth; whom the world cannot receive; for it beholdeth him

[23] John xvi. 13.
[24] John xiv. 17; xv. 26; xvi. 12.
[25] I Cor. xii. 4-11.
[26] Gal. v. 22.
[27] Rev. i. 4.

not, neither knoweth him; ye know him; for he abideth with you, and shall be in you." [28] In the last clause of the citation a question of the text arises. W H read *is* (ἐστίν) in you for *shall be* (ἔσται) in you, which is placed in the margin. The English and American Revisers retain the future, and the weight of the evidence appears to be in their favour. The phrase *with you* denotes the presence of the Spirit in the company of the disciples; *in you,* signifies his dwelling in the heart of the individual believer. And he is with them only as he is in them, for the heart of man is the home of the Spirit of God, who dwelleth not in temples made with hands, but in the living temples which he himself has fashioned for his abode.

The Father is God above us, the Son is God with us, the Spirit is God within us. We must constantly remind ourselves indeed that distinctions of this kind between the Persons of the Trinity are relative, not absolute. The province of Father, Son, and Spirit cannot be rigidly defined, as though each of them possesses attributes or exercises functions in which the other Persons have no part. The Father, too, is with us; "If a man love me, he will keep my word: and my Father will love him, and we will come unto him, and make our abode with him." [29] Paul represents him as "God and Father of all, who is over all, and through all, and in all." [30] The Son is not only with his people unto the end of the world, according to his promise, [31] but he dwells in their hearts through faith, [32] is in them the hope of glory, [33] so that Paul exclaims "It is no more I that live, but Christ liveth in me." [34] He abides in the believer and the believer in him as the vine in the branch and the branch in the vine. The vine abides in the branch by imparting to the branch its life; the

[28] John xiv. 16, 17.
[29] John xiv. 23.
[30] Ephes. iv. 6.
[31] Matt. xxviii. 20.
[32] Ephes. iii. 17.
[33] Col. i. 27.
[34] Gal. ii. 19.

branch abides in the vine by receiving from the vine its life.

But while this is true, yet the distinction which has been drawn is not without foundation. Predominantly both in the Old Testament and the New the Father is represented as dwelling in heaven. This is the way in which Jesus habitually spoke of him, and he taught men to pray to "Our Father, who art in heaven." When he addressed the Father, he lifted his eyes toward heaven.[35] He came from the Father into the world, he leaves the world that he may return to the Father.[36] The only title of majesty that Jesus ever gave the Father is, Most High.[37] When he speaks, he speaks from the heights of heaven.[38] Jesus must leave his disciples and ascend to heaven that he may prepare for them a place in the Father's house.[39] The Father is the transcendent God.

The Son promised to be with his people for ever, and the name given him before his birth is Immanuel, God with us. In him God came down from heaven to earth that he might dwell among us.[40] God is with us in him. The work of the Son for us was wrought in the power of the Spirit; the work of the Son in us is wrought in the Person of the Spirit. The Father dwells with men in the Person of the Son, the Son dwells within men in the Person of the Spirit. Distinctions of this nature are traced in the Scripture, and while we must beware of drawing rigid lines of division between the Persons of the Trinity and their peculiar offices, yet we must endeavour to ascertain and to express the differences which the Scripture indicates as clearly as the poverty of our knowledge and our speech may permit.

The sphere of the Spirit's ministry is carefully de-

[35] John xvii. 1.
[36] John xvi. 28.
[37] Luke vi. 35.
[38] Matt. iii. 17; Luke xii. 28.
[39] John xiv. 2.
[40] John i. 14.

fined. Jesus does not say as his words are rendered in A. V., "He will guide you into all truth," but as they are correctly translated in the Revised Versions, "He shall guide you into all the truth." The promise is not general but specific. There is a definite sphere within which the guidance of the Spirit is given, a certain definite body of truth to which his teaching is confined. The disciples are to be sent out into the world upon a particular mission, with a sharply defined message, and it is the content of that message to which Jesus refers in the phrase *all the truth*—all the truth that they are sent to teach, the truth in which they themselves have found life eternal, and which they are to commend to their fellowmen. It is true, of course, that God is the fountain of truth, and that all knowledge and wisdom in men are begotten of his Spirit; but that is not the thought of Jesus here. He speaks, as always, directly to the condition and needs of his hearers. He is not concerned with philosophical or theological definitions of truth; but thinks of his disciples, of the work for which they have been chosen and appointed, and suits the promise to their particular need. In the truth you need that you may worthily fulfil your ministry, you shall have the Holy Spirit as your guide. It is important to bear this specific reference of the words in mind if we would reach a true conception of the nature of apostolic inspiration. Beyond the limits of their commission no peculiar guidance of the Spirit was promised, and they shared the common opinions and errors of the time. There is a distinct and definite sphere of truth, with limits clearly marked, beyond which they have no assurance of a peculiar aid of the Spirit outside that which is accorded to all believers. Within the assigned boundaries they are the inspired, infallible guides and teachers of the church of God; outside those limits the Spirit exercises for them no peculiar office. The guidance of the Spirit is manifest not only in unfolding and interpreting to them the truth that they were commissioned to proclaim, but also in restraining them from venturing beyond the limit of their commission, and teaching men what they had not been taught of God. As he directed their activity, so he controlled their speech, and brought every thought into captivity to the obedience of Christ. Therefore though in themselves they were weak and ignorant as other men, yet in the discharge of the office entrusted to them they enjoyed the unfailing guidance of the Spirit of God; and their teaching contains no mixture of error with truth, but they spake as they were moved by the Holy Spirit, and speak to the church in every age with final and infallible authority. The Spirit guides them into all the truth and restrains them from all error. They believed much that was erroneous, like other men; they taught only what was true. Their teaching did not stray beyond the limits of their commission, and within those limits they were the organs of the Holy Spirit.

Jesus defines with care the sphere of truth to which the promise is confined. It is the truth as it is in him, the truth embodied in his Person and work. He who is the truth is the sphere of the Spirit's ministry and the substance of the Spirit's message. This embraces, in the words of Peter, "All things that pertain unto life and godliness." [41] This Paul recognized: "I determined not to know anything among you, save Jesus Christ, and him crucified"; [42] "whom we proclaim," [43] and John. [44] The Son reveals the Father, the Spirit reveals the Son, the Spirit who "searcheth all things, yea, the deep things of God," which "none knoweth, save the Spirit of God." [45]

[41] II Peter i. 13.
[42] I Cor. ii. 2.
[43] Col. i. 28.
[44] I John i. 1-4.
[45] I Cor. ii. 10, 11.

"He shall guide you into all the truth," "he shall teach you all things," this is the promise in general terms which is defined in two particulars.

(1) He "shall bring to your remembrance all that I said unto you." [46] Much of his teaching they failed to comprehend, and he often rebuked them for their slowness of understanding and hardness of heart. The central truth of the kingdom of God, foreshadowed in the Old Scripture, that the Christ must suffer for the sins of men, they could not grasp, though he set it before them again and again in the most explicit terms. The spiritual nature of his kingdom so clearly portrayed in his teaching, as in the Sermon on the Mount, made no appeal to their carnal hearts; and in the very hour of his ascension, though he had appeared unto them "by the space of forty days, speaking the things concerning the kingdom of God," [47] they were still dreaming with the Jews of a temporal reign of the Christ as the king of Israel: "Lord, dost thou at this time restore the kingdom to Israel?" [48] He rebuked them, and turned their thoughts to the power of the Spirit of God, with which they should be clothed. Thus the true nature of the kingdom is again declared.

It is the office of the Spirit to recall to the minds of the disciples the teaching of Jesus, much of which they had forgotten, had been unable to comprehend, or had entirely misunderstood; and interpret it to their understanding and apply it to their hearts, that his words might become to them spirit and life. [49] Certain specific instances are noted in which sayings of Jesus that carried no meaning to the disciples at the time, or were erroneously understood, were recalled at a later time, and their significance disclosed. When he said, "Destroy this temple, and I will raise it up in three days," "he spake of the temple of his body," but

---

[46] John xiv. 26.
[47] Acts i. 3.
[48] Acts i. 6.
[49] John vi. 63.

the reference was understood neither by friends nor foes. But when "he was raised from the dead, his disciples remembered that he spake this, and they believed the Scripture, and the word which Jesus had said." [50] When he entered Jerusalem in triumph, "These things understood not his disciples at the first: but when Jesus was glorified, then remembered they that these things were written of him, and that they had done these things unto him." [51] When Peter asked in wonder, "Lord, dost thou wash my feet?" he answered, "What I do thou knowest not now, but thou shalt understand hereafter." [52] When Peter and John found the tomb of Jesus empty, the truth at last broke upon their minds: "For as yet they knew not the Scripture, that he must rise again from the dead." [53] It was not simply the fact that convinced them, for others found in the empty tomb only fresh occasion for unbelief; [54] but the fact interpreted to faith by the Holy Spirit. When Peter told the story of his visit to Cornelius, he said, "As I began to speak, the Holy Spirit fell on them, even as on us at the beginning. And I remembered the word of the Lord, how he said, John indeed baptized with water; but ye shall be baptized in the Holy Spirit." [55]

It was by the Spirit that the words of Jesus were recalled to their remembrance, and the significance of his teaching made plain.

(2) Not only shall the Spirit recall and interpret the words of Jesus, but he shall teach them truth that Jesus had left unspoken. "I have yet many things to say unto you," said the Master, "but ye cannot bear them now." [56] They were prepared neither to understand nor to obey. The Spirit does not simply repeat the teaching of Jesus, and interpret it; he leads them

[50] John ii. 19-22; cf. Luke xxiv. 8.
[51] John xii. 16.
[52] John xiii. 6, 7.
[53] John xx. 9.
[54] Matt. xxviii. 11-15.
[55] Acts xi. 15, 16.
[56] John xvi. 12.

beyond the point to which Jesus had led them, unfolding to them new aspects of the truth, which Jesus had not presented, or had merely suggested. Much is of necessity reserved for the guidance of the Spirit, because it could not be apprehended until Jesus had completed his redeeming work. But here, too, the nature and limits of the Spirit's teaching are clearly indicated. It is always the truth as it is in Jesus that forms the sphere of his ministry, the burden of his revelation. The truth into which he shall guide them is the truth that finds its centre and circumference in the Person and work of the incarnate Son, who is, in the magnificent phrase of Augustine, *quo itur deus, qua itur homo*—as God the goal, as man the way. Or from another point of view we may say that the Father is the goal, the Son is the way, the Spirit is the guide. The Spirit guides to the Father by way of the Son. He does not speak of himself, but as he hears he speaks, conveying to men the revelation of the Father which is given in the Son. "He shall take of mine, and declare it unto you." The immeasurable significance of the phrase *of mine* is disclosed in the words that follow. "All things whatsoever the Father hath are mine: therefore said I, that he taketh of mine, and shall declare it unto you." [57] All the fulness of the Godhead dwells in the incarnate Son, and of his fulness the Spirit ministers to the children of God, supplying every need according to his riches in glory in Christ Jesus. [58]

Thus carefully is the doctrine of the guidance of the Spirit guarded against the excesses of fanaticism and the vagaries of mysticism. There are those in every age of the church who profess to receive special revelations of the Spirit. Every believer should be a mystic in the sense that he enjoys a profound experience of the immediate presence of God. But the danger which

[57] John xvi. 15.   [58] Phil. iv. 19.

always haunts the mystic is that he divorce the inward experience from the outward revelation, separate himself from historical Christianity, and the church that is built upon the foundation of the apostles and prophets. He has no standard by which to measure but his own experiences, shifting as the winds, unstable as the sea. He makes himself the measure and the norm of truth, and has nothing beyond himself by which he may test and verify his judgments and impressions. Rejecting the rule which God has given, he is thrown back upon his own strength, which is weakness, his own wisdom, which is folly.

A test is furnished here which may be applied to all alleged revelations of the Spirit. Do they centre in the Son, and present him as he is pictured in the Word? Are they in harmony with his teaching, his life, his character? Is it their aim to declare him, to glorify him? If the experience is not in accord with the revelation, if it does not spring out of the revelation as its natural fruit, it is not of the Spirit. This thought John emphasizes in his First Epistle. All professed revelations must submit to this test, do they conform to the testimony of Scripture regarding Jesus? "Beloved, believe not every spirit, but prove the spirits, whether they are of God; because many false prophets are gone out into the world. Hereby know ye the Spirit of God: every spirit that confesseth that Jesus Christ is come in the flesh is of God: and every spirit that confesseth not Jesus is not of God." [59] The teaching of the Spirit must accord with the teaching of the Gospel. Therefore it is said, the Son is the truth, the Spirit is the truth. [60] He is the truth because he bears witness to the truth as it is in the Son. And the witness that he bears is this, "God gave unto us eternal life, and this life is in his Son." [61]

[59] I John iv. 1, 2.   [60] I John v. 7.   [61] I John v. 11.

The sole purpose of the Spirit's work is to glorify the Son by making him known to men in the plenitude of his grace. Apart from Jesus the Spirit has no message. Truth is of the Father, revealed in the Son, interpreted and applied by the Spirit.

(3) But the ministry of the Spirit is not bounded by the past and the present; "He shall declare unto you the things that are to come." [62] The promise does not mean that the Spirit shall unroll before them the map of the future by which they shall direct their course and shape their lives. Prophecy is not given to be our guide; the law is our guide, and prophecy is a glimpse of the goal. The Old Testament depicts the first and second coming of the Christ, and sometimes blends them in a single view; while sufficient notes of person and time and place and circumstance were given, that men might be prepared for his coming, and might be able to recognize him when he appeared, nor be deceived by false prophets and false Christs. But no attempt is made to trace the long course of the history and mark the successive steps by which he makes his way to Bethlehem and Calvary and Olivet. The eternal laws and forces of the kingdom are disclosed by which the course of history is determined and directed toward the divine consummation. The New Testament portrays the final coming of Christ to judge the world. That he shall come again is plainly taught, but the time and mode and purpose of his coming are questions which have divided the church from the beginning; and the various stages and epochs of history which shall precede and prepare the way for his coming are not disclosed except in vague and fragmentary revelations. Still the word of Jesus stands— "It is not for you to know times or seasons, which the Father hath set within his own authority." [63]

Jesus gave his disciples hints and glimpses of the

[62] John xvi. 13.   [63] Acts i. 7.

life beyond the grave, of heaven and hell. But his teaching was fragmentary, incomplete. Just as we begin to look, the curtain falls. This, too, is embraced within the scope of the *things that are to come,* of which the Spirit shall give a fuller and clearer revelation.

The ministry and the writings of the apostles evince the fulfillment of the promise, which entered the sphere of historical achievement in Peter's sermon on the day of Pentecost. The men who had been pupils, slow and dull during the ministry of Jesus, became the inspired teachers of the church through the power of the Holy Spirit. In many particulars their teaching goes beyond the teaching of their Master as it is recorded in the Gospels. Jesus never named the church but twice, though he ordained the apostles to be its leaders, and gave the sacraments to be a badge of discipleship, a bond of union, a means of grace. The scattered hints and suggestions which the words of Jesus contain Paul unfolded and enlarged, especially in the Epistle to the Ephesians, and gave us the picture of the church as the pillar and ground of the truth; the temple of God, in which each individual believer is a living stone; the bride of Christ; the body of Christ, the fulness of him that filleth all in all. And John in his visions on Patmos rolls back the gates of heaven, and bids us look upon the hosts of angels, the innumerable company of the redeemed, the glory of God and of the Lamb. The very foundation of the gospel, the atoning sacrifice of the Son of God, is brought to light and developed in the letters of Paul with a logical fulness and power which has no parallel in the records of Jesus' life. But though the apostolic teaching thus develops, unfolds, enlarges, the truth which is contained in the gospel records, it adds nothing that is essentially new. As the truth embodied in the life and work of Jesus is the sphere of the Spirit's ministry, it is the theme of apostolic teaching. No doctrine, no experience, is of the Spirit of truth which does not spring from the revelation which is given in the Son, through whom alone men come to that knowledge of God which is eternal life.[64] The teaching of the apostles, the doctrine of the church, the experience of the believer are all determined by the revelation of truth and grace which is given in Christ Jesus.

It is the ministry of the Spirit to the apostolic company of which Jesus particularly speaks; but the promise is not confined to them, but finds a larger and continuous fulfillment in the history of the church. "Now there are diversities of gifts, but the same Spirit." There are many gifts in the church, "but all these worketh the one and the same Spirit, dividing to each one severally as he will." [65]

In view of the place which the Spirit holds in this discourse, of the supreme importance of his ministry as it is represented here, it may appear remarkable that the prayer which immediately follows, recorded in chapter xvii, the only extended prayer of Jesus which has been preserved, contains no allusion to the Spirit, no reference to his work, no petition that he may be sent to those who were in such need of him. The same singular omission occurs in the Lord's Prayer, though in Luke's report immediately after Jesus had given his disciples this form of prayer he added, "If ye then, being evil, know how to give good gifts unto your children, how much more shall your heavenly Father give the Holy Spirit to them that ask him?" [66] But it must be borne in mind that Jesus was about to return to the Father, and from the Father send the Spirit. And it is evident that every petition which he offered for his disciples involves of necessity the work

[64] John xiv. 6; xvii. 3.   [65] I Cor. xii. 4-11.   [66] Luke xi. 13.

of the Spirit in their behalf. Of these petitions there are four. (a) Keep them from the evil one.[67] While Jesus was with them he kept them in the name of the Father, that revelation of the Father which was given them in him.[68] The Spirit shall take his place, another Helper, and by the Spirit they shall be kept. (b) Sanctify them in truth.[69] To sanctify is to set apart, to *consecrate,* as we read in the margin of the Revised Versions. That this is the thought here is plain: "For their sakes I sanctify myself, that they also may be sanctified in truth." [70] Here the word evidently means, I devote myself to the work appointed. This consecration or devotion on the part of men requires spiritual cleansing. Sanctification in the New Testament is the condition of service, service is the fruit of sanctification. Men are never commanded to justify or save themselves; that is the work of God. But they are constantly commanded to sanctify or purify themselves both in the Old Testament and the New.[71] The text of I John v. 18 is uncertain, and it is difficult to determine whether we should read with the Authorized Version and American Revised Version and margin of English Revised Version, "We know that whosoever is begotten of God sinneth not; but he that was begotten of God keepeth himself, and the evil one toucheth him not": or with W H, the English Revisers, and the margin of the American Revision substitute, "He that was begotten of God keepeth him," where the subject is not the believer, but Christ. In the first clause, "Whosoever is *begotten* of God," the word is γεγεννημένος while in the second clause, "he that is *begotten* of God," γεννηθείς is used: and this difference is in favour of the reference of the second

[67] John xvii. 11, 15.
[68] John xvii. 12.
[69] John xvii. 17.
[70] John xvii. 19.
[71] Lev. xi. 14; II Cor. vii. 1; Jas. iv. 8; I Peter i. 15; I John iii. 3.

clause to Christ. Both thoughts are Scriptural; the believer is said to purify himself, and to be purified. But the believer purifies himself not by his own strength, but only through the power of the Spirit who works within him. "Work out your own salvation with fear and trembling; for it is God who worketh in you both to will and to work, for his good pleasure." [72] To work out your own salvation is not to work out a salvation of your own. The new life is a gift of God, but man must live it.

The prayer is that they may be sanctified in the truth, and the nature of the truth is indicated: "Thy word is truth," the revelation that has been supremely given in the Son. And it is the peculiar office of the Spirit to guide them into all the truth, this sanctifying word of God. The Spirit cleanses by the truth. The words of Jesus are spirit and life,[73] and through them the disciples are already clean,[74] like men who are bathed; yet as they traverse the dusty highway their feet are soiled, and must be washed, that they may be altogether clean.[75] But it is not the mere word addressed to the outward ear that purifies the soul; for there are those who hear, and do not comprehend; those who hear, and do not remember; those who hear, and do not obey. "He that hath an ear, let him hear." The word avails only as it is brought home to the heart, and this is the office of the Holy Spirit.

Jesus prays that the disciples may be cleansed as the branch is pruned, that they may bring forth fruit. Two kinds of fruit the believer should bear, the fruit of character, which is the fruit of the Spirit,[76] and the fruit of service. It is this which Jesus has particularly in mind here: "that ye should go and bring forth fruit" [77] evidently refers to their apostolic ministry.

[72] Phil. ii. 12, 13.
[73] John vi. 63.
[74] John xv. 3.
[75] John xiii. 10.
[76] Gal. v. 22.
[77] John xv. 16.

He prays for the disciples that they may be conse-
crated, devoted, in holiness and truth to their high
mission as he gave himself to his. It is the ordination
prayer of the Master. And as he through the eternal
Spirit offered himself to God,[78] through the Spirit
alone is the consecration of the disciples accomplished.
(c) Unite them in love. This he prays for the little
company of the disciples,[79] and for "them also that
believe on me through their word." [80] "That they may
be one, even as we are one," [81] one in the possession of
a common life and in the bonds of mutual love. And
this life is begotten of the Spirit, and this love is the
fruit of the Spirit. Therefore we are enjoined "to
keep the unity of the Spirit in the bond of peace." [82]
For as there is one head, Christ, and one body, the
church, so there is one Spirit, animating and controlling, who binds all the members together in the bonds
of love. The Spirit is the soul of the church, as the
church is the soul of the world. (d) Glorify them with
me. "Father, I desire that they also whom thou hast
given me be with me where I am, that they may behold
my glory, which thou hast given me." [83] It is not a
fleeting or barren vision for which he prays. Elsewhere the purpose and effect of this beholding are
plainly declared. "We all, with open face beholding as
in a mirror the glory of the Lord, are transformed into
the same image from glory to glory, even as from
the Lord the Spirit." [84] The verb rendered *transformed* (μεταμορφούμεθα) is the same that is used in
Matt. xvii, 2: Jesus "was transfigured before them."
We might read here—"shall be transfigured into the
same image." We behold as in a mirror, the mirror
of the Word, the truth into which the Spirit guides us,
and are transfigured from glory to glory, from one

[78] Heb. ix. 14.
[79] John xvii. 11.
[80] John xvii. 20, 21.
[81] John xvii. 22.
[82] Ephes. iv. 3.
[83] John xvii. 24.
[84] II Cor. iii. 18.

degree of glory to another. The work of atonement was accomplished once for all on Calvary; the application of that atonement in its regenerating, sanctifying, transforming power by the Holy Spirit shall continue to the end of time. The Spirit may never say with Jesus, It is finished, until the number of the elect is accomplished, and all the ransomed are gathered home.

John tells us, "We know that if he shall be manifested, we shall be like him; for we shall see him even as he is." [85] When Jesus prays that his disciples may behold his glory, he prays that by the vision they may be transfigured into his likeness.

Thus it appears that while Jesus does not name the Spirit in his prayer, every petition that he offers involves the ministry of the Spirit, and may be fulfilled through him alone. The apostles chosen by the Son are sanctified by the Spirit, through whom the Son himself was sanctified, that they may be prepared for the service to which they are appointed.

It is evident that in the thought of Jesus the revelation of truth and grace which has been given in him is complete and final. The Spirit guides into the truth, and all the truth finds its centre, its life, in him. Under the ministry of the Spirit there will be a continuous unfolding of the truth, a fuller disclosure, a deeper experience of its power. But the larger truth into which the Spirit leads the people of God is always the truth as it is in Jesus. There is given in him a divine standard by which every doctrine and experience may be tried. He is the truth, and nothing is true which is out of harmony with him. He is the way in which the Spirit leads. Each new discovery of the truth must accord with that system of truth which is expressed in his Person, his word, his work; as every new star that the telescope brings to the eye of the astronomer

[85] I John iii. 2.

takes its proper place in the established order of the
universe; for the world of truth as the world of nature
is a harmonious and ordered whole, and each separate
truth is bound to every other, and contributes to the
stability, the dignity, the beauty of the system to
which it belongs. Every revelation of the truth that
is given to men through the Spirit of God is an interpretation of Jesus in his redeeming and transfiguring
power; for it is the office of the Spirit and the office
of the church to bear witness to him by whom alone
men draw near to God.

In the light of this survey of the work of the Spirit
on behalf of the disciples, we may catch the meaning
of words of Jesus which they must have found it hard
to understand, so that he prefaced them with the
solemn assurance that he told them the truth: "It is
expedient for you that I go away." [86] He must go
that the Spirit may come, and the Spirit shall take
up and complete his work. He offered himself a sacrifice for the sins of men; the benefits of his sacrifice
are made known and applied to men by the Spirit.
The promise of the Spirit was fulfilled at Pentecost,
and the change wrought in the disciples was so great
as almost to transcend belief. In a single hour the
Spirit wrought in them a transformation that three
years of fellowship with Jesus had not affected. As
we cross over from the Gospels to the Acts we enter
a new world. These men who had been timid as sheep
are brave as lions. They had been ignorant and slow
of comprehension; they declare the word of God with
a mouth and wisdom which all their adversaries were
not able to withstand or to gainsay. [87] They were
narrow-minded Jews; they enter with full sympathy
upon the world-wide mission to which Jesus called
them. We look upon them with wonder. To what
height of mental and spiritual stature they have grown.

[86] John xvi. 7.   [87] Luke xxi. 15.

We say, Is this John? Can this be Peter? In them the promise finds its initial fulfilment, "Behold, I make all things new." He who rebuked Jesus for speaking of the cross and said, "Be it far from thee, Lord; this shall never be unto thee," [88] now preaches the crucified and risen Christ with such passion and force that three thousand souls are turned to God, the greatest display of the convicting and converting power of the Spirit which the history of the church records. After his resurrection Jesus told them "not to depart from Jerusalem, but to wait for the promise of the Father," the Holy Spirit whom he would send; and said, "Ye shall be baptized in the Holy Spirit not many days hence." [89] They went forth in the power of the Spirit, and their enemies bore witness that they turned the world upside down.[90]

[88] Matt. xvi. 22.   [89] Acts i. 4, 5.   [90] Acts xvii. 6.

CHAPTER XII

THE HOLY SPIRIT IN THE TEACHING
OF JESUS—VII.

4. RELATION OF THE HOLY SPIRIT TO THE WORLD

The world (κόσμος) fills a large place in chapters xiv.-xvii. The word occurs thirty-six times. Twice it is used in a physical sense—"before the world was," [1] "before the foundation of the world," [2] equivalent to "the earth." [3] In every other instance it is used in the ethical sense, and designates mankind alienated from God, sinful and condemned.[4] The prominence here given to the world is characteristic of Jesus' teaching throughout the Fourth Gospel, where the word occurs seventy-nine times, while it is found only nine times in Matthew, twice in Mark, three times in Luke. It occurs also twenty-three times in I John, almost always in the ethical sense.[5] This Epistle we may term a series of meditations on the words of Jesus, as they were recalled to the memory of the apostle and interpreted by the Holy Spirit. Or if the phrase be not too formal, we might call it a doctrinal exposition of the gospel history. As we pursue our study of Jesus' words, we shall note how constantly his teaching regarding the world is reflected in the teaching of the disciple.

[1] John xvii. 5.
[2] John xvii. 24.
[3] John xvii. 4.
[4] Westcott, add. note on John i. 10; Burton on *Galatians,* p. 514; Sermon of F. W. Robertson on "Worldliness," I John ii. 17.
[5] See Huther on I John ii. 15.

The word represents the whole body of mankind except those whom Jesus has called out of the world; and the distinction is clearly and sharply drawn. The disciples of Jesus are distinguished from the world by their knowledge of God. The world knows neither the Father—"they know not him that sent me." [6] "O righteous Father, the world knew thee not" [7]—nor the Son—"they have not known the Father, nor me"; [8] nor the Spirit, "whom the world cannot receive; for it beholdeth him not, neither knoweth him." [9] The disciples know the Father, [10] the Son, [11] and the Spirit. [12] Knowledge is not the mere intellectual understanding, but the sympathetic and appropriating apprehension of the truth by mind and heart and will, the response of the whole nature to the word of God. [13] Men have by nature a certain knowledge of God, [14] but it is not a saving knowledge. The world sees the Father and the Son, but only to hate them. [15] Men see God in nature, but do not know him in the true sense of the term. Saving knowledge is imparted by the Holy Spirit; and the conditions on which it may be received are noted by John in his First Epistle as obedience: "Hereby we know that we know him, if we keep his commandments"; [16] righteousness: "whosoever sinneth hath not seen him, neither known him"; [17] and love: "everyone that loveth is begotten of God, and knoweth God." [18] Here as always John followed the teaching of the Master: "Blessed are the pure in heart: for they shall see God"; [19] "If any man willeth to do his will, he shall know of the teaching, whether it is

[6] John xv. 21, *cf.* I John iii. 1.
[7] John xvii. 25.
[8] John xvi. 3.
[9] John xiv. 17.
[10] John xvii. 25, 26.
[11] John xvii. 8, 25.
[12] John xiv. 17.
[14] Rom. i. 18-23.
[15] John xv. 24.
[16] I John ii. 3.
[17] I John iii. 6.
[18] I John iv. 7.
[19] Matt. v. 8.
[13] Lightfoot on Gal. iv. 9; Westcott, Add. note on John ii. 24, *Cf.* my *Teaching of the Gospel of John,* p. 241.

of God, or whether I speak from myself." [20] To know
God in his Son is eternal life,[21] because he is the fountain of life, and to know him is to enter into that
fellowship with him through which the divine life
is imparted to the soul.

As the world does not know God, it is under the
dominion of Satan, "the prince of this world." [22]
Paul calls him "the god of this world." [23] As believers
are in Christ, so "the whole world lieth in the evil
one." [24]

What is the relation of the world to the disciples?
The world hates the Father, and the Son whom he
hath sent;[25] and it hates the disciples also. The world
loves its own;[26] but they are not of the world, have
not the spirit of the world, do not conform to the ways
of the world, bear witness against the sins of the world.
The world hates the disciples as it hated the Master.
"If the world hateth you, ye know that it hath hated
me before it hated you." [27] As it persecuted him, it
will persecute them.[28] "They shall put you out of
the synagogues: yea, the hour cometh, that whosoever
killeth you shall think that he offereth service unto
God." [29] This prediction found a conspicuous fulfilment in Saul of Tarsus; "I verily thought with myself that I ought to do many things contrary to the
name of Jesus of Nazareth." [30]

The attitude of the world toward the disciples is
plain: hatred and persecution. What shall be the
attitude of the disciples toward the world? It is a
relation of inevitable and unending antagonism and
conflict. In so far as the church and the world are
at peace, it is because each has tempered the other.

[20] John xvii. 17.
[21] John xvii. 3.
[22] John xiv. 30; xvi. 11.
[23] II Cor. iv. 4.
[24] I John v. 19.
[25] John xv. 23, 24.
[26] John xv. 19.
[27] John xv. 18.
[28] John xv. 20.
[29] John xv. 2.
[30] Acts xxvi. 9.

In the world is the leaven of religion, in the church is the leaven of worldliness. But in proportion as each is true to its own nature, they must always be at war. The church strives to lift the world to heaven, the world strives to drag the church down to earth. They are animated by different motives, seek different ends: and are in perpetual conflict. "If any man love the world, the love of the Father is not in him." [31] "Know ye not that the friendship of the world is enmity with God?" [32]

To the disciples is given the assurance of victory. "In the world ye have tribulation: but be of good cheer; I have overcome the world." [33] He has vanquished the prince of the world, broken his power, delivered men from the bondage of sin. "To this end was the Son of God manifested, that he might destroy the works of the devil." [34] And the victory of the Master is repeated in the experience of each individual believer. "For whatsoever is begotten of God overcometh the world: and this is the victory that hath overcome the world, even our faith. And who is he that overcometh the world but he that believeth that Jesus is the Son of God?" [35] Faith unites the believer to him, so that he shares the conflict and the triumph of his Master. The victory that Jesus won for us by his life of obedience and atoning death he wins again in every one who puts his faith in the Son of God. He conquered for us, and in him we conquer.

There is then a perpetual antagonism between the church and the world, and they can never be at peace. But the world seeks to overcome the church in order to destroy it; the church seeks to overcome the world in order that it may be saved. The world is the enemy of the church, but Jesus taught his disciples,

[31] I John ii. 15.
[32] Jas. iv. 4.
[33] John xvi. 33.
[34] I John iii. 8.
[35] I John v. 4, 5.

"Love your enemies, and pray for them that persecute you." [36] The disciples are sent into the world upon the same errand as their Master: "As thou didst send me into the world, even so sent I them into the world." [37] After his resurrection he said to the eleven, "As my Father hath sent me, even so send I you." [38] He sanctified himself for the sake of his disciples, they must be sanctified for the sake of the world.[39] He prayed not that they should be taken out of the world,[40] for the believer needs the discipline of the world, and the world needs the witness of the believer.

Through the church as his spiritual body Christ carries on his redeeming work in the world. The church is the organ and instrument through which his Spirit works. The Spirit "will convict the world in respect of sin, and of righteousness, and of judgment." [41] The Spirit is not limited or restricted, but works as he will; yet his chosen method of working, the method which he ordinarily employs, is through men in whom he dwells. His work of conviction is accomplished mainly through the church. That is indicated by the very form of the promise: "I will send him *unto you*. And he, when he *is come,* will convict the world." This thought of the church as the chosen medium of the Spirit's operation pervades the New Testament. The church is the pillar and ground of the truth,[42] for by its witness the truth of the Gospel is established, preserved, conveyed to men. The world owes its knowledge of the truth to the church. And not on earth only, but in heaven also the church is the witness of Christ: "to the intent that now unto the principalities and the powers in the heavenly places might be made known through the church the manifold wisdom of God." [43]

[36] Matt. v. 44.
[37] John xvii. 18.
[38] John xx. 21.
[39] John xvii. 17, 18.
[40] John xvii. 15.
[41] John xvi. 8.
[42] I Tim. iii. 15.
[43] Ephes. iii. 10.

The mysteries of redeeming love are known by experience to the redeemed alone. There is a rapture the angels may not share, a song the angels may not sing.

This passage is of special interest and value because it is the only passage in the New Testament in which the world-wide ministry of the Holy Spirit is clearly and explicitly taught. The truth of course is recognized elsewhere, as notably in the baptismal formula of Matt. xxviii. 19. But as in the Old Testament the ethical work of the Spirit is almost entirely confined to Israel, so in the New Testament it is almost entirely confined to the church. There are manifestations of his power beyond these boundaries under both economies, but with the rarest exception they are not referred directly to him. He appears in his own Person only in the church, and through the church performs his office in the world. This is suggested by the words of Christ, Ye are the salt of the earth, ye are the light of the world. When we put together these great words, I am the light of the world, ye are the light of the world, the truth is plain that the world sees the light of Christ reflected in his disciples, sees him as it sees him in them. The Son is sent into the world, the Spirit is sent to the disciples, the disciples are sent into the world as the witness of Christ and the organs of his Spirit.

In the Old Testament it was predicted that the world shall come to the church: "And it shall come to pass in the latter days, that the mountain of Jehovah's house shall be established on the top of the mountains, and shall be exalted above the hills and all nations shall flow unto it";[44] in the New Testament the church is sent to the world.

With these thoughts in mind we are prepared to grasp the true significance of Jesus' words, "I pray

[44] Isa. ii. 2; Micah iv. 1.

not for the world." [45] Was the world forgotten, when
he was just about to bear the sin of the world, to
offer himself a propitiation for the whole world,[46] when
the Father in his infinite love for the world had sent
him to save the world? The prayer must be as broad
as the sacrifice. The eleven for whom he prayed, and
those who believed on him through their word, who
had a place with them in his petition,[47] were all gathered from the world. The church is continually re-
cruited from the world. What then is the meaning
of these words, I pray not for the world? The prayer
pursues a logical order. First he prays for himself,
that his service and sacrifice may be owned and
accepted by the Father. Then he prays for the little
company gathered with him in the upper chamber,
that they may be kept from sin, sanctified for service,
united in love, glorified with him. But they are only
the first-fruits of the spiritual harvest. He prays for
the church, for all who through the witness of the
apostles shall be led to faith in him. And this is in
effect a prayer for the world, for from the world believers are chosen and called. If the world were forgotten, the church would expire with the last of the
apostolic company. But he goes further. Why are the
disciples called, why is the church established? "That
the world may know that I love the Father, and as
the Father gave me commandment, even so I do";[48]
"that they all may be one; even as thou, Father, art
in me, and I in thee; that they also may be in us:
that the world may believe that thou didst send me.
And the glory that thou hast given me I have given
unto them; that they may be one even as we are one;
I in them, and thou in me, that they may be perfected
into one; that the world may know that thou didst

[45] John xvii. 9. [47] John xvii. 20.
[46] I John ii. 2. [48] John xiv. 31.

send me, and lovedst them even as thou lovedst me." [49] That the world may know, that the world may believe, is the ultimate purpose of the Son of man.

"I pray not for the world" therefore is not to be taken in an absolute sense, as though the world had no place in his thought or prayer. He prays first for the disciples, because it is through them that he purposes to lead the world to faith in him. The sanctification of the disciples must precede and prepare for the salvation of the world. He prays for the disciples for the sake of the church, he prays for the church for the sake of the world. The spirit of Jesus' prayer in this respect is reflected throughout the New Testament. Nowhere in the Gospel or Epistle of John is love to the world enjoined, but always love to the brethren. Yet when he bids us, "Love not the world," [50] it is obvious that he does not forbid us to love wicked men, for that would be out of harmony with the plainest teaching of the Master; but he enjoins us not to set our affections on the things of the world, its riches, pleasures, honours, and make these the main concern of our lives.

The prayers contained in the New Testament are offered almost entirely on behalf of the church. Nowhere does a specific petition for the world appear. The prayer of Paul for Israel in Rom. ix. 4; x. 1, may appear to be an exception; but it must be borne in mind that Israel was the people of God, to whom belonged the adoption and the glory, and the covenants, and the giving of the law, and the service of God, and the promises, and the fathers, and the Christ,[51] and whom he has not finally cast off.[52]

But Israel under the old covenant and the church under the new are chosen to be God's ministers to

[49] John xvii. 21-23.   [51] Rom. ix. 4, 5.

[50] I John ii. 15.   [52] Rom. xi. 1.

mankind. Christ made the world, he loves the world, he died for the world, the world is his by sovereign right. He rules the world, though Satan is suffered to exercise a limited power for an appointed time; he shall redeem the world. His relation to the church must not obscure his larger relation to mankind. His purpose to save the elect is part of a larger purpose which embraces the universe. "For it was the good pleasure *of the Father* that in him should all the fulness dwell; and through him to reconcile all things unto himself, having made peace through the blood of his cross; through him, *I say,* whether things upon the earth, or things in the heavens";[53] "Making known unto us the mystery of his will, according to his good pleasure which he purposed in him unto a dispensation of the fulness of the times, to sum up all things in Christ, the things in the heavens, and the things upon the earth."[54] These passages declare that the universe shall be restored[55] by him who saith, "Behold, I make all things new."[56]

The words of Bishop Lightfoot are true and weighty:

> This creative and administrative work of Christ the Word in the natural order of things is always emphasized in the writings of the apostles, when they touch upon the doctrine of his Person. It stands in the forefront of the prologue of St. John's Gospel; it is hardly less prominent in the opening of the Epistle to the Hebrews. His mediatorial function in the church is represented as flowing from this mediatorial function in the world. With ourselves this idea has retired very much into the background. Though in the creed common to all the churches we profess our belief in Him as the Being through whom all things were

[53] Col. i. 19, 20.
[54] Ephes. i. 9, 10; *cf.* Rom. viii. 19-22.
[55] Acts iii. 21.
[56] Rev. xxi. 5.

created, yet in reality this confession seems to exercise very little influence on our thoughts, and the loss is serious. How much our theological conceptions suffer in breadth and fulness by the neglect, a moment's reflection will show. How much more hearty would be the sympathy of the theologians with the revelations of science and the developments of history, if they habitually connected them with the operation of the same divine Word who is the centre of all their religious aspirations, it is needless to say. Through the recognition of this idea with all the consequences which flow from it, as a living influence, more than in any other way, may we hope to strike the chords of that "vaster music," which results only from the harmony of knowledge and faith, and reverence and research.[57]

The precise nature of the ministry which the Spirit executes in the world through the disciples is indicated; "And he, when he is come, will convict the world in respect of sin, and of righteousness, and of judgment." He guides believers into all the truth, he convicts the world of error. The truth as it is presented by the disciples he brings home to the hearts and consciences of men. For the word is the sword of the Spirit, which pierces even to the dividing of soul and spirit, and is quick to discern the thoughts and intents of the heart. There is given to the disciples the promise of a mouth and wisdom, which all their adversaries shall not be able to withstand or to gainsay.[58]

The word ἐλέγχω, of which the future is here rendered, *shall reprove* in the Authorized Version, and *convict* in the Revised Versions, occurs seventeen times in the New Testament, and is employed in two dif-

[57] *Com. on Colossians,* Intro. III.   [58] Luke xxi. 15.

ferent though closely related senses. (a) To rebuke, reprove. This is the most frequent signification of the term, and is found in Matt. xviii. 15; Luke iii. 19; John iii. 20; I Cor. xiv. 24; Ephes. v. 11, 13; I Tim. v. 20; II Tim. iv. 2; Titus i. 13; ii. 15; Heb. xii. 5; Rev. iii. 19. (b) To convict, to prove guilty: John viii. 46; Titus i. 9; James ii. 9; Jude 15.

To rebuke or reprove is to charge with guilt, to convict is to prove guilty. Rebuke or reproof may be just or unjust; conviction carries the truth of the charge. Jesus was rebuked, reproved; but his challenge was never answered, "which of you convicteth me of sin?" [59]

Many scholars give to the word a third sense, to convince.[60] But it cannot be shown that the word conveys this meaning anywhere in the New Testament. And it is not required, or even appropriate, here. To reprove is to accuse, to convict is to prove guilty, to convince is to persuade of guilt. He is convicted who is shown to be in error, he is convinced who owns himself in error. Reprove in this passage is too weak, convince is too strong, to express the proper meaning of the term. The Spirit does not simply accuse the world of error, he demonstrates that the world is in error. But *convince* would indicate that the world is brought to see and own its error, and this is not affirmed. The error is made plain, but whether it shall be recognized and acknowledged is not foretold. In fact the world is divided; all are convicted, but not all are convinced. There are those who recognize and confess their error, and there are those who in spite of the demonstration of the Spirit still hold fast to it. They resist the revelation of the Spirit as they close their eyes and hearts to the revela-

[59] John viii. 46.
[60] Trench, *Syn. N. T.*, 4; Hare, *Mission of the Comforter*, note 1; Smeaton, *Doct. Holy Spirit*, p. 186.

tion of nature: "For the invisible things of him since the creation of the world are clearly seen, being perceived through the things that are made, even his everlasting power and divinity; that they may be without excuse; because that, knowing God, they glorified him not as God, neither gave thanks; but became vain in their reasonings, and their senseless heart was darkened." [61] In both revelations the truth is demonstrated, but in both cases while all are convicted there are those who refuse to be convinced. The Spirit so presents the truth to men that they ought to believe; whether they do believe the word does not indicate. To convict is a matter of argument, to convince is a matter of experience. Convict is therefore to be preferred, because it denotes the nature, while convince would indicate the result of the witness of the Spirit. The world is universally convicted of error, but the world is convinced only in part.

The convicting power of the truth as it was proclaimed by the apostles is abundantly illustrated in the New Testament. With such clearness and force was it presented, with such power was it driven home to the hearts of men by the Spirit, that no answer was possible, no excuse for not accepting it could avail. Yet there were those who refused to be convinced, to recognize and acknowledge their error, and hardened themselves in unbelief. The day of Pentecost was the most conspicuous manifestation of the convicting power of the Spirit, when under the preaching of Peter the multitude were pricked in their heart, and three thousand souls were led into the kingdom of God. But the apostolic message did not always convince and convert. When Peter and the apostles preached to the Sanhedrin the crucified and risen Christ, "they were cut to the heart, and were minded to slay them." [62] The Jews "were not able to withstand the wisdom and

[61] Rom. i. 18-21.   [62] Acts v. 33.

the Spirit" by which Stephen spake;[63] but they stoned him to death. When Paul "reasoned of righteousness and self-control and the judgment to come, Felix was terrified," but he kept him in prison and hoped for a bribe."[64] Paul speaks for the whole company of the apostles: "But thanks be unto God who always leadeth us in triumph in Christ, and maketh manifest through us the savour of his knowledge in every place. For we are a sweet savour of Christ unto God, in them that are saved, and in them that perish; to the one a savour from death unto death; to the other a savour from life unto life."[65] Jesus came not to condemn the world, but to save the world; and for this purpose the Spirit is sent, for it is his office to fulfil the work of the Son. The end sought in conviction is conversion. The truth is made plain to men, not that they may be hardened and condemned, but that they may be persuaded and redeemed. The purpose of the Spirit's witness as of the ministry of Jesus is salvation; the result of his witness as of the ministry of Jesus is that some believe and are saved and others believe not and are condemned.

The witness of the Spirit convicts the world of error. By the world is not meant simply the Jews, as Godet interprets it. The word is never used by Jesus or by John in this restricted sense, nor indeed anywhere in the New Testament. In John i: 10, 11 the world and the Jews—his own—are distinguished. The world is the mass of mankind, alienated from God, and hostile to his Son. There is no distinction between Jew and Gentile in sin, "for all have sinned, and fall short of the glory of God";[66] nor in salvation, "for there is no distinction between Jew and Greek; for the same Lord is Lord of all, and is rich unto all them that

[63] Acts vi, 10.
[64] Acts xxiv. 25, 26. See also Acts xix. 9; xxviii. 24.
[65] II Cor. ii. 15, 16.
[66] Rom. iii. 23.

call upon him.[67] The witness of the Spirit is as wide as the preaching of the apostles who were commanded to make disciples of all the nations.

The Spirit convicts the world of error in three matters of primary importance. It is shown to be mistaken in its view of sin, of righteousness, and of judgment. The world is marching steadily toward the judgment-seat of God, and men shall be justified or condemned as righteousness or sin has ruled the life. Yet the world is fatally in error regarding the judgment which lies before it, the righteousness that shall justify, and the sin that shall condemn.

In each of these respects the world is convicted of error, not by force of argument but by the witness of the Spirit to a conspicuous and outstanding fact. Over against the error is set the countervailing truth, by which it is exposed and overthrown. The error of the world is contrasted with the truth of God.

1—In respect of sin, "because they believe not on me." It is not said that the Spirit shall convict the world of the sin of unbelief, but of sin through its unbelief. The world's estimate of sin is wholly false; for men conceive of sin as consisting in outward transgressions, and do not recognize that the seat and origin of sin is lack of faith in God, that faith by which the soul is united to him. The Spirit makes plain to men the true source and nature of sin by pressing upon them the fact of their unbelief. This is the crowning and convicting evidence of the sin of the world, that when God reveals himself most clearly and fully in the Person of his Son, he is rejected and crucified. The sinfulness of the world is brought to light by its attitude toward Christ. Since the heinousness of sin is measured by the degree of knowledge enjoyed, lack of faith in him in whom dwelleth all the fulness of the Godhead bodily is the height of sin. The Spirit will make

[67] Rom. x. 12.

manifest to the world its sin by pressing upon it the fact of its unbelief.

This conception of unbelief as at once the root and the climax of sin is presented elsewhere in the Gospel with equal plainness. "For God sent not the Son into the world to judge the world, but that the world should be saved through him. He that believeth on him is not judged: he that believeth not hath been judged already, because he hath not believed on the name of the only begotten Son of God." [68] "If I had not come and spoken unto them, they had not had sin: but now they have no excuse for their sin"; "if I had not done among them the works which none other did, they had not had sin: but now have they both seen and hated both me and my Father." [69]

2—In respect of righteousness, "because I go to the Father." The term is used in the broadest sense. The world's judgment regarding the nature and source of righteousness is as mistaken as its estimate of sin. This is the only instance of the use of the word in the Fourth Gospel. Three times it is found in the First Epistle of John, in the phrase "doeth righteousness," [70] or "doeth not righteousness." [71] Jesus uses the word eight times in the earlier Gospels, seven times in Matthew,[72] and once in Luke, [73] always in the broad general sense of the holy character and conduct which God requires. The thought of the imputed righteousness of Christ which some scholars have discerned in this passage [74] is nowhere explicitly set forth in the Gospels, though it is intimated in Mark x. 45: "to give his life a ranson for many" (λύτρον ἀντὶ πολλῶν), and

[68] John iii. 18, 19.
[69] John xv. 22, 24.
[70] I John ii. 29; iii. 7.
[71] I John iii. 10.
[72] Matt. iii. 15; v. 6; x. 20; vi. 1, 33; xxi. 32.
[73] Luke i. 75.
[74] Hare, *Mission of the Comforter,* note W.

should not be introduced here. Scripture usage, therefore, as well as the whole tenor of the passage requires us to give to the word the largest meaning. It is righteousness in general, the world's whole conception of the nature of righteousness, which Jesus has in mind. Here again the world looks upon the surface, and as it discovers sin only in the acts of transgression, so it discovers righteousness only in the acts of well doing. But in truth as sin is want of conformity to the will of God, springing from the root of unbelief, righteousness is obedience to his will. The world's estimate of righteousness as its estimate of sin is false because it finds no place for God as he is revealed in his Son. When perfect righteousness was manifested in him, the world did not recognize it, but counted him a sinner and condemned him as a malefactor. The world's estimate of sin is false because it takes no account of unbelief as the root and origin of sin; the world's conception of righteousness is false because it does not know him who alone is righteous. Jesus thus presents himself as the example, the norm, of righteousness. He is the Righteous One,[75] as the apostles delighted to call him.[76]

As the world's estimate of sin is shown to be in error by the fact of unbelief, so the world's estimate of righteousness is shown to be in error by the fact of the ascension of Jesus to the Father, which is established not only by the witness of those who on Mount Olivet saw him carried up into heaven,[77] but by the outpouring of the Spirit and the ministry of the disciples. True righteousness, the full measure of conformity to the will of God, is found in him alone; and the crowning proof of his righteousness is that God has received him. The world crucified him, God has

[75] Acts iii. 14; vii. 52; xxii. 14; I John ii. 1, 29; iii. 7; I Peter iii. 12.
[76] On Jas. v. 6 see Mayor and Ropes, *in loc.*
[77] Luke xxiv. 5.

exalted him to his own right hand. His resurrection was the first step in his ascension. "God raised him from the dead," [78] and thereby declared him to be his Son. [79] Jesus and the resurrection formed the theme of apostolic preaching, beginning with Pentecost. [80] The earliest creed contained two articles: Christ died for our sins according to the Scriptures, and was raised on the third day according to the Scriptures. [81] Though the passage does not teach the doctrine of imputed righteousness, it is in entire harmony with it; for if Christ alone is righteous, the righteousness of men must rest upon him. There are indeed only two conceivable forms of righteousness—man-made righteousness and God given righteousness; [82] and every man who seeks after righteousness must work out a righteousness of his own, or receive the gift of righteousness from God.

Jesus adds the tender words, with a touch of sadness in them, "And ye see me no more." The occasion of the discourse is never absent from his thoughts, and the love that fills his heart continually overflows. The return to the Father of which I speak means that I am about to leave you.

3—In respect of judgment, "because the prince of this world hath been judged." As the world is in error regarding sin and righteousness, its standards of judgement are of necessity false. It judged and condemned the righteous, it approves and obeys the wicked one, its prince. But Jesus is exalted to the right hand of God, and the wicked one is judged already. Jesus regards his work as finished, the victory is won. "The prince of this world hath been judged." His sentence has been pronounced, his power is broken, though his complete and final overthrow may be long delayed.

[78] Acts ii. 24, 32; xvii. 31. [81] I Cor. xv. 3, 4.
[79] Rom. i. 4. [82] Phil. iii. 9.
[80] Acts xvii. 18.

The death of Jesus appeared to be the hour of Satan's triumph—"this is your hour, and the power of darkness";[83] yet through death he brought to nought him that had the power of death, that is, the devil.[84] In his death Jesus conquered; in his victory Satan was condemned. The world has judged and condemned the Righteous One; he has judged and condemned the prince of the world.

How is this judgment of the prince of the world made manifest? How shall the world know that its sovereign has been condemned? The proof is furnished by the triumphant ministry of the disciples, which rests upon the finished work of Christ. When the seventy returned with joy, exclaiming, "Lord, even the demons are subject unto us in thy name," Jesus answered, "I beheld Satan fall as lightning from heaven." [85] In the casting out of evil spirits he read the evidence of the overthrow of their chief. For "how can one enter into the house of the strong man, and spoil his goods, except he first bind the strong man?" [86] Every soul that is turned from darkness to light and from the power of Satan unto God is a witness that the power of the prince of the world has been broken.

The world lies in the wicked one, its prince,[87] and is judged in him, but it is not finally condemned. The world is in sin, between the righteousness of Christ and the judgment of Satan, and must take its place on this side or on that. With these words should be compared the similar passage in John xii. 31, 32: "Now is the judgment of this world: now shall the prince of this world be cast out. And I, if I be lifted up from the earth, will draw all men unto myself." It is plain that the judgment pronounced upon the

[83] Luke xxii. 53.
[84] Heb. ii. 14.
[85] Luke x. 18.
[86] Matt. xii. 29.
[87] I John v. 19.

world is not absolute and final, for Christ lifted up upon the cross will draw all men unto himself. The words can mean nothing less than that the great majority of mankind, the world that is judged, in Satan, shall be redeemed in Christ. The race that fell in Adam shall be restored in Christ, and the long conflict that began in Eden shall issue in the triumph of the Kingdom of God; and a multitude that no man can number shall lift the song of redeeming grace in the paradise above. Jesus' drawing all men to himself is the proof that the power of the prince of the world has been broken.

Thus a divine standard is given in Christ by which sin and righteousness and judgment may be determined. In respect of each of them the world is convicted of error by a cardinal fact: in respect of sin, by the fact of unbelief; in respect of righteousness, by the exaltation of Christ; in respect of judgment, by the condemnation of Satan. Three great truths are made clear, and pressed upon the hearts and consciences of men through the witness of the disciples and the Spirit; the sin of the world, the righteousness of Christ, the judgment of Satan. The sin of the world is shown by its unbelief; the righteousness of Christ is shown by his exaltation; the judgment of Satan is shown by the saving power of the gospel in the ministry of the disciples. The world is convicted, Jesus is glorified, Satan is condemned. In these solemn words is indicated the whole course of human history; they illuminate the first promise that followed immediately the first sin: "I will put enmity between thee and the woman, and between thy seed and her seed: he shall bruise thy head, and thou shalt bruise his heel." [88] The heel of the seed of the woman was bruised when Jesus was nailed to the cross; the head of the serpent

[88] Gen. iii. 15.

was crushed when Jesus rose from the dead and sent forth his Spirit to convict the world.

Jesus' teaching regarding the Holy Spirit in the Fourth Gospel is brought to a fitting close by the words addressed to his disciples when he first appeared to them after his resurrection. Two gifts he conferred upon them, the gift of peace and the gift of the Spirit, and he enjoined upon them a mission. These we shall treat in the order which they hold in the record of John xx. 21, 22.

(a) The gift of peace. In the parallel passage in Luke xxiv:36 the words, "and saith unto them, Peace be unto you," are regarded by W H as an early interpolation.[89] This is the order of events as indicated by the comparison of Luke's narrative with John's: Jesus appeared to the disciples with the salutation, "Peace be unto you." They were terrified and affrighted. To convince them that he is their Master, and not a spirit, as they supposed, he showed them his hands and feet and side, with the wound-prints of the nails and spear. Then they were glad, assured that he was risen indeed. Again he saluted them:—"Peace be unto you"—and set them apart to the service of the kingdom.

"Peace be unto you" was a common form of salutation among the Jews.[90] Peace was a conspicuous feature of the Messiah's kingdom.[91] The Messiah is called Prince of peace,[92] and in his days shall "abundance of peace" prevail, "till the moon be no more." [93] When Jesus sent forth the twelve upon their first missionary journey, he bade them search out in every

[89] See Plummer, *in loc*.
[90] Gen. xliii. 23; Judg. xix. 20; I Sam. xxv. 6; Ps. cxxii. 7; Dan. x. 17.
[91] See *Lexicon* of Brown, Driver and Briggs, Art. "Shalom."
[92] Isa. ix. 6.
[93] Ps. lxxii. 7. See also Isa. xi. 6-9; lv. 12; Micah iv.

village who in it was worthy, and abide with him. "And as ye enter into the house, salute it." The mode of salutation is indicated by the words that follow: "and if the house be worthy, let your peace come upon it: but if it be not worthy, let your peace return to you."[94] When he appointed the seventy and sent them to prepare the way before him, he commanded them, "And into whatsoever house ye shall enter, first say, Peace be to this house." [95] The term expresses the sum of the blessings which belong to the Messianic kingdom that they were sent to proclaim.

On the lips of men this is a friendly salutation, a pious wish; on the lips of Jesus it is a gift, as when God said to Gideon: Peace be unto thee; fear not; thou shalt not die." [96] Jesus renews and confirms the gift of peace already conferred upon them.[97]

Two senses of the word *peace* are clearly evident in the doctrinal teaching of the New Testament.

(a) Peace with God, the peace of reconciliation. This denotes the change of relation to God which is brought about by justifying faith in Christ. By nature men are alienated from God, and the relation between them is one of antagonism. But Christ becomes our peace by reconciling us to God. Peace with God is that state of justification in which the law no longer condemns. The word thus designates not an experience, but a relation, a change in the attitude of God and man toward each other.

This is the peace of which Paul speaks in Rom. v. 11. The text of the verse is uncertain. The weight of manuscript authority favours the reading, "Let us have peace" (ἔχωμεν), but the indicative (ἔχομεν), "we have peace," is evidently more in keeping with the course of the apostle's argument; and in view of

94 Matt. x. 11-13.
95 Luke x. 5.
96 Judg. vi. 23.
97 John xiv. 27; xvi. 33.

the facility with which o and ω are interchanged [98] the American Revisers have done well to retain the indicative in the text with marginal note: "Many ancient authorities read *let us have;* while the English Revisers follow the text of W H and read, "Let us have peace," with marginal note, "Some authorities read *we have.*" It seems obvious that Paul here uses the term in the forensic sense, denoting the new relation upon which we have entered through faith in Christ; and if this be true he cannot say, Let us have peace. We have it at once and forever as soon as by faith we lay hold upon the Saviour.[99]

(b) The peace of God, which is the sense of security, of rest, of tranquil contentment, that flows from justification. When our sins are forgiven, a relation of peace is established between the soul and God. And this is accompanied and followed by that inward state of serene, tranquil satisfaction which Paul terms "the peace of God" that "shall guard your hearts and your thoughts in Christ Jesus." [100] Peace with God is that state of justification which we enter through faith in Christ; the peace of God is the inward experience of his saving grace.

It is in this second sense that the word is here employed. "My peace I give unto you," said Jesus;[101] the peace which dwelt in his heart shall be theirs. This peace which is the gift of Christ is the fruit of the Spirit.[102] The peace which he confers is imparted through the Spirit.

On the whole subject see the Lexicons and Commentaries and Arts. "Peace" in *HBD.* and *HDCGS.*

---

[98] Robertson, *Gr. Gk. N. T.,* p. 200.
[99] For the indicative see Meyer and Hodge and Godet; for the subjunctive, Sanday and Headlam.
[100] Phil. iv. 7; *cf.* Col. iii. 15.
[101] John xiv. 27.
[102] Gal. v. 22.

Both of these articles refer to a sermon of F. W. Robertson entitled "Human Race." No such sermon is known, and the reference is apparently to a discourse on Col. iii. 15: "Unity and Peace."

2—The mission enjoined. "As the Father hath sent me, even so send I you." With these words he commended them to the Father: "As thou didst send me into the world, even so sent I them into the world."[103] By nature they are in and of the world; by grace they are called out of the world; and by grace when they are sanctified they are sent into the world. Saved, sanctified, sent, is the divine order. By nature they are born into the world, by grace they are sent into the world. They are sent upon the same errand as their Master, and he lives in them and works through them as his spiritual body. It is their office to proclaim to men the salvation which he has provided for them, and without their ministry his work would be unfinished. Paul puts the argument in conclusive fashion: "Whosoever shall call on the name of the Lord shall be saved. How then shall they call on him in whom they have not believed? And how shall they believe in him whom they have not heard? And how shall they hear without a preacher? And how shall they preach except they be sent? Even as it is written, How beautiful are the feet of them that bring glad tidings of good things. . . . So belief cometh of hearing, and hearing by the word of Christ."[104] In this sense Paul affirms that he fills up in his flesh that which is lacking of the afflictions of Christ for his body's sake, which is the church.[105] Christ labours and suffers again in his disciples, and his spiritual body like the body of his flesh bears the marks of the nails and the spear; for the believer is crucified with his Lord.

Thus again it appears how large a place the world holds in the thought of Jesus, the world which God so

[103] John xvii. 18.   [104] Rom. x. 13-17.   [105] Col. i. 24.

loved that he gave his Son to redeem it. He sanctifies himself for the sake of the disciples, the disciples are sanctified for the sake of the world. He purposes to save the world through them, as they convey to men the gospel of redeeming grace.

This is John's representation of the great commission which Matthew records, and differs from it in two main respects. (1) it is couched in general terms, while Matthew portrays the nature of the mission in detail. (2) it compares the mission of the disciples with the mission of their Lord. This is implicit in the word of Jesus, "All authority hath been given unto me in heaven and on earth: go ye therefore"; but it is not directly affirmed in Matthew as in John. The disciple is sent into the world upon a definite errand, like his Master; upon the same errand as his Master, to bring a lost world home to God.

(c) The gift of the Spirit. "He breathed on them, and saith unto them, Receive ye the Holy Spirit." The breathing was a symbol of the imparting of the Spirit. The gift of the Spirit was not only promised, but actually conferred, as the word *Receive ye* (λάβετε) plainly indicates. The immediate purpose of the gift was to prepare them for the fuller and richer outpouring of the Spirit which came upon them at Pentecost. It was the Spirit who interpreted to them the significance of Jesus' resurrection; who gathered the company of the disciples together with one accord in one place; waiting according to the Master's command for the promise of the Father. Their apostolic ministry began with the gift of the Spirit at Pentecost; and that they might be prepared to receive him this preliminary measure of his power and grace was granted them by the risen Lord. This was the first-fruits of Pentecost, as Pentecost in turn is the first-fruits of a richer and fuller blessing yet to be bestowed.[106]   As

[106] Rom. viii. 23.

the vision of the Son which believers now enjoy [107] shall be followed by a brighter vision of his grace and glory,[108] so the exercise of the Spirit's grace and power which is now granted to the children of God shall be followed by a deeper experience of his renewing and transforming ministry. It is the office of the Spirit to prepare men to receive him in ever increasing measure. The gift of the Spirit here was not therefore directly to equip them for their ministry, but to prepare them to receive him when he should come upon them in the plenitude of his power. It was the cleansing, quickening power of the Spirit that is here conferred; in them he prepares his home. This gift is conferred that through it they may be qualified to enter upon their ministry. It is the first step in their preparation for the work to which they are called, so that as they are sent upon the same errand as their Master, they are clothed with the same power. They receive from him the Spirit by whom he was sanctified that they too may be sanctified for their ministry. But the endowment of the Spirit is not yet complete; and they must stay in Jerusalem until they shall be baptized in the Holy Spirit.[109]

This preliminary and prophetic gift of the Spirit is accompanied by a specific grant of power: "Whosesoever sins ye forgive, they are forgiven unto them; whosesoever sins ye retain, they are retained." The apostles were empowered not simply to proclaim the conditions of salvation, but to determine and declare in specific instances whether those conditions had been fulfilled; and this power they exercised, as in the case of Ananias and Sapphira,[110] and Elymas the sorcerer.[111] A similar authority was granted to Peter by name: "I will

[107] John i. 15; II Cor. iii. 18.
[108] I John iii. 2.
[109] Acts i. 5.
[110] Acts v. 1-5.
[111] Acts xiii. 8; cf. I Cor. v. 1-5; I Tim. i. 20.

give unto thee the keys of the kingdom of heaven: and whatsoever thou shalt bind on earth shall be bound in heaven; and whatsoever thou shalt loose on earth shall be loosed in heaven";[112] and to the company of the twelve.[113] Authority was given them to declare and to execute the judgment of God upon men through the guidance of the Holy Spirit. The question whether and how far the powers vested in the apostles have been transmitted to the church does not fall within the scope of our inquiry.

It is evident that in the symbolic act of breathing Jesus did not simply foretell the gift of the Spirit: the gift was actually bestowed. But as he commanded them not to depart from Jerusalem, but to wait for the promise of the Father, and said, "Ye shall receive power, when the Holy Spirit is come upon you," [114] it is no less evident that the Spirit was not conferred in the fulness of his power. The gift was an anticipation and an earnest of the greater gift which they were soon to receive.

Jesus sent the little company of the apostles upon a world-wide mission with his own peace enthroned in their hearts, and clothed with the power of his Spirit. Here at the close of our study the Persons of the Trinity are again brought together, as the church is charged with a world-wide ministry: the Father sends the Son, the Son sends the disciples, and the Spirit clothes them with power.

Since the Son is the only Saviour of men, it is the office of the Spirit to make him known, and this work he accomplishes ordinarily through the disciples of Jesus, the church which he purchased with his blood. They are his witnesses, and the office of the witness is to testify of him with such clearness and power that

[112] Matt. xvi. 19.
[113] Matt. xviii. 18.
[114] Acts i. 4, 5.

they may say to those who hear them, as Paul said to the Galatians, Before your eyes Jesus Christ hath been openly set forth crucified. When he who was lifted up on the cross of Calvary is exalted by the witness of disciples who are clothed with the Spirit, the promise shall be fulfilled that he will draw all men unto himself.

INDEX OF SUBJECTS AND AUTHORS

A

Abbot, Ezra: on John i:18, 123; on John iii:3, 260.

Abbott, T. H.: on Col. ii:12, 247.

Africanus, Julius: on Gen. vi:2, 118.

Allen, W. C.: 54, 75, 79, 86, 102, 222, 231.

Alexander, J. A.: 47, 284, 324.

Alford, H.: 234.

Ambrose: on John iii:6, 272.

Andrews, S. J.: on genealogies of Christ, 73.

Angels: place in Scripture and in Protestant theology today, 109 ff.

Anthropomorphism of O. T. and N., 32.

Apamea, enrolment of: 63.

Apocryphal writings, Jewish: 189.

Apostles' Creed: 55, 311.

Aquinas, Thos.: 301.

Aristides: on virgin birth, 55.

Athanasian Creed: 311.

Athanasius: 308, 313.

Augustine: on Gen. vi:2, 118, 119, 154; on the Spirit as a dove, 156, 190; on inspiration, 216, 265, 288, 301, 304; on the procession of the Spirit, 308, 337.

Augustus: history of reign obscure, 59; enrolments made by, 62; relation to Herod, 65.

B

Bacon, Francis: 103, 171.

Baptism: of John and Jesus, 133; origin of baptism of John, 134; of proselytes, 134; significance of, 136; in N. T., 137; signified by *water* of John iii:5, 261.

Basilides: accepted virgin birth, 56.

Bengel, J. A.: on I John v:6, 267.

Blasphemy: 199.

Book of life: 167.

Box, G. A.: on John i:13, 75, 85.

Briggs, C. A.: on use of Ruach in O. T., 24, 38; on Ps. ii:7, 12, 119, 148; David not author of Ps. cx, 220.

Broadus, J. A.: 102, 123, 134, 220, 224.

Brooke, A. F.: on *Paraclete*, 322.

Brown, Driver and Briggs, Lexicon: 24, 33, 367.

Bunyan, John: sin against the Holy Spirit, 206.

Burkitt, F. C.: 54.

Burton, E. D.: 57, 77; sons of God in O. T., 117; Fatherhood of God, 119; *spirit* in N. T., 132; on baptism, 249, 257.

Burton & Goodspeed, Harmony Syn. Gs.: 88, 91, 105, 106.

C

Calvin: 261, 267, 278.

Carpocrates: rejected virgin birth, 56.

Cerinthus: rejected virgin birth, 56.

Charles, R. H.: 83, 133, 251, 276.

Chase, F. H.: 231.

Christ: names of in O. T., 22; relation of his teaching to O. T., 24; Servant of Jehovah, 42; representations of in O. T., 46; date of birth, 67; Son of God, 120; scene of his baptism, 149; significance of his baptism, 151; temptation, purpose of,

INDEX OF TEXT

Passages discussed are marked with an asterisk (*)